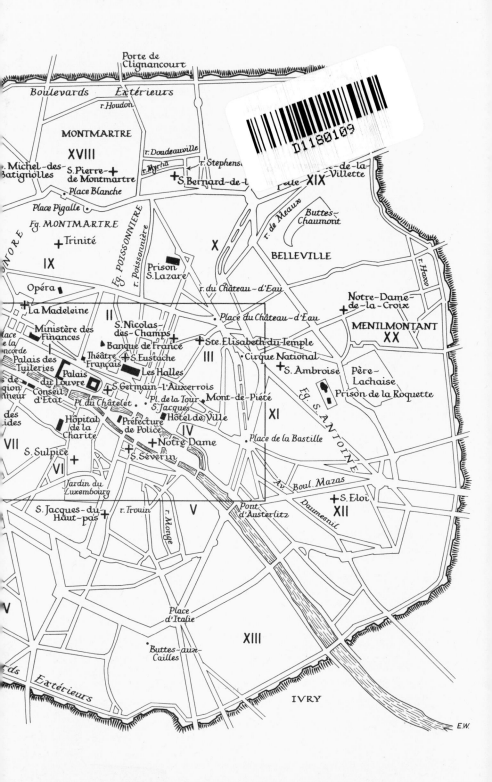

Porte de
Clignancourt

Boulevards Extérieurs

r. Houdon

MONTMARTRE

XVIII

r. Doudeauville

. Michel-des-
Batignolles   S. Pierre-   r. Myrha   r. Stephens.   —de-la-
                     de Montmartre   S. Bernard-de-l. Rue XIX Villette

. Place Blanche

Place Pigalle .

Fg. MONTMARTRE   r. de Meaux   Buttes-
                                                                      Chaumont
+ Trinité

IX   X   BELLEVILLE   r. Haxo

Opéra .   Prison
            II   S. Lazare   r. du Château-d'Eau
                                                                    Notre-Dame-
+ La Madeleine   de-la-Croix

ONORE   Ministère des   S. Nicolas-   . Place du Château-d'Eau   MENILMONTANT
lace   Finances   des-Champs   XX
e la   . Banque de France + Ste. Elisabeth-du-Temple
ncorde   Théâtre   + S. Eustache   III   . Cirque National
Palais des Français   Les Halles   Père-
Tuileries   Palais   + S. Ambroise   Lachaise
ion   du Louvre   S. Germain-l'Auxerrois   Prison de la Roquette
nneur   Conseil   Pl. de la Tour . Mont-de-Piété
            d'Etat   Pl. du Châtelet
des   . S. Jacques   Fg. S. ANTOINE
ides   Hôpital   Préfecture Hôtel de Ville
VII   de la   de Police   XI
            Charité   IV
S. Sulpice   + Notre Dame   . Place de la Bastille
    +   . S. Séverin
VI
        Jardin du   Av. Boul. Mazas
        Luxembourg   + S. Eloi
V   S. Jacques-du-   r. Trouin   Pont   Daumesnil   XII
    Haut-pas   V   d'Austerlitz

                                                      IVRY

V   Place
                        d'Italie

                              XIII
            . Buttes-aux-
              Cailles

    ds Extérieurs   E.W.

THE WOMEN INCENDIARIES

Edith Thomas

The
Women
Incendiaries

Secker & Warburg
London

Originally published in France as
LES PETROLEUSES
Copyright © 1963, Editions Gallimard
English translation by James and Starr Atkinson

First published 1966 by
George Braziller, New York, U.S.A.
Copyright © 1966, George Braziller, Inc.

In this first British edition published 1967 by
Martin Secker & Warburg Limited
14 Carlisle Street, London W.1
some amendments by Roger Greaves have been made to
the Atkinson translation
Copyright © 1967, Martin Secker & Warburg Limited

Type set by Gloucester Typesetting Co. Ltd
Printed in Great Britain by
Western Printing Services Limited, Bristol

❧

CONTENTS

CONTENTS

✤

PLATES

MAPS

INTRODUCTION

MY INTEREST IN the women of the Commune was dictated, not by chance or whimsy, but by a firm conviction that a study on the subject was necessary and overdue.

'History'—which, in the sense that its movements affect both women and men, is one and universal—is almost exclusively the work of men. Judging from the results, they have nothing to be proud of. Women, at all events, hardly ever figure in it, except in minor roles or as victims.

The fact that 'feminism'—or rather 'feminine humanism,' of which feminism is merely the nineteenth-century avatar—is thought today to be outmoded, is a means of dodging the problems it raised, which are still very far from being solved. To confirm this one need only look at the composition of the committees that run political parties, ministerial councils, and meetings of the United Nations. Despite declarations concerning the political and social equality of men and women, this equality more often than not remains illusory. But that the principle has been accepted is already a considerable achievement; a century ago, it would have seemed foolish and outrageous.

So the history of half the human species, which has almost always been enacted on the fringes of History, raises its own questions, peculiar to itself. In France, from Christine de Pisan to Louise Labé, from Marguerite de Valois to Marie de Gournay, from Mme du Châtelet to Mme de Coicy, from Olympe de Gouges to Mme de Staël, we never lose sight of its hidden continuity: all of them demand that women be considered as human beings. From 1830 onwards, the Saint-Simonians, Fourier and his disciples, Cabet and Marx raised the problem simultaneously with that of the proletariat: what was involved was the liberation of all humanity, whatever be the

form of servitude by which it had hitherto been fettered. Claire
Demar, Flora Tristan, Pauline Roland, Jeanne Deroin, Daniel
Stern, George Sand and many others passionately discussed the
conditions of this liberation: education, career, marriage,
position under the law, political rights, and so on.

Though women had participated in the great battles of the
1789 Revolution, they were even more active in that of 1848,
from which they hoped for recognition of their rights. But the
men of 1848 did not seem disposed to grant them these rights,
any more than did their 'great forebears' of 1789. The shooting
started afresh in 1871, on the occasion of the Commune.

The history of women, considered as a branch of social history, is generally held to be insignificant. For 'serious' historians,
it deserves to be taken no more seriously than any other 'ladies'
fancy-work.' An historian of the Commune has recently
written: 'Inevitably there were feminine demonstrations
instigated by the petty bourgeoisie. They may have been the
rowdiest of all, but the essential point does not lie in that; it lies
in the fact that the working women of the Commune shattered
the illusion according to which the emancipation of their sex
was to occur as a side effect of the class struggle.' Now this
emancipation is by no means an illusion. The women who
today have access to intellectual professions (university professors, doctors, engineers), in the capitalist countries as well as
in the socialist states; who earn a living without a protector,
either lover or husband; who are directly engaged in society—
these women are infinitely more 'free' than their grandmothers
would have dared to dream. So it seems that the liberation of
women is not necessarily fused with that of the proletariat. The
two do not move at the same rate. The fact that many Marxist
historians and most bourgeois historians are in agreement on
this issue merely proves that the former are as subject to
masculine bias as their colleagues, although for them it is more
a question of political tactics.

The other tradition also denies that the problem exists.
Women hold no interest for these historians except in their
amatory relations—that is, they matter only as objects. Bed-

room histories will always be best-sellers. Mme de Pompadour and Mme du Barry are found as scandalous as ever, and re-emerge periodically, accommodating themselves to the tastes of the day. Mme de Staël is more interesting for her lovers than for the struggle she waged against Napoleon. Flora Tristan and Pauline Roland interest nobody.

It appears, then, that the history of feminist movements has to contend with a total lack of sympathy, and universal opposition. Also, here even more than in other fields, large vague syntheses have preceded the precise, necessarily limited studies which would have allowed the former to be compiled with some degree of accuracy. My ambition is solely to do a little clearing of a terrain that is still covered with brush, to pursue a task of analysis so that there can be a subsequent attempt at a real synthesis—which is impossible given the present state of our knowledge. In short, I seek to establish a few modest truths. Studies on the women of 1848, on Pauline Roland and on George Sand, led me logically to the Commune.

Contemporaries were struck by the importance of women's participation in the 1871 Revolution. I shall summon a few before the jury, to justify my having taken on this task.

Maxime du Camp: 'The weaker sex behaved scandalously during those deplorable days, and, as a sequel to *Le Mérite des Femmes*,* one might write a quaint book called *On the Role of Women During the Commune*. The story of their folly ought to titillate the talents of a moralist or alienist. They tossed much more than their caps over windmills; not stopping at this minor detail, all the rest of their clothing followed. They bared their souls, and the amount of natural perversity revealed there was stupefying. Those who gave themselves to the Commune— and there were many—had but a single ambition: to raise themselves above the level of man by exaggerating his vices. There they found an ideal they could achieve. They were venomous and cowardly. . . . They were all there, agitating and squawking: inmates from Saint-Lazare out on the spree;

---

* A reference to a pitiful attempt at poetry by Gabriel Legouvé (1801). Intended to glorify womankind, it was often cited by feminists.—*Trans.*

the natives of little Poland and greater Bohemia; the vendors of *modes à la tripe de Caen*; the gentlemen's seamstresses; the gentlemen's shirtmakers; the teachers of grown-up schoolboys; the maids-of-all-work; the vestals of the Temple of Mercury, and the Virgins of Lourcine. What was profoundly comic was that these absconders from the workhouse unfailingly invoked Joan of Arc, and were not above comparing themselves to her. . . . During the final days, all of these bellicose viragos held out longer than the men did behind the barricades. . . . Many of them were arrested, with powder-blackened hands and shoulders bruised by the recoil of their rifles; they were still palpitating from the overstimulation of battle. . . .'[1]

And from Dauban, also an extreme reactionary: 'The women were like the men: ardent, implacable, frenzied. Never had they turned out in such great number, braving peril and defying death. They dressed the horrible wounds made by case-shot, shells, and cylindrical bullets; they ran to the side of those who, under the pressure of unheard-of tortures, were howling, sobbing, and bellowing with pain and rage; then, their eyes filled with blood, their ears full of those cries torn from the last living shreds of flesh, they resolutely took up the chassepot and ran toward the same wounds and the same agony. And what dauntlessness at the barricades, what ferocity in combat, what presence of mind, against the wall, before the firing squad. . . .'[2]

From Dumas *fils*, this final word: 'We shall say nothing about their females, out of respect for women—whom these resemble once they are dead.'[3]

On the other side is Benoît Malon: 'One important fact among all those brought to light by the Paris revolution is the entry of women into politics. Under the pressure of circumstances, and through the spread of socialist ideas and the propaganda of the Clubs . . . they felt that the co-operation of women was indispensable to the triumph of the Social Revolution now in the fighting stage; that woman and the proletariat, those ultimate victims of the old order, could not hope for their emancipation except by forming a strong union against all the

forces of the past. Then again, they recalled that the women of
Paris had been responsible for the 5th and 6th of October, one
of the finest chapters of the Revolution of 1789, as well as for
many other glorious moments. They passionately put themselves
at the service of the Commune's Revolution. . . . Impressive
numbers were always to be found in group activities, and
many of them gave their lives for the revolutionary cause. A
number of these daring yet modest heroines helped to hold
the advanced posts, some in the uniforms of the National
Guard. One could no longer keep track of the *cantinières*
who distinguished themselves. Ten or more had been killed,
and the survivors were no less brave.'[4]

From Lissagaray: 'That woman who greets and accompanies
you is the valiant, the true Parisian woman. The androgynous
scum risen out of the filth of the Empire have followed their
clientele to Versailles, or are working the Prussian army at
Saint-Denis. The woman who comes forward now in the
streets is strong, loyal, tragic; she knows how to die as she loves,
because of that pure and generous vein which, since 1789, has
run richly through the heart of the people. She who was before
a partner in life and work now wishes to share her man's
association with death. "If the French Nation were composed
of nothing but women, what a terrible nation it would be,"
writes the correspondent of *The Times*. . . . She does not hold
her man back; on the contrary, she thrusts him into battle,
bringing soup and linen to him in the trenches as she did when
he was out at work. Many women do not want to go back home,
but take up a rifle. . . .'[5]

Finally, from Marx: 'The tarts had picked up the scent of
their protectors, who had gone to ground—those men of family,
of religion, and especially of property. In their stead, the real
Parisian women had come to the surface: heroic, noble, and
devoted, like the women of Antiquity.' And again: 'The women
of Paris joyfully give up their lives on the barricades and
execution grounds. What does this prove? It proves that the
daemon of the Commune changed them into Megaeras and
Hecates.'[6]

I could go on amassing evidence but this would be pointless. It is not very important that the critics of the Commune called the women who participated in it 'females' and 'viragos,' and that the supporters of the Commune exalted those 'pure heroines.' From these contradictory opinions one certain fact can be extrapolated: the massive, extraordinary, momentous participation of women in the Commune. The parliamentary inquiry into the insurrection of the 18th of March, moreover, confirms this officially: 1,051 women were arraigned before the Councils of War. Others—how many will never be known— were killed at the barricades and in the great slaughter during the Bloody Week.

Who were these women? What did they do? What did they want? What did they think? Were the *pétroleuses* a myth or a reality? All of these questions demand the historian's attention.

The documents that allow history to be retraced—here, apart from newspapers and memoirs, the dossiers of the Councils of War in the Archives of the Ministry of War, and the reprieve dossiers in the National Archives—remain so much dead and meaningless paper, unless they be selected, criticized, interpreted, and organized by the historian who uses them. In this confrontation the historian's personality must necessarily be apparent. Historical method is a science, and a rigorous one. But objectivity is a decoy, particularly when we are concerned with periods that are near to us and touch upon problems that are still burning issues. One's view of the Commune varies according to whether one considers it as the revolt of a people rightfully inflamed by defeat and social injustice, or as an undertaking of criminal subversion against the established order. In the former instance, one will tend to consider the women and men of the Commune as pure, sympathetic heroes; in the latter, as common criminals.

We shall endeavour to avoid this naïve Manicheism. Despite its mistakes and shortcomings, the Commune embodies a significant moment in revolutionary history and in the progress of justice. And the cause of justice is not upheld by choirboys and Girl Guides.

Nor do I believe that an historian can speak about things which he has not himself experienced, or understand actions that are utterly alien to him. I agree that it is not safe to trust analogies in history: nothing ever repeats itself exactly. But Mathiez realized that what had made him able to understand the legality of the revolutionary tribunals was having served on military tribunals during the First World War. This 'bourgeois' historian, brought up during a period of relative social calm, could not have understood the imperatives of exceptional justice without this experience.

What allows me, perhaps, to understand the women of the Commune is that during the Resistance, I took part in the co-ordinating committee of the Union des Femmes Françaises, edited their tracts, and helped them to plan the women's demonstrations against the Vichy government and the Nazi occupation; the barricades of 1944 replied to the barricades of 1871.

But if the historian has the right to be impassioned, and to be —whether as man or as woman—committed to his time, under no circumstances does this passion entitle him to pass in silence over awkward documents, nor to conceal truth, which, like Janus, always has two faces.

A final word about the title.* The term '*pétroleuses*' was coined in 1871 to designate the women who were accused of having set fire to Paris. I am using it in a much wider sense: it applies to all the women who were involved in the revolutionary movement of 1871. In no way is its use pejorative.

---

* The original French title is *Les Pétroleuses*, here rendered as *The Women Incendiaries.—Trans.*

I

WOMEN DURING THE SECOND EMPIRE

AT THE OPERA BALL, the most fashionable courtesans—
Marguerite Bellanger, Blanche d'Antigny, Cora Pearl, La
Paîva, and others of lesser renown—were waltzing with the
men of the hour. Dressed in silk, embroideries, lace, and furs,
the *dames aux camélias* were in their glory. The crinoline had
come into fashion, and was becoming a symbol. A gown called
à la Béguine, of Chantilly lace and Indian cashmere, was made
of 250 yards of fabric and cost 10,000 francs.[1] On the Market,
speculators built fortunes one day and lost them the next. A
new-moneyed luxury, a petty depravity, an invariable bad
taste, characterized the zenith of a class whose motto remained,
more than ever, Guizot's saying: 'Get rich.' (The full advice, it
seems, was 'Get rich by work and by thrift.' By *whose* work was
open to interpretation.) Never had money been so fashionable, never had it taken the place of everything else quite so
much.

Two distinct classes, then: the rich and the poor. This division was carved into the very stones and asphalt of the city for
everyone to see. Reconstructing the old Paris, Baron Haussmann had built new thoroughfares which could easily be
swept by cavalry charges from north to south, west to east.
Thus no more barricades. No more would people see those
citadels of the poor which had caused the authorities so much
bother in 1830, 1848, and 1851. No longer were the same
houses divided perpendicularly, as in the eighteenth century,
between bourgeois and artisans. The workers were pushed back
toward the north and east of Paris, to Belleville, Ménilmontant,
and, beyond the fortifications, toward the suburbs that were
emerging into the ugliness of industrial anarchy (called
'freedom').

All along the new streets sprang up the expensive houses of the eminent banking and business families. Two different worlds, each filled with hatred and fear—or at best, ignorance —of one another.

For the condition of the workers had scarcely improved since 1830. Wages were still beneath the level that would allow a man to live like a human being. Yet within the proletariat itself, a distinction must be made: women were the more exploited. At Lyon and in the Nord, women worked in factories, where their daily wages were relatively high: 3 fr 50 for a weaver, 3 or 4 francs for a warper.* But most women could earn a living solely by doing the needlework which had given Paris an international reputation. These masterpieces provided them with little more than a starvation wage. Certain working women (tailors' seamstresses, for example) might manage to make 4 fr 50 but others got no more than 50 centimes. Seamstresses earned, on the average, 1 fr 70; embroiderers, 1 fr 71; dressmakers, 1 fr 98. A high-quality linen-draper might get 5 or 6 francs, but most received barely 2 or 2 fr 50 for an eleven-hour working day. Out of 112,000 working women, 60,000 were employed in needlework, and 6,000 made the artificial flowers that were so much in fashion during the Empire: 'The most skilful are veritable artists, who study natural flowers lovingly and reproduce them more faithfully than do the best painters.'[2]

I still have boxes of those fuchsias, roses, and ivy-leaves which my great-grandmother made during the Second Empire, and which are masterpieces of their kind. The 'veritable artists' earned 3 francs for eleven hours of this work.

Le Journal des Demoiselles called the attention of young ladies of the bourgeoisie to the lot of their unfortunate sisters: 'Among the poor girls who ply the needle, there is a scale of wages which goes from 5 francs down to 15 centimes per day. The

---

* A rough approximation of contemporary (1871) comparative money values: a franc, consisting of 100 centimes, equalled 9½d. Thus there were 25 francs to the pound. For prices during the siege of Paris, see p. 31.— Trans.

average comes to 2 francs earned for a thirteen-hour day . . . and the thread or silk used by the worker must still be deducted from this sum.'[3]

The highly paternalistic Jules Simon calculated as follows the budget of a working woman living alone on the streets of Paris: if she was very skilful, she earned 2 francs per day, not counting Sundays, holidays, and the off-season, which was very important in the fashion trades. Her earnings added up, then, to about 500 francs per year, if she was not ill a single day. First, she must have a place to live. When Haussmann's thoroughfares were laid out, numerous workers' dwellings were destroyed. For a tiny seventh-floor garret, one had to allow 100 to 120 francs on the left bank, 150 francs on the right; for an actual room, 20, 30, or 40 francs more. In 1851, inspectors reported a woman 'entombed rather than accommodated in a hole five feet deep and three feet wide'; another who, in order to breathe, had to break the pane of her attic window. Jules Simon calculated 115 fr 50 for clothing. As for heat, a coalman would fill the foot-warmer with charcoal and ashes for 5 centimes. Light was a wick steeped in oil, consuming 10 centimes' worth of oil for every three hours. That makes 36 francs for light and heat. Thirty-six francs for laundry. Assuming the rent to be a minimum of 100 francs, the total comes to 287 fr 50; 212 fr 50 were left for food—that is, 60 centimes a day, enough not to die of hunger. Many working women ate only bread and milk. If illness came along, there was no way of paying for a doctor and medicaments. And of course many of these wretches did not earn as much as 2 francs a day.[4]

The convents gave the linen-drapers and dressmakers great competition, for the handiwork of the convent sewing-rooms did not cost much. A nun, 'who is not rushed by anything, works slowly and works well.' Thus the religious orders could supply excellent work at prices 25 per cent lower than those of working women.[5] This competition was not, perhaps, irrelevant to the anticlericalism of the Commune women.

Since it was almost impossible for a working woman to live off her wages alone, she found a mate, legal or not. A shoe-

stitcher, Victorine Brochon, to whom we shall turn for witness
on more than one occasion, describes the life of a working-class
family in these terms:

I have seen poor women who work 12 or 14 hours a day for ludicrous
wages, forced to leave aged parents and children and to shut themselves up for long hours in unhealthy workrooms, beyond the reach
of air, light, or sunshine—for they are lit by gas. Droves of women
are crammed into factories to earn the modest sum of 2 francs a day,
or even less, and nothing on Sundays and holidays. On Saturday
night, having finished their day's work, they spend half the night
mending the family clothing; they also go to the public wash-
house to soak their linen, then go back to wash it on Sunday
morning.[6]

To get away from the hovel they lived in, her husband spent
all his time and three-quarters of his pay in taverns. Sometimes
he beat his wife, and she would have to protect the children from
his blows. She had to ask for credit from the butcher, coalman,
and grocer; to pawn her pitiful possessions at the Mont-de-
Piété,* that poor man's bank. For the woman, there was no
rest, since she went out to work and kept house into the bargain.
For the man, there was the tavern. This description bears out
the inquiries of Villermé, or Michelet's Le Peuple.

What good was it, among such poverty, to invoke traditional
morality? 'The words honour, virtue, faith, ring false in the ears
of these outcasts. For them, they are hollow phrases, void of
meaning.'[7]

Prostitution, then, appeared as a normal, and often indispensable, means of supplementing one's wages, or of earning a
living when regular employment was unobtainable. In 1867,
the Lyon Academy proposed the following subject, suggested
by a former Saint-Simonian, Arlès-Dufour: 'How to raise
women's wages to the same level as men's, when the work they
do is equal, and to make new careers available for women.'
A girl named Julie Daubié won the prize with her study

* The Mont-de-Piété was—and is—a sort of city-owned pawnshop.
In 1871 the mother-house at 55 rue des Francs-bourgeois had 22 branches
throughout the city.—Trans.

Women and Poverty in the Nineteenth Century. She, like Jules Simon, emphasized the economic character of prostitution:

The inadequate pay of the urban working-woman sometimes drives her, even during a period of industrial prosperity, to complete her budget by the sale of her body; this is called the fifth quarter of the day. During periods of unemployment, this kind of right to work fills the entire day. In various cities, according to the testimony of the inspectors of the public morals brigade, women who have decidedly not lost all conception of honour are forced into ignominy because they lack means of subsistence. . . . Generally the poverty of these women is such that among 6,000 registered in Paris, only 2,000 had any resources. One woman can be mentioned who struggled for three days against the tortures of hunger, before giving in. . . . [8]

In any case, marriage in the eyes of the law and of God was not the rule in the working-class family. But these irregular unions were often of long duration, and displayed a much greater fidelity than many legitimate marriages.[9] This 'concubinage,' which outraged the chaste Councils of War and seemed to them one more charge against the women of the Commune, was indeed considered scandalous by all right-thinking people. The Catholic Association of Saint-François-Régis made it its business, although in vain, to facilitate the marriage of women. Generally, people were a good deal more indulgent toward courtesans who had succeeded in climbing up into the *demi-monde* than toward the poor girls of the rue Quincampoix and the Faubourgs.

Thus the morality of the working class was not, as a rule, that which reigned among the bourgeoisie. It had other laws: the foremost virtue was that of solidarity; the ideal to be blindly pursued was that of justice.

In 1864 the International Working Men's Association was founded in London; its inaugural address was drafted by Marx, and its French section organized by Tolain, Fribourg, and Charles Limousin. These men were Proudhonians, and it is known that Proudhon, who got on well with the Empire, was resolutely hostile to the idea of women going out to work. Consequently, the French section of the International drew up a statement against the participation of women in industry. However, this did not prevent their belonging to the International. Victorine Brochon took part in the meetings and brought her husband to them. She wrote: 'Even though Frankel was a Hungarian, he was as much a compatriot of ours as if he had come from Montmartre.'[10] She helped set up a co-operative bakery in the quarter of La Chapelle.[11] A third of the profits went to the members of the co-operative, a third made up the reserve fund, and the final third was lent without interest to establish another co-operative. But in 1867, the bread problem became so acute that they could not deny workers credit; that was the ruin of the undertaking.

Nathalie Lemel, a bookbinder, started another food co-operative, *La Marmite*, with the worker Varlin. Born in Brest in 1826 of a well-to-do family—her parents owned a café—and well-bred Nathalie Lemel was highly respected in the town. At first, she ran a bookshop with her husband in Quimper. But their business became rather shaky, and the Lemels went to live in Paris, where she worked in several binderies. She belonged to one of those mutual-aid societies which the police kept under constant surveillance because they could easily turn into resistance groups. In 1866, Nathalie Lemel became a member of the First International. She was a militant who read 'evil newspapers' aloud. By virtue of her intelligence and 'the luminous clarity of her mind,' she exercised an undeniable influence over her fellow workers. But her independence and her political opinions separated her from her husband who, moreover, had started to drink.

La Marmite, whose aim was to 'furnish workers with food at a low price,' was an institution authorized by the government. Thanks to the activity of Nathalie Lemel, who was its treasurer, the society developed rapidly. Taking up Jeanne Deroin's former project for the federation of the trade unions, they created an organizing committee which was to integrate the various catering, supply and production co-operatives. There too, Nathalie Lemel, who took on its secretarial duties, played an important role. This banding together for solidarity had two goals, political education and propaganda for the International,[12] which were what separated the co-operatives of working-class origin from similar efforts established by the charitable segment of the bourgeoisie. The former societies were only palliatives, moving toward social revolution; charity was an end in itself.

Yet another supply co-operative, with the strange name of the *Société des Equitables de Paris*, was set up by another woman, Marguerite Tinayre. She belonged to a middle-class family from Issoire, where she was born in 1831. She was a good student and in 1856 received her qualifying certificate at Lyon as an elementary school teacher. She married a notary clerk, and first ran a private school in Issoire. Then, 'giving vent to her reckless imagination and having always professed advanced ideas' (so reads a police report in the inimitable style of documents of this type), she 'went up' to Paris and ran private and 'protestant' schools in Neuilly, Bondy, Noisy-le-Sec, and Gentilly. She was a woman 'of unusual energy and vitality who was 'morally' irreproachable—what a pity!—were it not for the fact that she shared her family's subversive ideas: those of her brother Antoine Guerrier and her brother-in-law Jules Babick, a slightly crazy adherent of the Fusionist religion. Along with some former Saint-Simonians who, unlike most, remained faithful to the ideals of their youth, Marguerite Tinayre then organized *Les Equitables de Paris*. The meetings were held in the rue des Vieilles-Haudriettes, at the home of a shoe-maker, Henry, who was their chairman. Marguerite Tinayre, a member of the executive, allied the co-operative with the International and the *Fédération des Sociétés Ouvrières*. She took the floor at political meetings, organized from 1868 onwards, to defend 'socialist and antireligious ideas.' A dangerous woman, in short, and one who would bear watching.[13]

But Marguerite Tinayre was also a novelist, putting herself under the patronage of George Sand, to whom she dedicated

her first work, *La Marguerite*, in 1864. Naturally, like George
Sand and Daniel Stern, she took a masculine pseudonym, and
her novels may be found in the Bibliothèque Nationale under
the name of Jules Paty. These ill-starred novels have not had
a single reader in the course of a century; I had to cut their
pages.[14] Their fault lies in being long-drawn-out and full of
pathos. But, good or bad, a novelist never conceals himself in
his works: even if he believes that he is objective, traces of his
personality can always be found. This is why I would have felt
I was remiss had I not tried to know Marguerite Tinayre a little
better through the novels of Jules Paty. The Council of War
that made me aware of this identification was right. Jules Paty
took as his setting the Auvergne and Issoire, where Marguerite
Tinayre was born. His novels are dated from Noisy-le-Sec,
where Marguerite Tinayre once ran a school. Jules Paty cites as
an epigraph a sentence from a certain Jean Guerrier (*Œuvres
Inédites*), who must have been some distinguished member of her
family, since Marguerite Tinayre's maiden name was Guerrier.
These little games of internal criticism are diverting for the
researcher; the reader will forgive me if they bore him.

In her first work, *La Marguerite*,[15] the edifying story of the
devotion of a Sister of Charity towards her nephews, Marguerite
Tinayre describes for us some peasants from the Allier who come
to Paris to try to make their fortune. The coalman of the rue des
Amandiers manages to earn a decent living, but the laundress of
the rue des Blancs-Manteaux wears herself out bringing up her
four young nephews. Illness is a catastrophe which throws budgets
as precarious as hers into confusion. There is no meat for a stew
even on Sundays, and they take the few rags they possess to the
Mont-de-Piété. In Paris, 'being poor is a hundred times worse
than anywhere else.'[16] All these common people are described
precisely and lovingly. We shall meet them again among the
participants in the Commune. In this novel, the Sisters of
Saint Vincent-de-Paul appear as good angels, showing that
Marguerite Tinayre was not at this time at all anticlerical—or
rather, that her anticlericalism admitted of just discrimination.
Everything ends happily, as in the novels of George Sand: the

uprooted peasants, unable to adjust to Paris, return to their village—a conclusion that obviously contains nothing subversive.

But in her second novel, *Un Rêve de femme*,[17] Marguerite Tinayre frees herself from the influence of George Sand. She displays a disabused scepticism that is rarely found in her mentor's work, and that seems rather surprising coming from a revolutionary temperament. Marguerite Tinayre must have been a woman without illusions—which still did not keep her from participating in a revolution. In literature, she wished to be neither classical (she acknowledged only the rule of common sense), nor romantic (she did not dream of the Middle Ages, 'that monstrous usurpation of justice by force, which delivered the nation's masses, like vile matter, over to the iron gears of feudalism'), nor eclectic ('the rule of choice is still a rule'). A realist, then? Yes, 'if realism consists in seeking the ideal of art in the sincere imitation of nature, particularly if this inquiry into the physical order should lead to the discovery of social harmonies and equilibriums of which religion and morality are merely formulas brought within the scope of a human understanding obscured by ignorance, tainted by passion, or atrophied by poverty.'[18]

So Marguerite Tinayre was above all a moralist, but a moralist who distrusted current morality and religion: it is in this that she was revolutionary. She adds that her book is not for the eyes of young people. An advocate of absolute liberty in art, she wants art to be no more chaste than nature. Yet be reassured: despite these warnings, *Un Rêve de femme* seems today very decorous. What Marguerite Tinayre wanted was to put women on their guard against 'their pointless aspirations, their groundless worries,' and to draw their attention to the necessity of 'physical harmony' in marriage, a delicate subject that was scarcely spoken of in 1860. A pure young girl, Valentine de Rochebrune, whose father is a ruined nobleman, marries a wealthy young marquis, Gustave de Bergonne. Under the influence of his wife and his secretary Artona, a poor country youth, Gustave sets up a factory which gives work to the peasants, and creates a model city with houses for the workers, a day nursery, a school, and a hospital. But alas, with the couple Valentine and Gustave, 'the laws of nature were reversed,' 'the natural protector was the protected,' the woman superior to the man. One day, Valentine gives herself to Artona, who, unlike the finer-bred Gustave, is handsome, strong, stalwart, and so forth. This mistake brings terrible ills upon all these equally noble and generous beings. Gustave goes mad, abandons the factory and village, refuses to recognize his son, and shuts up his wife, who finally commits suicide.

Marguerite Tinayre also depicts a loathsome businessman, the typical newly-rich bourgeois, whom she despises. But she does not, on the other hand, show herself as the dupe of revolutionary phraseology. The Clubs of 1848 in Issoire seem to her 'political pasquinades,' and she cannot have too much sarcasm for the bands of imbeciles who overrun the tribune. 'In this second dawn when liberty illuminated the rights of the common people, showing them the duties attached to universal emancipation, the peasants, brutalized by fifty years of ignorance, hoped for no progress but the repeal of the tax on drink, and knew only one political duty: the abolition of that toll by force or otherwise.'[19] The women, massed outside, listened to the orators and exchanged stupid remarks about the 'tarts of that harsh Rollin (Ledru-Rollin), la Mennais (Lamennais), and la Martine (Lamartine).' But this description, which seems to accord with that of the detractors of the Revolution of 1848, is not a right-wing criticism. Artona, the author's spokesman, explains, in fact: 'The folly of individual interests possesses this mass . . . But let the light shine into all darkened minds, and you will see to what heights man can rise.'[20]

Thus, for Marguerite Tinayre, there had to be, first and foremost, a task of education among the masses. The mutual-aid societies and the supply co-operatives, in which she actively participated, were the means of this education.

The 'political' activity of women first appeared in these various supply co-operatives; and this follows tradition. Women are much closer to everyday realities than men are. Feeding the family is a part of their age-old role. The price of bread has been their business for centuries. Thus, before seeking to involve themselves in truly political activity, they tried to attend to 'material administration,' upon which they could act directly. It is from this angle that those of them with the greatest awareness hoped to come to grips with social reality.

But that was obviously only one aspect of the question.

It was not just the working women who had complaints to make of an order that excluded women from society. A century ago, a woman could scarcely exist socially without a protector, either husband or lover. The education she received was mediocre or non-existent. The Law of 1850 had indeed ordered the creation of a girls' school for every commune with a con-centrated population of more than 800. But the law was a dead-letter. Out of 48,496 public schools, 18,732 schools were for boys, 11,836 schools were for girls, and the others were mixed. It is true that the private schools re-established the balance to some extent. But, generally, one child in five never went to any school, because he was in rags and was dying of hunger. The men and women who taught in elementary schools constituted a decently-dressed proletariat. More than 4,000 schoolmistresses earned less than 400 francs a year. Almost 2,000 earned 100 to 200 francs.[21] We have seen that the minimum budget of a Parisian working woman came to about 500 francs.

The liberal professions were virtually closed to girls of the bourgeoisie. When Julie Daubié sat for her baccalaureate, despite the opposition of the rector of Lyon, and passed the examination, the Minister of Public Education refused in his turn to give her her diploma, for fear of 'forever holding up his ministry to ridicule.' This incident marks the starting-point of a revolution, and people today tend to forget that this revolution is the outcome of a persistent struggle.

This demand for equal education, which the aged Christine de Pisan had already made in the fifteenth century, this passion for culture, this feeling of frustration—we meet them all during the Empire, among those penniless schoolmistresses who 'went up' to Paris to escape being swallowed by the provinces, to initiate themselves into the culture that the provinces refused them, to transcend the destiny that was imposed upon them by tradition. Marguerite Tinayre had come from Issoire; Louise Michel came from Audeloncourt. Let us look more closely at this girl who was to become a symbol.

On the 28th of May 1830, at the Château de Vroncourt in the Haute-Marne, a young servant, Marianne Michel, gave birth to a little girl whom she named Louise. The father was perhaps the owner of the château, Charles-Etienne Demahis; more likely his son Laurent, who, some days later, left the family home and settled down at a nearby farm. The servant remained at the Château de Vroncourt with the baby, Louise, who was brought up by Charles-Etienne Demahis and his wife, whom all her life she called 'grandfather' and 'grandmother,' with an unfailing care and tenderness. On the paternal side of her family were members of the legal profession brought up on Voltaire and Rousseau, who had welcomed the 1789 Revolution sympathetically. On her mother's side were decent and upstanding peasants who had taught themselves how to read. Louise Michel was raised on a compromise between the Voltairian rationalism of her Demahis grandparents, and the popular Catholic mysticism of her mother's family. She went to the village school, where she attracted attention because of her gaiety and her unmalicious mischievousness. She read all the books her cousin brought home from the *collège*, and also read, under her grandfather's guidance, Corneille, Lamartine, and Lamennais, who had a decisive influence upon her. During the long winter evenings, her grandmother sang, and her grandfather read or recounted the legends and epic struggles of the First Republic. But she also loved the rough games of boys, and long windy walks. She knew of the poverty of the peasants, and tried to assuage it. She gave away fruit from the garden and money she stole from her grandfather; he offered to give her a small amount every week for her charities. 'I refused,' she says, 'thinking that I lost too much by accepting.' Her lack of a sense of property and her impulsive generosity were features she retained all her life. But she also learned that charity was not enough: 'I was beginning to understand,' she says, 'the agrarian revolts of ancient Rome.' Her pity extended even to animals mistreated by the peasants.

Her sensibility and her intelligence were apparent in her early poetry, which she sent to Victor Hugo. The poet answered, and encouraged her. Later, in 1870, they met, and Louise Michel figures briefly in the *Carnets intimes*.[22]

Although—despite her stunning eyes and forehead—she was not pretty, the girl who was called 'Mlle Demahis' in the country was twice asked for in marriage by substantial country bourgeois. She mockingly turned them down. She could not accept the condition of women, any more than she could bear the misery of animals or the poverty of peasants. Chrysale's* theories exasperated her. She wanted to find a love based on admiration, a man whom she could admire, whose ideal she could share, with whom she could devote herself to the same cause. But such a man cannot be found every day, at Vroncourt or elsewhere.

Twice, then, Louise Michel rejected the classic destiny of women. Her grandfather died in 1845, her grandmother in 1850. Laurent Demahis' wife turned her out of the château as a 'bastard'—the first time this word had been hurled at her— and forbade her to use the name of Demahis. Her grandfather had arranged a small dowry for her, but Louise had turned down the option of marriage. So it was necessary for her to earn a living. Today, a girl like Louise Michel would enroll at a university; in 1850, she had no solution but that of becoming a schoolteacher. She got her diploma at Chaumont and took a job at Audeloncourt, so as not to be separated from her mother.

The 2nd of December *coup d'état* threw her into the ranks of the opposition. Her students sang *La Marseillaise* and left the church when prayers were said for Napoleon III. The schoolteacher was denounced. She had to go to Chaumont to give an explanation to the inspector who, as an old liberal, admonished her

* A character of well-intentioned, but dull and plodding commonsense in Molière's comedy *Les Femmes Savantes.—Trans.*

paternally and asked her to promise to be more prudent. But Louise Michel relapsed; she published a violent article in one of the local newspapers.

Domitian was ruling. He had banished the philosophers and the wise men from Rome, raised the praetorians' pay, reinstated the Capitoline games, and people were admiring the merciful emperor while waiting for somebody to assassinate him. The apotheosis comes earlier for some and later for others; that's all there is to say. We are in Rome, in A.D. 95.

This time she had gone too far. The *préfet* threatened to send her to Cayenne. Insolently she replied that she would go there willingly, at the government's expense, to establish a school.

The affair went no further for the time being. But Louise Michel found provincial conformity stifling. She longed for a dynamic, intellectual atmosphere. Paris lured her, as it did so many provincials, from Julien Sorel to Rastignac. But Louise Michel did not leave as they did, impelled by a lust for power. She wanted, not to 'arrive,' but to fulfill her destiny.

We find her first as assistant headmistress in the school of Madame Vollier, at 14 rue du Château-d'Eau; then—because schoolteachers in the State system had to swear an oath to the Empire—she directed a private school at 24 rue Oudot. She used remarkably bold methods, which presaged the methods of the New Education a century later. She opened the minds of her pupils to concrete objects, flowers and stones, and taught them to know and to love animals. Later she declared before the Council of War: 'The ethics I taught was this: the development of awareness to such an extent that there could exist no reward or punishment apart from the feeling of having done one's duty, or having acted badly. As for religion, that was left to the parents' wishes.'[23]

She taught herself at the same time she was teaching the children. She eagerly attended the night school in the rue Hautefeuille, run by Jules Favre, Eugène Pelletan, etc.

The women who, during the Empire, were young schoolteachers or were preparing to be, were greedy for that knowledge in which women can share only insofar as they snatch out at it with both hands; they came to the rue Hautefeuille to quench their thirst for knowledge and liberty. A passion for knowledge possessed us. I believe that more often than not we seemed like students, not like schoolteachers.[24]

She took up the study of physics, chemistry, and natural history. In Darwin's *Origin of Species*, in Claude Bernard's *Introduction à la Médecine Expérimentale*, she discovered the foundations of scientific method and of determinism. Louise Michel declared herself an atheist and a materialist. But 'although the individual does not survive in a personal form, he still exists in the extent to which he has been able to devote himself to the human community.' In politics, she joined the International.[25]

This education of women, however mediocre it may have been, was carried on in the professional schools founded by Elisa Lemonnier. At the school in the rue Thévenot Louise Michel taught literature and ancient geography.[26] She also turned her attention to the immediate relief of working women's poverty, by founding *La Société Démocratique de Moralisation*, whose goal was to help women live by, or return to, work done 'in duty.' The declaration specifies that what mattered was not theoretical problems, but furnishing workers with bread and jobs.[27]

None of all this went very far. It was the condition of women itself that had to be transformed; and, at the same time, the whole of society.

2

THE FEMINIST CONTROVERSY

THE INGLORIOUS ATTITUDE which relegated women to the status of objects was justified by the 'thinkers' of the period: Auguste Comte, Michelet, Emile de Girardin, and particularly Proudhon.

Whereas most socialist theorists—Saint-Simon and the Saint Simonians, Fourier and his disciples, Cabet and Marx—were proclaiming that women, like the proletariat, had the right to be considered as free and equal human beings, Proudhon fell into step with the most reactionary theorists, in this realm as in others. His influence on the French working class was too profound, at that time, for us not to linger a little over his lucubrations.

In *Amour et Mariage*, Proudhon sets out to demonstrate woman's triple inferiority from the physical, intellectual, and moral standpoints. Physically, woman is an instrument of reproduction and nothing more. Therefore she cannot exist in society without a 'protector'—father, brother, husband, or lover. With pseudo-scientific pedantry he declares that if man's physical strength be given the factor 3, that of woman will have the factor 2. It is not known upon what investigations Proudhon based these mathematical conclusions, but no matter.

From the intellectual standpoint, woman cannot, he says, sustain man's 'cerebral tension.' Her intellectual frailty affects not only the quality, but also the duration and intensity of her activity. Woman has a mind that is essentially full of error, and the error is irremediable. Her mind is neither critical nor synthesizing. Without man, she would be incapable of transcending the state of bestiality. For intelligence is a function of strength, as much in the physical sense as in the intellectual sense. Therefore in this realm also, man has the right to the factor 3, and woman 2.

One might at least hope that woman would recover ground on the moral plane. Even many misogynists have acknowledged this. But Proudhon, lucid spirit that he is, sees what no one else has perceived: virtue is also proportional to strength. Thus woman's awareness, insofar as it concerns justice, is inferior to that of man. Her only insight bears on charity. In politics, woman is reactionary; for her, the true social order is represented by the aristocracy. Her character is weak and inconsistent: she whines, weeps, and wails. These facts, expounds the latter-day Chrysale, are generally observable. Moreover, woman is immodest, for chastity is a corollary of justice.

From these irrefutable observations are derived precise measurements. Woman $= 2 \times 2 \times 2$, man $= 3 \times 3 \times 3$. Q.E.D.

According to these eminently scientific revelations, the subordination of women is therefore inevitable, and entirely justified. Woman has only the choice between 'housewife or whore': marriage alone can keep her from falling into evil ways. Moreover, it is obvious that in marriage the authority and power of command revert to man. Divorce, of course, is prohibited. In *La Pornocratie*, Proudhon confirms the preceding observations. Women do not know how to walk; they are meant for dancing or for the solemn gait of a procession. Women who meddle in serious matters become ugly. If, by ill luck, it should happen that he, Proudhon, marry a lady author, he would offer her this heartfelt address:

Madame, you have appeared against my will at the meeting of the Academy. You are choked by vanity, and it will be the downfall of us both. But I shall not drink the cup to the dregs. At the first act of disobedience, wherever you may run for refuge, I shall reduce you to such a helpless state that you can never re-appear and get yourself talked about.

What a pity it is that Proudhon never tried his hand as a playwright; he would have had a great success on the boulevards. He advises a young man thus: 'If you want to get married, understand at the outset that the prime requisite for a man is to dominate his wife and be the master.' And this other advice, unparalleled in baseness: 'If she brings you money and you have none yourself, you must be four times stronger than she is.' That's *real* socialism for you!

If it serves any purpose to pause a moment over these idiocies, it is because Proudhon was, during the Empire, the leading light of the French proletariat. Therefore it is no wonder that in 1866 the French section of the International presented a memorandum against work for women. Nor, under these circumstances, is it any wonder that women did not always join forces with the proletariat, as Flora Tristan once did, nor that they waged war on their own ground—even those who, from the political point of view, claimed kinship with the Republic, socialism, and democracy. When it came to the problem of women, reactionaries and progressives often fell into agreement about keeping them subservient.

Jenny d'Héricourt, in *La Femme Affranchie* (1860), led the attack, with violence but with wit. She had no wish to reply to those who claimed that, because woman had been the first to sin, God had willed that she be submissive; instead, she answered the others—Michelet, Proudhon, Emile de Girardin, Auguste Comte—who carried on the debate at the level of reason and justice. Malicious jokes, slander, and insults were lavished upon women who defended their rights. 'Vain hopes. The time when we could be intimidated is no more.' Woman, it was said, cannot have the same rights as man, because her intellectual faculties are inferior to his. This means that 'you consider yourselves all to be equal in ability, and each as intelligent as any of the others.' How absurd! Yet men considered themselves all to be equal before the law; the law, then, is not based on ability. The proof is the same as far as function is concerned: woman performs only inferior functions. 'Then you have to prove that the functions each of you performs individually are equal; that Cuvier, Geoffroy Saint-Hilaire, Arago, Fulton, and Jacquard did no more for civilization than an equal number of manufacturers of pin-heads.' It remains to be proven that the jobs of motherhood and housekeeping are not as useful to humanity as those of 'manufacturers of jewellery or children's toys.' It also remains to be proven that school-mistresses, dressmakers, and milliners do not perform functions equal to those of schoolmasters, tailors, or hatmakers. If the law is not based upon function, why speak of the value of function when women are concerned?

Woman could not be man's equal before the law, it was said, because she was temperamentally unsuited to enter certain careers. But then, by the same argument, a man unfit for bearing arms would be excluded by the law. 'If a woman had written anything so silly, she would be trumpeted as a fool from one end of the world to the other.' Woman could not be man's equal before the law because he protected and fed her. 'Then acknowledge the rights of grown-up daughters and of widows whom you do not feed or protect.' It was also said that women laid no claim to their rights. But 'was it necessary to wait for the whole male population to lay claim to the vote before it was given them?'

Today this whole debate seems founded upon truisms. But it took almost a century for these common-sense assertions to cease being considered scandalous and ludicrous paradoxes. Jenny d'Héricourt warned the democrats of the consequences of their ostracism of women. If women drifted away from the Revolution of 1789, it was because they saw that the Declaration of the Rights of Man had nothing to do with them. History repeated itself in 1848. 'I tell you this in all sincerity: all your struggles are in vain, if women do not march with you.' Indeed, it was women who inculcated children with their earliest ideas: 'You are blind not to understand that if woman is on the one side and man on the other, humanity is doomed to do the task of Penelope.' And, in a last appeal to the democrats who were condemning women to eternal subordination, she cried:

Woman is ripe for civic liberty, and we declare to you that, from this time on, we shall regard as an enemy of progress and of the Revolution anyone who comes out against our legitimate claim, just as we shall rank among the friends of progress and of the Revolution those who speak out for our civic emancipation—even if they be your enemies.

The hat was in the ring. A young friend of George Sand, Juliette Lamber (Mme Edmond Adam), attacked Proudhon in particular with an essay entitled *Idées anti-proudhoniennes sur l'amour, la femme et le mariage* (1858). The tone was calmer, but the criticism was as far-reaching.

Proudhon's theories on love are too anachronistic to awaken the slightest response. But his opinions on women are much more dangerous, 'for they express the general feeling of men who, whatever party they belong to, progressive or reactionary, monarchist or republican, Christian or pagan, atheist or deist, will be delighted to have found a means of pandering to their egoism and soothing their conscience at the same time.' Proudhon's crime is having tried to prove that man's superiority to woman is at once necessary and legitimate. Juliette Lamber reviews and refutes Proudhon's pseudo-arguments each in turn. She insists upon the necessity of giving women an education which will enable them to earn a living. They have to become 'productive,' for work alone can establish their freedom. She recognizes the importance of motherhood; but maternal concerns do not occupy all of a mother's time, and, besides, many women have no children. Women's wages are often indispensable to the livelihood of the family, and indispensable, too, if prostitution is to be kept within bounds. 'Giving women access to careers with free and decently paid work amounts to closing down the brothels. Is that what you men want or not?' And that was of course the most important aspect of the problem. Men's attitude to prostitution was, in general, ambiguous. They pretended to be outraged by it, expressing their scorn for the very prostitutes who would not have existed without the use to which they put them. Concerning marriage, Juliette Lamber demands for women the right to divorce, and the possibility of marriage contracts allowing them the administration of their own property. These aspirations, shocking a century ago, are today written into the law.

Louise Michel attacked Michelet: 'The great man makes

woman into an idol—and a poor idol, since her husband, a
pretty puny specimen, has had to create her in his own image.'[1]

But women were not content with writing. In answer to
Barbey d'Aurevilly, who in an article on *Les bas-bleus* had
insulted 'clever women,' a well-bred young girl, Maria
Deraismes, decided to overcome the timidity that was due to
her over-nice upbringing. At the request of two editors of
L'Opinion Nationale, she agreed to participate in the conferences
held in 1865 at the Grand-Orient.* Even though the reporter
from Emile de Girardin's newspaper *La Liberté* was very hostile
to the preferment of women, he wrote: 'I was greatly surprised
when I saw a girl of twenty-four or twenty-five walk in, with a
rather pale face, great distinction of form and bearing, a simple
elegance; neither foolishly timid nor insolently poised.' Maria
Deraismes became famous overnight.

From 1866 to 1870, before an increasingly large audience,
she spoke on the emancipation of women and on free thought.
Wisely and knowledgeably, she examined the historical, legal,
and familial condition of women. 'The inferiority of women is
not a fact of nature; it is a human invention and a social fiction.'
The belittlement of women lowered the potential of the whole
of society. And after the proclamation of the Republic on the
4th of September 1870, she warned the republicans: 'If the
democrats do not have women on their side, their triumphs will
be merely superficial and transitory.' The education of children
would pass out of their hands, and women would constantly be
preparing for reaction.[2]

In 1868, the Empire granted freedom of assembly. The
people, who had been silent for so long, awakened. The
conferences at Vaux-Hall were directed at a public much more
of the working-class than those at the Grand-Orient. The cycle
of conferences began with 'Work for Women.' Women's wages,
always lower than those of men, had decreased with a 'terrifying
rapidity,' and would end up 'permitting no other alternative

* The Grand-Orient, in the rue Cadet, was a public hall which also
housed the Grand-Orient Lodge of Freemasons. Vaux-Hall was in the rue
de Château-d'Eau.—*Trans.*

but prostitution or suicide to women who have only work to live by,' stated a great number of speakers.[3] But a strong Proudhonian current existed in the International. For these followers of Proudhon, woman, as we have seen, was mere 'receptivity' and consequently incapable of creating anything by herself, 'a housewife or a whore,' etc., etc. It was on these premises that the discussions were based.

Maria Deraismes, Paule Minck, and André Léo spoke in defence of the political rights of women. Much notice was taken of Paule Minck, founder of the *Société Fraternelle de l'Ouvrière*, and editor of a little paper called *Les Mouches et les Araignées*. Her father, Jean Népomucène Mekarski, a former aide-de-camp in the Polish army, had emigrated to France in 1831. Her mother, Jeanne Blanche Cornelly de la Perrière, belonged to the lesser nobility. Their children, Paulina Mekarska (Paule Minck) and her brother Jules, a quantity-surveyor, caught the attention of the police because of their 'dangerous and extravagant opinions.' (Jules Mekarski was to become commissioner of police during the Commune.[4]) Paule Minck was 'a little, very dark woman, somewhat sarcastic, who spoke with great energy.' Of this language teacher, linen-draper, and occasional journalist (for none of these occupations gave her enough to live on), it was said that she was 'as skilful at plying the needle as at giving lessons.'[5]

André Léo, too, was one of the more prominent speakers. She was already known for her novels; *Un mariage scandaleux* had attracted critical attention. 'This novel is one of the most remarkable works that has come to light during recent years,' we read in *Le Siècle* for the 4th of September 1863. And in *Le Constitutionnel* for the 28th of July 1863: 'There are passages that are as beautiful as the best of George Sand: the same strength, the same scope and the same simplicity; less idealism and lyricism, perhaps, but a better conceived plot and more exact observation.'

Un mariage scandaleux is, indeed, as good as George Sand's best novels (which, in my opinion, is a compliment). The story is well constructed and well handled. The descriptions of the countryside are pleasant, and one feels that the sensibility behind them is very much attuned to trees, earth, the sky, and the seasons. Peasants and bourgeois appear, delineated with a sharp, sometimes almost cruel, pen—one that is, in any case, without illusions. The subject-matter itself—the marriage of a poor girl of the bourgeoisie to an intelligent young peasant—comes directly from George Sand. Love overthrows social barriers; happiness is possible when it is removed from considerations of rank and money.

In *La Vielle Fille*, André Léo returns to the theme of the girl who prefers spinsterhood to a second-rate marriage. But in the end, it is the obstacle of age which she has to surmount; the marriage will be happy, even though the thirty-five-year-old girl is wed to a boy of twenty-five.

In *Un Divorce*, André Léo studies the consequences of divorce with great objectivity. One might expect this bold woman to defend a right which did not yet exist in the France of her day, and which was being demanded by the socialists and the republicans. Not a bit of it. With great lucidity she portrays the unhappiness of children torn between their father and their mother. Although divorce is legitimate when the marriage is sterile, it solves no problem at all when there are children. Instead, then, one must go to the root of the evil: marriage without love—marriage which, too often, is nothing but an alliance 'between pride and cupidity.' This 'moralization' of marriage and this defence of the family come from Pierre Leroux, to whom George Sand also owed many of her ideas. Indeed, André Léo (Léonide Béra), born in 1832 at Champagné-Saint-Hilaire in the Vienne, the daughter of a naval officer, had married a follower of Pierre Leroux, Grégoire Champseix. After the 2nd of December *coup d'état*, they lived in Switzerland (most of André Léo's novels take place in that country). Their marriage was happy. They had two children, André and Léo, whose names made up their mother's pseudonym. Back in France after the amnesty, Grégoire Champseix died in 1863. His wife had to support herself and her children with her pen. But she also engaged in political activity, particularly the

struggle for women's rights. It was at her house that the plat-
form of the *Société des Droits des Femmes* was discussed.[6]

In her study *La Femme et les Mœurs*, she refutes, in her turn,
the various arguments of the antifeminists. Physical inferiority?
Woman was, in point of fact, the 'first beast of burden,' and
even today one could see the chores women assumed in the
country. Were the toils of pregnancy and labour, and the care
devoted to children, also to count for nothing? The fact that
woman's physical resistance was different from man's did not
imply that she was inferior to him. As for the false ideal of the
pale, vapourish woman, André Léo reduced it to what it was:
a passing fashion. 'When nerves are no longer in fashion, they
will be put to much less use,' she remarked sensibly. History has
proved her right. The vapours, the swoons, the flacons of smell-
ing salts—all of which were the exclusive preserve of women of
'quality' during the eighteenth and nineteenth centuries—have
disappeared completely. Intellectual inferiority? Women had
never been given the possibility of training their intelligence.
Let education be as complete for woman as for man, and it
would be seen what would happen to that pretext of inferiority.
Motherhood was the only role she was credited with. But woman
would be more capable of raising her children if she were less
ignorant, less denigrated as a moral and intellectual being.
Besides, the duties of motherhood only occupied her for about
fifteen years. And what about those who had no children?
Actually, they were denied the right to acquire knowledge and
to work because society wanted to deny them independence,
because society wanted to keep them in a state of subordination.
Revolutionaries became conservatives on this question. Socialists were divided. Proudhonians were hostile. For them the
family was to be 'an absolute monarchy' in which the father
was to reign uncontested. But 'a woman in slavery can raise
nothing but slaves.' Democracy proclaimed that freedom was
necessary to 'the dignity and the morality of the human being.'
But when it came to women, freedom was 'an object of suspicion
and of terror.' Democracy proclaimed humanity's redemption
through knowledge, but knowledge for women would be a

noxious thing. Democracy believed in the virtues of fellowship, but marriage was supposed to be based upon obedience. And, taking up the arguments of Jenny d'Héricourt, André Léo recalls that even if woman's inferiority were admitted (and it has still to be proven), the social contract is not to be based upon the principle that might is right. Even if woman's inferiority were admitted, was the voting-slip 'a doctoral diploma'? Either the principles of democracy were false, or else one had to grant women the same rights as men or risk repudiating those very principles.

It must be agreed that these were strong arguments. But, the working-class public at the Vaux-Hall remained unmoved according to Gustave Lefrançais. A friend of Pauline Roland, Gustave Lefrançais was to be a member of the Commune. He was not a Proudhonian, and acknowledged the justice of these criticisms. But, he claimed, they were relevant only to conditions in the bourgeoisie:

What does it matter to working-women who ply the needle or the burnisher, or who bloody their fingers fashioning stems for paper flowers, whose health is being ruined by twelve or thirteen hours' work that still does not earn them enough to live on—what does it matter that they are not voters, that they may not administer the property they do not possess, and that they cannot deceive their husbands on an equal basis?[7]

A wave of the hand and the problem is conjured away once again. This passage throws light admirably on a certain 'socialist' mentality, which denies all importance to the problem of women in society. This mentality, obsessed with the plight of the working class to begin with, is not interested in other forms of social injustice. Unfortunately this was a rather common attitude among certain leaders of the workers' parties, for whom the Revolution was nothing more than an almost ritualistic custom, void of all its content of truth and justice. We know where this was to lead.

An orator began his speech with '*Citoyennes et Citoyens.*' This appeal to the *citoyennes* produced an 'extraordinary effect' on the audience. But be assured that he immediately added that the political rights claimed by women were entirely 'secondary.' If women had the right to vote and to be elected, would they 'be any the less considered as exploitable material in all forms by the capitalist exploiters?'[8] This was a sophism current in that day. Even under capitalist regimes, the issue of universal suffrage emerges as an instrument of protest claimed by the working class. Why, then, not claim it also for women? Furthermore, the subordination of women existed long before the capitalist system. The disappearance of the latter does not necessarily imply the disappearance of a situation which has existed for thousands of years. In reality, the old latent anti-feminism, almost biological, was behind all this. The schism cut not only through the classes, but also through the sexes. And it is with scorn that the revolutionary Gustave Lefrançais speaks of the ladies and their 'rhetoric.' Yet the Vaux-Hall discussions ended in a vote of principle that recognized the right of women to work, and as a result, to enjoy social equality.[9]

In the hall at Pré-aux-Clercs, debates on marriage, divorce, and *union libre** took place between Catholics and socialists, in the presence of the forces of law and order. Olympe Audouard was called to order by a police commissioner for having declared that divorce would guarantee 'family morals.' She replied that this opinion was taken from the *Idées napoléoniennes* of Louis-Napoléon Bonaparte, written during his imprisonment in the fortress of Ham. Olympe Audouard had run *Le Papillon* and then *La Revue Cosmopolite*, but the board of directors had not let her change that publication into a political newspaper, for this authorization could be granted only to a French man.[10] She was a vigorous opponent, who did not hesitate to attack. In *Le luxe effréné des hommes* (1865), she neatly parries the criticism generally levelled at women. In *Guerre aux hommes* (1866), she portrays the relentlessness men employed to quash any woman showing promise in the arts, science, or literature. 'For a woman to succeed in any career whatever, she must

* An *union libre* is the approximate equivalent of 'common-law' marriage in Anglo-Saxon law.—*Trans.*

have ten times as much talent as a man, for *he* finds a spirit of co-operation ready to aid and sustain him, while *she* has to struggle against a stubborn attitude of ill will.' What she asked for was simply that the law and society treat her like an intelligent being, not like a child.

This whole movement culminated in the *Société de la Revendication du Droit des Femmes*—which brought together André Léo, Maria Deraismes, Louise Michel, Noémie Reclus, Mme Jules Simon, and others—and in the newspaper *Le Droit des Femmes*.

But politics does not consist solely of written or verbal manifestoes. It is a driving force. The movement which impelled women to demand their rights as adult, equal, free human beings, is inseparable from the total political situation. Thus we find women participating in the struggle of the republicans and the socialists. On the 1st of November 1868, there was a demonstration at the grave of the deputy Baudin. Victorine Brochon, who, as we have seen, had joined the International and participated in the organization of co-operatives, was there, and succeeded in eluding the police.[11] Pierre Bonaparte's assassination of the reporter Victor Noir threw the people of Paris into a turmoil. A huge meeting took place in Belleville. 'We must put a stop to this,' they said, and agreed to meet again the next day. 'Women everywhere,' Jules Vallès noted. 'A good omen. When women get embroiled, when the housewife gives her man a push, when she rips her black flag of revolution down from the kitchen to raise it in the streets, it means that the sun will rise over a town in revolt.'[12] The next day, the 12th of January 1870, two hundred thousand Parisians, men and women, swarmed over the Champs-Elysées. André Léo, and the schoolteacher Louise Michel—dressed like a man, 'so as not to bother or be bothered by anyone,' and dreaming of Harmodius—mingled among the crowd. Louis Michel had a dagger hidden in her clothes. 'Almost everyone who turned up at the funeral expected to go home again as members of a republic, or not to go home at all.'[13] The police were at

every corner, ready to intervene. But old Delescluze and
Rochefort prevailed over Flourens and the Blanquists: Victor
Noir's body was carried directly to the cemetery to avoid an
ill-prepared demonstration, which would have given the police
a pretext for a bloody repression.

But the decaying Empire needed military adventure. War
was declared against Prussia, under the worst imaginable
conditions. A part of the people, deceived by official propaganda, raised the cry: 'To Berlin!' But the workers of the
Corderie* demonstrated in favour of peace; a dynastic war did
not concern the people.[14] Louise Michel, who certainly had
moments of poetry, but was a bad poet when writing in verse,
expressed this state of mind:

> Since they want war, since fighting must be done,
> People—your heads bowed down, and sad of heart—
> Against the tyrants you must fight as one,
> And crush them both, William and Bonaparte.[15]

The disasters of this war became known immediately. The
French Army withdrew. On the 14th of August, the Blanquists
Eudes, Granger, Brideau, and Flotte tried to seize weapons from
the barracks in La Villette: the Empire had to be overthrown.
They were arrested and condemned to death on the 29th of
August. Louise Michel, André Léo, and Adèle Esquiros—the
wife of Alphonse Esquiros, and herself the author of several
rather bad novels—circulated a letter from Michelet in the
prisoners' favour. Thousands of signatures were soon appended
to this letter. As often happens in this sort of appeal, a few
nervous people wanted to withdraw their names: 'I admit that
I refused to delete two or three timid signatures,' records Louise
Michel. But this petition had to be got through to General
Trochu. It was not easy to reach the Governor of Paris, but the
three women did not let themselves be intimidated. They
entered the general's antechamber; orderlies requested that

---

* In other words, the members of the Federation of Syndicated Workers'
Chambers, which was located at 6, Place de la Corderie; this soon became
the Paris headquarters of the International.—*Trans.*

they retire. They declared that, 'coming on behalf of the people', they would not leave without an answer, and settled down on the benches. In view of their stubbornness, a secretary went to get someone who claimed to represent Trochu. The bulk of the petition seemed to impress him, and, to get rid of the intruders, he stated that their submissions would be taken into consideration. Louise Michel was under no delusion: 'His promise would have counted for little, had the Empire not fallen.'[16] No matter. That some virtually unknown women had taken it upon themselves to carry the petition of thousands of Parisians before the Governor of Paris was an extraordinary act, bordering on scandal.

These intercessions on behalf of Eudes and his friends had at least one result: they were granted a stay of execution on the 2nd of September. On the 4th of September, the Empire fell and the Republic was proclaimed. 'The proclamation of the Republic, that dream dear to my childhood, was going to come true. I was so happy,' wrote Victorine Brochon in her memoirs.[17] But Louise Michel, much more of an extremist, was not to be duped; the Empire had desecrated *La Marseillaise* that the crowd was singing. The real song of the workers was that of Jacques Bonhomme:

> Bonhomme, bonhomme,
> Get an edge on your scythe.
> We are rebellion, rebellion we'll have.[18]

From that day on, an almost unbridgeable gulf existed between the bourgeois and the socialist Republics.

3

THE SIEGE OF PARIS

BY A TWIST OF FATE of which we have seen other examples, those who had rejected war found themselves, when the *Patrie* was invaded, fighting in the front ranks. When the Prussians were at the gates of Paris, the people, who in 1870 had hardly shown enthusiasm for a dynastic war, decided to fight. By contrast, caught between two problems—the Prussians on the one hand and the people on the other—the men of the 4th of September* preferred, for the most part, to negotiate with the former as soon as possible. Thus they would have been free to re-establish order—their own order. The newly-proclaimed Republic was of the bourgeoisie, and it was understood that it would remain so. As in 1830 and 1848, the bourgeoisie had triumphed over the working class.

When Paris was besieged on the 19th of September, there emerged a strange antagonism between a people which believed in the possibility of defence and victory, and a government which did not, and which organized a few absurd, bloody sorties as red herrings. This siege has become part of the folklore of Parisian families. When I was a child, my grandmother showed me a piece of 'bread from the Siege' that had been kept as a symbol. Since then, the French have certainly known other suffering, but never has Paris been cut off, as it was then, from all its surrounding territory, without which it is nothing but a desert of stone and asphalt, and reduced to asphyxiation and slow death. Cold, hunger, queues at the doors of shops—my generation has known all that. But in 1871 our grandmothers experienced much worse. An egg cost a franc then. Butter rose

---

* Those who proclaimed a Republic and set up a provisional government, called the Government of National Defence, with reactionaries as its most powerful members.—*Trans.*

from 6, to 20, to 28 francs a pound. In the Faubourg Saint-Germain, a rabbit cost 45 francs, a cat 20, a dog's leg 6 francs a pound. There was no milk for the children. Animals from the Jardin des Plantes appeared at the butchers' under the name of 'fancy meats.' The trees of Paris were cut down, but the green wood smoked and gave off no heat.[1]

From the 19th of January onwards people had to produce rationing-cards to get any bread: 300 grams for adults, 150 for children.[2] Even so it was an indescribable concoction in which straw and paper were to be encountered.

Women suffered more than men: it was they who had to stand in queues for hours at a time, in mud, snow, and cold, trying to feed their families. 'All food became so repugnant that to think of eating brought one almost to despair.'[3] And one did indeed despair seeing children die of hunger and cold, despite the women's efforts. To the tune of the ballad of Fualdès,* they sang:

Not a single shop or store
Has got anything on show,
And whatever way you go,
Knock at each and ev'ry door,
It won't do you any good,
There's not even any wood . . .

A poor mother, so they say,
Out of wood and lacking coal,
In the cold at the bread-dole
Had queued up for a whole day.
In her arms, where he did doze,
Her first son to death was froze. . . .[4]

Nathalie Lemel and her *La Marmite* carried out the difficult job of feeding hundreds of starving people. Louise Michel organized a soup kitchen for her pupils.[5] They were dining well at Brébant.

There was no work. At the ramparts of the town, the National Guard earned 1 fr 50 a day, plus 75 centimes for their wives.

* Fualdès was a magistrate assassinated in 1817; the subsequent trial created a great stir, and formed the basis of a popular ballad.—*Trans.*

This did not go very far when an egg cost a franc. Work, then, had to be given to women. But what work, except making soldiers' equipment? Victorine Brochon wrote:

I signed up at the *Mairie* of the 7th arrondissement, since I was from that district. They gave me a soldier's tunic to make; they were satisfied with it. I was paid 4 francs for my work, but they only gave out three jackets a week to each of us, which was fair, in that more people were kept in work. This gave me 12 francs a week, for four people. However, we managed. Thousands of people did not have that much.[6]

Mme Poirier (Sophie Doctrinal), whose husband was president of the 18th arrondissement Vigilance Committee, ran a workshop where clothing was made, and employed seventy or eighty women. She persuaded the mayor of Montmartre, Georges Clemenceau,* to requisition her further premises at 64 Boulevard Ornano. This attempt was socialistic in inspiration, for the women did not earn a salary, but instead shared in the profits. After the 10th of March, Sophie Poirier, having no more work to give out, changed her workshop into a medical centre.[7] From this it can be seen how difficult it is to clear a logical path (work for women, medical centres, etc.) amid a ceaselessly shifting reality, in which all activities are commingled and in which one encounters the same people under various aspects. It is a characteristic of revolutionary periods that the vitality of circumstances breaks down social functions and categories.

Workshops of this sort were organized in every *mairie*. Work for women was one of the goals of the *Comité des Femmes* on the rue d'Arras, founded by Jules Allix. He was a peculiar fellow, slightly mad, although the organization and goals of his committee do not seem to be at all mad: work, education, social welfare, and rights for women. Jules Allix advocated the establishment of communal workrooms, in which women might find some work and be fed during the length of the Siege. The Education Committee organized meetings to propagandize on

* The same Clemenceau who was to lead France during the last years of World War I.—*Trans.*

behalf of the social Commune. One could sign up for work, for nursing, for first aid, or even for the women's brigade 'being formed on the ramparts.' Moved from 3 rue d'Arras to 14 rue Notre-Dame, where the treasurer, Geneviève Vivien, lived, the Committee seems to have been greatly expanded during the Siege, since it comprised an under-secretariat to each arrondissement, 160 district committees, and more than 1,800 members. Except for André Léo and Elizabeth Dmitrieff, a member of the organizing committee, scarcely any of the women who were in it participated in the Commune. I noticed, in passing, the name of a Juliette Drouet in the 9th arrondissement, without having been able to ascertain whether it was she who was Victor Hugo's sweetheart.[8]

But the women of the bourgeoisie were more frequently found in the *Société de Secours Pour les Victimes de la Guerre*. On an equal social basis, they became much more openly involved than the men of their class; perhaps because they were more naive, and in any case less vulnerable to political wheeling and dealing. 'Those members of the National Defence, who did so little defending, had heroic wives,' acknowledged Louise Michel.[9] The International Convention of Geneva, still quite new, hastily organized the training of nurses; but General Trochu preferred nuns to these suspect laywomen. Victorine Brochon was accepted into the 7th Company of the 17th Battalion of the National Guard. She wrote, 'I was happy, not because of the sorrows that burdened France, but because I believed in the accord of a national feeling of humanity. I thought that the problems and differences of opinion would dissolve in the face of imminent danger.'[10] This illusion quickly disappeared before the absurdity of marches and counter-marches, the incoherence of the defence, and those ill-prepared sorties in which, despite the dedication of the ambulance nurses, many dead men remained upon the battlefield. 'It takes twenty-five years to make a man, and then he is killed. What a stupid role they have God play.'[11]

The snow fell. The artillery shells fell. In this war in which civilians mingled with fighters, in which there was neither front nor rear, and in which everyone found himself equally involved since the enemy was at the gates of the city, bombarding people's houses, it was normal for women to follow their men up to the ramparts, carrying their rifles, accompanying them, with their children, as far as possible. They cheered them on, but they also heaped sarcasms on them when they lost ground, as did those housewives from the Boulevard Ornano who jeered at the deserters from the 32nd Battalion.[12]

The women worked as ambulance nurses and carried food. Constance Boidard, a buttonmaker who had no children to take care of, brought provisions to the 160th Battalion, whose quartermaster-sergeant was her husband.[13] The day-worker Palmyre Thierry (*veuve* Delcambre), brought food to the Montrouge Volunteers, to which her lover belonged.[14] All these women thus served an apprenticeship in the common fight, shoulder to shoulder with their men. But some of them went further, demanding that a women's battalion be formed. André Léo dissuaded them from this: Paris did not lack defenders, and there was no need for a women's battalion.[15]

But the idea was in the air. On the 3rd of October, in *La Liberté*, one Félix Belly had suggested that ten battalions of 'Amazons' be armed. Green posters had been pasted up to help spread the idea:

In answer to the desire that numerous letters have expressed to us, and to the generous dispositions of a great part of the feminine population of Paris, there will be formed successively, in proportion to the resources given us for their organization and equipment, ten battalions of women, without distinction as to social class, who will be called the Amazons of the Seine.

They would, along with the garrison National Guard, be given the task of guarding the ramparts and the barricades, 'bringing the soldiers all the domestic and fraternal services that are compatible with moral order and military discipline,' and giving first aid to the wounded. They would be given small arms, and, like the men, would receive wages of 1 fr 50 per day. And—since at that time people loved colourful uniforms—it was provided that their uniform consist of black trousers with orange bands, a black wool cowled blouse, a black peaked cap trimmed in orange, and a cross-belted ammunition pouch. An enlistment office was opened at 36 rue Turbigo, where the applicants were to appear accompanied by a member of the National Guard, who would answer for their 'morality.' The battalion was to comprise eight companies of one hundred and fifty Amazons each, who would immediately be trained in how to handle a rifle.

To meet the expenses of this organization the 'originator and provisional head of the first battalion' appealed to the generosity of 'ladies of the wealthy classes.' They surely would not hesitate to offer their bracelets, necklaces, and other jewels—of which, in any case, they would be divested if the Prussians entered the city. Thus they would attest to their civic feeling (and their awareness of their own best interest), and would contribute to overturning the barriers that had for too long separated them from the working classes (Félix Belly thought of everything). A ladies' committee would, moreover, function as a 'family council.' A doctor, preferably female, would be attached to each battalion. The arms and weapon manufacturers were invited to submit models of weapons which would be examined by artillery officers. In short, everything was arranged. And, concluded the poster:

Every moment counts. Our women, too, feel that their country and their civilization need all their strength to resist the savage violence of Prussia. They want to share our perils, sustain our spirit, give us the example of fearlessness in the face of death, and thus be worthy of their emancipation and their civic equality. And may the whole of Europe learn with admiration that it was not only thousands of citizens, but also thousands of women, who, in Paris, defended the freedom of the world against a new Barbarian invasion.[16]

Women came to the rue Turbigo to sign up—fifteen hundred of them, Belly claims—but General Trochu put an end to this project: Jeanne Hachettes and Jeanne d'Arcs are all very well —but in the past.[17]

During the Siege, then, women served in the fighting only individually, as ambulance nurses or *cantinières*; but at the same time they were serving their apprenticeship in political life. Vigilance Committees were organized in various quarters; there were two in Montmartre, one for men, the other for women. Louise Michel participated in both at once: 'No one was very much bothered by the sex of those who were doing their duty. That silly problem was over and done with.'[18] The Women's Vigilance Committee of the 18th arrondissement had been set up by Louise Michel, Mme Collet, and Mme Poirier, who, as we know, ran a sewing workshop. 'This committee had the job of allocating work, receiving and distributing contributions, visiting the sick and the poor and caring for them in their homes,' explained Mme Poirier before the Council of War. 'I was given the title of president. Besides,' she added, 'I was better known than the two working-class ladies, and I was known by all those with whom we had to deal for the apportioning and use of relief funds to the sick.'[19] Mme Collet left for England on the 16th of March; Louise Michel, on the other hand, became twice as active. She wrote articles: 'When the country is in peril, we must point out danger wherever it is, and cowardice wherever it lurks. Let us be on our guard. . . . Here, in Paris, we breathe an odour of death. Treason is rampant. If Trochu follows Bazaine's footsteps, we must not let the people sleep. Let us be on our guard. . . .'[20] Often she presided over meetings, keeping discipline by brandishing an old hammerless gun at the 'men of order,' who, armed with bayonets, invaded the hall. At other times, accompanied by a member of the National Guard, she went collecting in the churches. 'I spent the finest hours of the Siege with the Montmartre Vigilance Committee and with the *Club de la Patrie en Danger*. One was a little more fully alive there, with the joy of feeling oneself in one's element, in the midst of the intense struggle for liberty.' The members of the Vigilance Committees went around enlivening the Clubs: 'Every night we would swoop down on Paris, sometimes demolishing a club of slackers, sometimes fanning the Revolution.'[21]

After the 4th of September, when the theatres were closed down, even more people were attracted to the Clubs. These Clubs, in which all opinions met and clashed, were of various leanings. Women brought their children along; there, at least, they were out of the cold, but they also attended out of political conviction, and did not hesitate to intervene in the proceedings. Nathalie Lemel took the floor at the *Club de l'Ecole de Médecine*,[22] Louise Michel, at the *Club de la Patrie en Danger* and elsewhere. Both the defence of Paris and the sending of delegations to the Hôtel de Ville were discussed. Faced with governmental inertia, they demanded mass sorties; faced with disparity in food provisioning, that measures be taken against the shopkeepers. In a hall in the Faubourg Poissonnière, they raised the question of *unions libres*, so prevalent among the working classes. The 'companion' of a National Guardsman should be accorded the same rights as a legitimate wife.[23] They discussed socialism: if men hesitated to form the Commune, it was the women who would show them the way to the Hôtel de Ville.[24] A speaker voiced doubts about the fighting spirit of the workers of Belleville: 'You could not find five hundred men determined to fight for the Commune,' he said. Women stood up: 'We will be the first to go; we will ask them for bread.'[25] Asking for bread is the primordial demand of women. On the 5th and 6th of October, 1789, it was the women who went to Versailles looking for 'the baker and the baker's wife and the baker's little boy.'* And once more, it was around the theme of hunger that women were organized against the Germans and the Vichy government, during the brutal winters of the 1940's. Women's politics begins with the distribution of essential goods, the just administration of things.

Women also participated in street demonstrations. On the 18th of September they took the initiative of a demonstration of sympathy with Strasbourg, which had been beseiged for more

* This alludes to what was something of a hunger march on Versailles by a mob of irate women to demand bread on the 5th of October 1789. On their return to Paris they sang this song; their demands had been met and the royal family had agreed to live in Paris.—*Trans.*

than a month. 'The idea came to some among us—or rather, some women among us, for we women were in the majority— to get weapons and set forth to help Strasbourg defend herself, and to die with her.'[26] Louise Michel and André Léo led a little group that set out for the Hôtel de Ville crying 'To Strasbourg!' Women—many schoolteachers, young people, and especially students—joined them along the way. They stopped before the statue of Strasbourg to attest to their involvement, then set off again for the Hôtel de Ville to demand weapons. To their great surprise, Louise Michel and André Léo were allowed to enter, but it was only to be locked up with two other 'prisoners,' a student and an old woman coming from the grocer's. She had no idea of what had happened to her, and she 'was trembling so much that the oil she had just bought spilled all over her dress.' They let the old woman go, but an officer interrogated André Léo and Louise Michel at great length: 'What can it matter to you if Strasbourg falls, if you are not there?' he concluded.[27] Such was the tone of the defenders of the Republic. The two women were released, thanks to the intervention of a member of the Government who arrived at the Hôtel de Ville.

At the end of November, some women wanted to go to the Hôtel de Ville to propose various means of defence and ask to be recruited. They appealed to Louise Michel and the Montmartre Vigilance Committee to back their mission. Louise Michel went with them, although she was not in agreement with this venture, which she considered 'more courageous than clear-sighted.' 'We went with them as women, in order to share their dangers, not as *citoyennes*,' she explains. Naturally, Louise Michel, who was beginning to be recognized and dreaded, was the one arrested as the instigator. Arguing insolently, she denied any responsibility. She could not organize a demonstration that appealed to a government she no longer recognized; when she came to the Hôtel de Ville on her own behalf, it would be 'with the people in arms.' Finally, Mme Meurice (speaking for the *Société des Femmes Pour les Victimes de la Guerre*), Ferré (in the name of the Clubs), and Victor Hugo intervened for her release.[28]

That day Louise Michel gave rendezvous to the people of
Paris. On the 22nd of January, in the square of the Hôtel de
Ville, that rendezvous was indeed kept. The capitulation that
was gradually being sensed in the provisional government's
ambiguous acts, in the endless hesitations of General Trochu, in
those ill-prepared sorties which, despite the men's courage, all
ended in failure—this capitulation (the word was pronounced
on the 20th of January, after the Buzenval sortie) was not
desired by the people of Paris. They had suffered four months
of hunger and cold and bombardment and misery; they had
buried their dead and not mourned them. These people, said
to be so fickle and inconstant, had borne everything with a
patience, abnegation, and courage that had won them the
admiration of all Europe. They wanted all these sacrifices at
least to have been of some use. Moreover, these intelligent
people did not understand how it was that their forces had
not been concentrated in battle all at once; that they had been
allowed to be nibbled away in little fragments, exhausted in
ludicrous sorties. These intelligent people did understand that
they had been deceived; that the famous Trochu 'plan,' with
which they had been mollified for so long, had never existed;
that the Government of National Defence had never been anything but a lure; and that the strong who rule the earth had,
perhaps, once more cheated them of their due. The replace-
ment of General Trochu by General Vinoy could not restore
their lost confidence. During the night of the 21st of January,
the delegates from the National Guard, the Vigilance Committees, and the Clubs agreed to gather on the 22nd at the
Place de l'Hôtel de Ville to oppose surrender. Those from the
National Guard were urged to arrive armed; women, to go
along to protest against the latest measures of bread-rationing:
people were still willing to put up with rationing, but only if it
were for victory.

An enormous crowd filled the square. A great number of
women were present, among them André Léo, Sophie Poirier,
Béatrix Excoffon, and Louise Michel (who was dressed in a
National Guard uniform). Deputations were received by the

assistant to the mayor, Chaudey, who lost his temper. Outside, people were shouting 'Death to the traitors!' From the windows of the Hôtel de Ville, Breton Mobile Guards fired into the crowd.* 'The bullets made the noise of a summer hailstorm.'[29] The National Guard returned the fire, but some of them said later that they had aimed only at the walls. 'I was not one of them,' wrote Louise Michel. 'So to act would mean eternal defeat, with its piling up of the dead, its long misery—it would even be treason.' But she felt no hatred toward those other men who were merely the helpless instruments of the Government:

Standing before those accursed windows, I could not take my eyes off the pale, savage figures who were firing upon us, emotionlessly, mechanically, as they would have fired upon packs of wolves. And I thought: 'We will have you one day, you scoundrels, for you kill, but you believe. They haven't bought you, they've tricked you. We need people who aren't for sale.' And the stories of my old grandfather passed through my mind, stories of those times when hero against hero, the peasants of Charette, Cathelineau, and La Rochejacquelin fought implacably against the Army of the Republic.[30]

This feeling of respect, of fraternity for the enemy, is rare and noble enough to note in passing. Yet at the same time, Louise Michel was giving herself wholly to battle: 'The first time you defend your cause with weapons, you live the battle so intensely that you are no longer yourself so much as a projectile.' This division into actor and spectator ranks very high on the scale of human values.

* The French Army consisted of conscripted recruits, serving seven years. The annual 'class' of eligible men was actually chosen by a lottery. Those receiving 'bad numbers' served, unless they were rich enough to buy substitutes. The Mobile Guard had been instituted late in the 1860's by Napoléon III's Minister of War, Marshal Niel, to reform and strengthen the National Guard by giving special training to its unmarried members. Although these goals were never fully achieved, the Mobile Guard was separate from, and elected the officers of, the National Guard. In the eyes of the Parisian National Guard, whose men were drawn mostly from working-class districts, the Mobile Guard consisted of the appointees of a deposed tyrant.—Trans.

Some people held the women responsible for the failure of the demonstration. At the *Club de Belleville*, remarks were made that set the room laughing: 'How do you expect to make virile resolutions in the midst of a bunch of women, children, and good-for-nothings who come here to digest their dinner? It is the Clubs that are ruining us. The enemy is immediately informed of our intentions.'[31]

But that was not the Government's opinion. On the contrary: they feared the Clubs' activity and ordered them to be closed down. They outlawed newspapers and sent out warrants for the arrest of the demonstrators, who were called 'foreign partisans.' After this, the Government had its hands free to sign the armistice. On the 28th of January, four hundred thousand armed men surrendered to two hundred thousand. It was easier to reach an understanding with the Prussians—men of order— than with the workers in Belleville. On the 29th of January the German flag was flying over the strongholds.

Now it was a question of electing an assembly. The provinces sent to Bordeaux all the ghosts of the *ancien régime*, the heirs of the Restoration, the opportunist politicians of the Second Empire, petty squires exhumed from their country seats— everyone who was as narrow, as out of date, as clerical, as rancid as could possibly be found; everyone who was ready to unite against that city, Paris, perennially disposed to rouse its rabble in the name of any imaginable sort of justice, liberty, or right. This *introuvable* assembly* found its leader, its symbol, and its style in Monsieur Thiers.

On the 26th of February the peace preliminaries were signed. France had to pay 5 billion francs and hand over the whole of Alsace, save Belfort, and a part of Lorraine, to the Germans. Paris felt, not vanquished, but betrayed. On the Place de la Bastille, where in former days the people had not left a single stone of the prison standing, the battalions of the Mobile Guard marched in parade. From time to time, a man would

* An allusion to the *Chambre Introuvable*, elected in 1815; Louis XVIII gave it this nickname because of his gratified amazement that such a pro-Royalist group could have been gathered.—*Trans.*

harangue the crowd, and women dressed in black would hang a tricoloured flag from the column: 'To the martyrs, from the women of the Republic.'[32]

The Assembly 'of Notables,' for its part, took the most reactionary measures possible: bills of commerce that had fallen due between the 13th of August and the 13th of November 1870, were immediately payable, the moratorium on rent payments and the National Guard's pay were cancelled. In Paris, where commerce and industry had been paralysed by the Siege, where famine was rampant, this meant that many people were rendered destitute.

But rumour had it that the German army was going to enter Paris. One thing, at least, that the Prussians would not have was the cannons. The Parisians considered these their property; they had paid for them by the subscriptions—from 10 centimes up—of the common people. Women and children went up the Faubourg Saint-Honoré toward the Parc Monceau. The guards opened the gates and 'these people whom a flick of the finger would have knocked over'[33] took away the cannons. On the 26th of February a singing crowd, an entire population—National Guardsmen, women, children, all together—triumphantly brought the cannons from the *beaux quartiers* back to Montmartre, Belleville, La Villette, and Les Buttes-Chaumont.[34]

On the 1st of March, the Germans entered a Paris in darkness, gloomy and deserted; they left again on the 2nd, and camped in the outlying districts.

4

THE EIGHTEENTH OF MARCH

IT WOULD NO DOUBT be an exaggeration to say that this day of revolution was the work of women. But they contributed a great deal, at least to the first part: the neutralization of the troops.

Matters had to be brought to an issue. At the order of Thiers, the army had entered Paris during the night. It had occupied the strategic points, and had effortlessly laid hold of the cannons at Les Batignolles. On Montmartre, a post of the 61st Battalion of the National Guard stood watch in the rue des Rosiers. Louise Michel had come there to deliver a message, when the National Guardsman Turpin was wounded by a bullet, in rather suspect circumstances. Louise Michel and a *cantinière* gave him first aid.[1]

The army had encountered no resistance, and it seemed that the whole business would quickly be taken care of. But General Vinoy had forgotten that, in order to move cannons, one has to have horses. He had forgotten the horses: a minor detail. The cannons from La Butte would have to be brought down by man-power.

During this time Montmartre had awakened. The housewives, who were going out to get their bread and milk, began to flock together and spread the news. Inquisitive groups formed about the soldiers. Around seven o'clock, the mayor of Montmartre, Clemenceau, climbed to the top of La Butte and asked to have the wounded man taken to hospital. General Lecomte refused. He strictly forbade 'the promenade of this corpse.' A military doctor was attending to the man.[2]

But the alarm had been given. The tocsin was ringing out from the churches of Paris. 'I went down, my rifle under my coat, crying "Treason," ' wrote Louise Michel. 'A column was

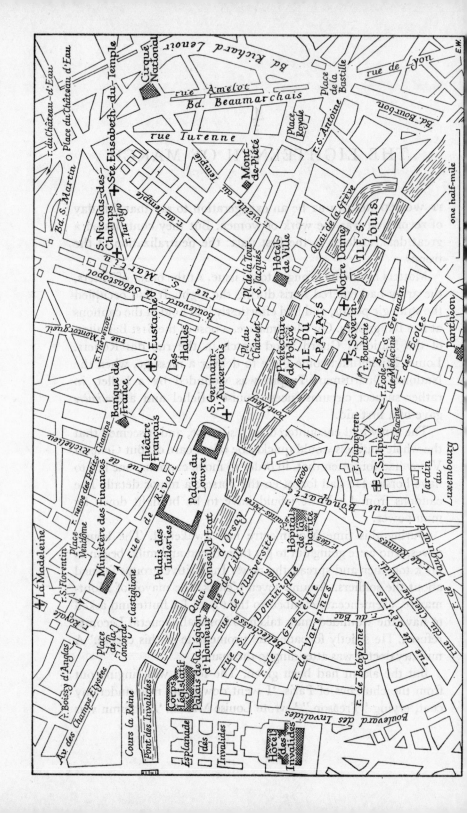

forming. The whole Vigilance Committee was there: Ferré, old Moreau, and the rest. . . . Montmartre was waking. The call to arms was sounding out. I was returning, indeed, but with others, to the attack on the heights of Montmartre; we ran up at the double, knowing that at the top there was an army in battle formation. We expected to die for liberty. It was as if we were lifted from the earth. . . .'³ And, since Louise Michel was gifted with the sensibility of poets for whom sky, sun, and night are in constant attendance upon the actions of men, she adds: 'La Butte was enveloped in white light, a splendid dawn of deliverance.' Suddenly, she saw her mother beside her—her mother, the old servant Marianne Michel whom she had never ceased, nor would cease, to love with utter tenderness: 'I felt an appalling anguish. Worried for us, she had come. All woman-kind was at our side, I don't know how.'⁴

The groups of housewives with their children—merely curious or bantering at first—had swelled and become threaten-ing. Now, between the soldiers of the 88th Battalion and the National Guard, they formed a 'veritable human barricade.'⁵ General Lecomte gave the order to fire. At this the women spoke to the soldiers: 'Will you fire upon us? On your brothers? Our husbands? Our children?'⁶ The statement of General d'Aurelles de Paladine on this subject is very significant:

The women and children came and mixed with the troops. We were greatly mistaken in permitting these people to approach our soldiers, for they mingled among them, and the women and children told them: 'You will not fire upon the people.' This is how the soldiers of the 88th, as far as I can see, and of another line regiment found them-selves surrounded and did not have the power to resist these ovations that were given them. People were shouting, 'Long live the line!'⁷

Faced with this unexpected intervention, the soldiers hesitated. A warrant officer stood in front of his company and shouted: 'Mutiny!'⁸ Thereupon the 88th Battalion fraternized with the crowd. The soldiers arrested their general.

Crowds of women had assembled in the rue Houdon. General Susbielle gave the order to charge. But, intimidated by the

46 THE WOMEN INCENDIARIES

women's cries, the cavalry 'backed up their horses,' which made people laugh.[9] Everywhere—in the Place Blanche, Place Pigalle, in Belleville, at the Bastille, at Le Château-d'Eau, and in the Luxembourg Gardens—the crowd, mostly composed of women, surrounded the soldiers, stopped the horses, cut the harnesses, forced the 'bewildered' soldiers to fraternize with their 'brothers' in the National Guard.

Disconcerted by this strange, this scandalous, victory of the people, General Vinoy ordered his troops to withdraw to the Champ-de-Mars. The field was left to the women. They had nothing to do but to go back home and get the dinner ready—which, for the most part, they did.

At the moment when, in the rue des Rosiers, they shot both General Lecomte, who that morning had given the order to fire into the crowd, and General Clément Thomas, who remained in the eyes of the Parisian people the slaughterer of the insurgents of June 1848, the housewives of that morning had disappeared from the scene. But other women had appeared, mingling with the crowd, which was escorting and insulting the prisoners.

Prostitutes, registered or not, came from the quarter of Les Martyrs, or out of hotels, cafés, and the brothels that were then so numerous along the old *boulevards extérieurs*. On the arms of line soldiers, accompanied by a legion of pimps, they had surged out, the pathetic spume of prostitution upon the revolutionary wave. There they were: getting drunk at all the bars, howling their beggarly joy over this defeat of an authority that, for them, was characterized by the prefecture of police and its spies. It was they, plus a few poor women demoralized by the deleterious effects of poverty, who, at the corner of the rue Joudon, cut up the still-warm flesh of the horse of an officer killed a few moments earlier. It was they who dragged the infantrymen along, hurling themselves upon the prisoners, uttering threats of death.[10]

This document is by neither Maxime du Camp, nor Jules Claretie, nor Dumas *fils*, but by a supporter of the Commune, Gaston da Costa, who was an assistant to the Public Prosecutor of the Commune and was condemned to death by the Council of War. This account does not deny the violence or the excesses inherent in every revolution, but it does give an explanation for them. For da Costa, the women who that morning had placed themselves and their children between the troops and the National Guard were not the same ones whose insults, that evening, escorted the two arrested generals. But 'this is not to say that the former cannot also suddenly become desperate Furies,' he adds.[11]

The harpies, with their screaming, yells and violence, had attracted the attention of the Commune's enemies, who had indeed seen only these women; meanwhile, the supporters of the Commune noticed only 'honest women of the people, and heroic *citoyennes*.' Often the two were the same. Both, in any case, fought side by side, and knew how to die with equal courage upon the barricades.

It is necessary, then, to introduce nuances into a subject which has few of them (Manicheism is the characteristic of revolutionary periods), and try to relate the behaviour of the masses to the only true reality: the quasi-biological facts about the individuals of whom the masses were composed; at least to the extent that it is possible to understand and explain them.

It was again women and children who, on the 19th of March, tried to wrest General Chanzy away from the escort that had taken him prisoner. In their eyes, every general was a traitor deserving immediate execution.[12]

Ten days later, when the Commune, elected on the 26th of March, moved into the Hôtel de Ville, a crowd that included many women joyously welcomed the new power—the power of the people, and of hope.[13]

This hope took an immediate concrete form in measures that were very simple, but went straight to the heart of the poor people made even poorer by war and siege: the remission of the quarter-day settlements of October 1870 and of January and April 1871; and the suspension of the sale of articles deposited at the Mont-de-Piété.

But the government, which had taken refuge in Versailles, could not tolerate that other power which was holding its own

in Paris. On the 2nd of April, Versailles attacked Courbevoie.
Hearing the cannons anew, Paris awakened from its dream.
Ever since the Commune had been established, they had been
living in an atmosphere of fervour, confidence, and hope. Was
a new siege beginning? The barricades went up again. The
cannons were dragged up on to the ramparts.[14] The women on
the boulevards formed the chorus of a Greek tragedy; their
cheers inspired the National Guard, who were going to the
outposts; their invective was heaped upon the idlers who stood
around and watched them go by.[15]

And the women decided to lead an action of their own. An
appeal to women was launched in several newspapers:

Let's go to Versailles. Let's tell Versailles what the Revolution of
Paris is. Let's tell Versailles that Paris has formed the Commune
because we want to stay free. Let's tell Versailles that Paris has made
ready to defend herself, because she has been slandered, because she
has been betrayed, because people tried to take her by surprise and
disarm her. Let's tell Versailles that the Assembly is not the law:
Paris is. Let's tell Versailles that the government has to answer for
our brothers' blood, and that we hold them responsible, before the
whole of France, for our bereavement. *Citoyennes*, women, let's go to
Versailles, so that Paris shall have made the last attempt at reconciliation. There can be no delay. Let us meet this very day at noon
on the Place de la Concorde, and make this important resolution
before the statue of Strasbourg.

The signature—'*Une Véritable Citoyenne*'—was anonymous.[16]

But let us listen to Béatrix Excoffon, whom we have already
encountered at the Place de l'Hôtel de Ville, and whom we
shall meet again on several occasions. Béatrix Excoffon was
born in Cherbourg on the 10th of July 1849. She was the
daughter of a watchmaker, Ange Euvrie, who had been arrested
for having opposed the 2nd of December *coup d'état*. Although
he was released, young recruits were forbidden to enter his
shop for a period of nine years.[17] (The ruling powers bear
grudges.) Béatrix was a nice young girl who had been living
for more than four years with a printer's compositor, François
Excoffon, by whom she had had two children. She bore his

name, although they were not married. We have seen that
unions libres—whether due to negligence, or distrust of bourgeois
law, or anticlericalism—were very frequent among the working
class.

On the 1st of April (Béatrix Excoffon was mistaken here about the
date: it was the 3rd that she was speaking of) a woman from my
neighbourhood, surprised to see me, asked me whether I had read
the newspaper announcement of a women's meeting on the Place de
la Concorde. They wanted to go to Versailles to stop the bloodshed.
I told my mother that I was leaving, I kissed my children, and off I
went. At the Place de la Concorde, at half-past one, I joined the
procession. There were between seven hundred and eight hundred
women. Some talked about explaining to Versailles what Paris
wanted; others talked about how things were a hundred years ago,
when the women of Paris had already gone to Versailles to carry off
the baker and the baker's wife and the baker's little boy, as they said
then.

These reminiscences of the Revolution of 1789 reappeared
everywhere during the brief reign of the 1871 Commune, even
to the use of the Republican calendar—just as the revolutionaries of 1789 had often draped themselves in the trappings of
the Roman Republic.

At the gates of Versailles, the women ran into freemason
parliamentarians, who, for their part, had seen their offers of
mediation refused. Worn out by the march, the *citoyenne* who
led Béatrix Excoffon's group suggested that they regather at the
Salle Ragache. Béatrix Excoffon was designated to replace her.
'They made me get up on a billiard-table and I said what I
thought: that although there were not enough of us to go to
Versailles, there were enough to go and tend the injured in the
Commune's marching companies.'[18] But like Fabrizio on the
battlefield at Waterloo, Béatrix Excoffon saw only one aspect
of these demonstrations. Even today, with newspapers and
memoirs, it is hard enough to reconstruct their chronology.
Other groups of women were stopped at the fortifications by the
National Guard, who dissuaded them from going farther for
fear that they would be gunned down.[19]

On the 4th of April, the demonstrations continued. A delegation of women dressed in mourning announced at the Hôtel de
Ville that 10,000 (*sic*) Parisian women were preparing to march
upon Versailles. Around three o'clock, some twenty women in
the Boulevard Richard-Lenoir railed against the men 'who
would rather hide than go and fight against Versailles.' They
said that 700 *citoyennes* had just left the Place de la Concorde,
with red flag unfurled, 'to march in the lead before the
men.'[20]

Around half-past three, a column of women carrying the
red flag did, in fact, leave from the Place de la Concorde, and
headed for Le Point-du-Jour. These were women of the people,
'very neatly dressed;' some of them even wore black silk dresses
and hats. Their bodices were adorned with red rosettes (the
Council of War was to consider red among one's clothing a
proof of allegiance to the Commune). About fifty street-urchins,
singing *Le Chant du Départ*,* went ahead of them. They declared
that 'they were going to Versailles to call upon the Government
to stop sending bombs down on Paris,' and they unsuccessfully
invited the women along the way to join them. But here once
again, the National Guard blocked their passage.[21] Around
seven o'clock that evening, a woman was haranguing the
crowd in the Place de la Bastille: 'The bloodshed has to
be stopped.' She gave rendezvous to all women for the 6th
of April.[22]

On the 5th, the watchwords—if watchwords there were, the
initiatives, in any case—became entirely contradictory. At the
Bastille, at Le Château-d'Eau, and at the Place de la Concorde,
the women declared that they had given up the project of going
to make the Versailles government listen to reason. It was
decided that all the women, no matter what their class, would
mingle among the National Guardsmen, thus avoiding bloodshed.[23] A utopian plan, some thought, for the presence of
women had certainly not hindered the shooting on the 2nd of
December.

---

* A famous patriotic song dating from the 1789 Revolution, written by
André Chenier's brother, Marie-Joseph.—*Trans.*

In front of the Hôtel de Ville, a girl suggested to the Fédérés*
that the wives of policemen living in Paris march in front of
them, so that the Versailles soldiers would hold their fire.
'Bareheaded, with beautiful blonde hair, and an intelligent and
dedicated face, she made a great impression on everyone around
her', said a bourgeois woman, Mme Blanchecotte, who was
passing by and whose sympathies were surely not directed
toward the Commune.[24] Another woman, 'also blonde, decently
dressed, serious and distinguished,' called, in her turn, for
resistance.[25]

From all these initiatives, one may conclude that on the 3rd,
4th, and 5th of April, the women were making an effort 'to do
something' to avoid the bloody clash between Versailles and
Paris. But these outbursts seemed neither organized nor coherent. They were divided among various currents, from conciliation to resistance.

On the 6th of April, in Jules Vallès, newspaper (*Le Cri du
Peuple*), a *citoyenne* (who may have been a *citoyen*) appealed for
calm. 'We have been to Versailles. We wanted to avoid bloodshed. In the name of the women of Paris, we bore our recent
mourning for our fathers, husbands, and children to Versailles.
We were not able to carry out our task of reconciliation and
humanity. The government has attacked Paris. Blood has been
spilled.'[26] What should women do from now on? Disband their
ranks, and stay 'calm and collected.' 'We have no politicking to
do, we are human and that is all. Since we cannot prevent
bloodshed, our primary mission is ended.' Thus, women were
to go back to their homes or, at the most, organize medical
stations. Any other initiative would hinder the military movements and the execution of the Commune's orders. And finally

* The Fédérés were the members of the 215 battalions, out of some 270,
who formed the Republican Federation of the National Guard on the 3rd
of March 1871. In the main, the members were from the working class or
lower-middle class; in opposing the Versailles government they were interested in preserving the Republic, and the autonomy both of Paris and of
the National Guard. Even today there is an annual May Day procession by
labour organizations to the *Mur des Fédérés* in the Père-Lachaise cemetery,
where the last remnants of the Commune died fighting.—*Trans.*

—an odd argument, which makes me think the passage was drafted by a man, or upon his advice—'Any inopportune step on our part would cast a slur on our men's dignity.' The women's attempt at action was sure to live on as a protest against the Versailles government, whom they held responsible for the blood that had flowed, and as an act of faith in the Commune, that 'honest, simple government,' made for all, which through liberty and work would bring 'a little comfort into every sort of poverty.' So let the women disperse, crying 'Long live the Republic! Long live the Commune!' and leave the men to take care of their own business. This document, worthy of the good Chrysale,* is signed *'Une Vraie Citoyenne.'*

But the women hardly seemed inclined to go back to their homes. Moreover, any popular government presupposes the participation and mobilization of the masses. The Commune had decided to hold national obsequies for the first men who died fighting in the defence of the Revolution. Courbet probably did not become involved in making the arrangements, as David had done earlier for the ceremonies of the other Revolution; nonetheless, the burials could not have been conducted with more ceremony. On the 6th of April, at two in the afternoon, a crowd gathered at the Beaujon hospital, where the victims' bodies were displayed. The wives and mothers, 'like Spartan women,' Lissagaray tells us, uttered 'cries of fury and vows of vengeance.' Then the three biers, draped in black cloth and red flags, and drawn by eight horses, moved slowly toward Père-Lachaise. At the head of the procession came the buglers, the muffled drums, the Vengeurs de Paris, and then the members of the Commune. Behind them, the dead men's wives and the ambulance nurses wore Geneva armbands and the red scarf of the Commune. All along the boulevards, 'the Sacred Way of the Revolution,' were thousands of sobbing women. There were two hundred thousand people at the Bastille. 'The men of Versailles can no longer say that we are a handful of malcontents.' And when they parted beside the graves, it was to the cries of 'Long live the Republic! Long live the Commune!'[27]

* See note on p. 13.

On the 9th of April, the guillotine was burned at the foot of the statue of Voltaire—the 'defender of Sirven and Calas.' The Commune wanted to show thereby that a new world had begun, one from which the death penalty was to be excluded, and in which justice would reign. Here again, at this symbolic ceremony, women were present.[28]

Any political system which demands the consensus of the masses and at the same time serves as the expression of the masses, must appeal to popular sentiment and organize a following. Religions, like political movements, need collective demonstrations. Women, who are more emotional than men, are doubtless even more susceptible to this communal appeal.

But the women also had good reasons for supporting the new regime. To be sure, the goals of the Commune, set forth in a Declaration to the French People, took no account of women's existence.[29] The men of the Commune did not foresee for a single instant that women might have civic rights, any more than did their 'great forebears' of 1789 and 1793, or the revolutionaries of 1848. But certain measures, like the remission of rent payments or the discontinuation of the sale of articles deposited at the Mont-de-Piété, affected women directly.* A decree of the 10th of April affected them even further. A pension of 600 francs was to be granted to the wife, legal or not, of any member of the National Guard who had been killed defending the people's rights, after an inquiry that would establish her rights and needs. Each of her children, legitimate or not, could collect a pension of 365 francs until he was eighteen. Orphans would receive the education necessary 'to make their own way in society,' at the expenses of the Commune.[30]

* The Commune decreed that any rent payments made during the Siege of Paris were to be deducted from future payments, that any tenant could cancel his lease during the next six months, and that he could not be evicted for the next three months. They also decreed that pledges left at pawnshops could not be sold until further decrees established regulations for dealing with these articles, especially tools—the loss of which would hinder a worker in finding new work.—*Trans.*

This was an implicit recognition of the structure of the working-class family, as it really existed, outside the context of
religious and bourgeois laws: the recognition of *unions libres*; of
the right of children, legitimate or natural, to subsistence, and
the disappearance of the old *macula bastardiae* of Roman Law,
the Church, and the Civil Code. In this, the Commune, which
never interfered with the Banque de France and did not venture
to make any inroads into private property, undoubtedly took
one of the most revolutionary steps of its brief reign. That this
measure outraged the bourgeoisie, and that it was received with
jubilation by the members of the Commune are indications of
its significance. Arthur Arnould, a member of the Commune
writes:

This decree, which raises woman to the level of man, which puts her,
in the eyes of morals and the law, on a footing of civic equality with
man, placed itself upon the plane of living morality, and delivered a
mortal blow to the religio-monarchical institution of marriage as we
see it functioning in modern society. It was an act of justice as well,
for it is time to have done with that iniquitous prejudice, that legal
barbarism, which—in what today is called concubinage, as opposed
to legal marriage—strikes only at the weak: the seduced woman and
the innocent child.

And defining the moral nature of *union libre*, he adds, 'The
union of man and woman must be a fundamentally free act
performed by two responsible people. In this union, moral
rights as well as duties must be reciprocal and equal. When a
man becomes a woman's lover and gives her a child, that woman
is his wife, those children are his children.' The society that did
not condemn the man had no right to condemn the woman, still
less the children. But this decree included a qualifying statement: in every arrondissement, a jury headed by a member of
the Commune was to ascertain that the illegitimate wife was
not an 'occasional prostitute.'[31] Another decree provided that
an alimony be granted any married woman who asked for legal
separation from her husband.

But the Commune could not hope to legislate for the future

if it did not first defend its own existence. After the attempts at conciliation, the illusions were shattered. The Commune had to fight. On the 11th of April, some *citoyennes* flung out a violent call to battle, in pure 1792 style.[32] 'Paris is being blockaded. Paris is being bombarded. *Citoyennes*, where are our children and our brothers and our husbands? . . . Do you hear the roaring cannon, the tocsin ringing out the sacred call? To arms! The *Patrie* is in danger!' Were these foreigners who were coming to attack Paris, threatening those triumphs called 'liberty, equality, and fraternity'? 'No, these enemies, these murderers of the people and of liberty, are Frenchmen.' And the women explained the meaning of the struggle: 'This is the final act in the eternal antagonism between right and might, between work and exploitation, between the people and the people's oppressors.' For what the Commune wanted was the end of man's exploitation of man. 'No more exploiters, no more masters; work and well-being for all; government of the people by the people.' And they recalled the noble watchword of the proletarian struggles: 'To live free, working, or to die fighting.' For fear of having to account for itself one day before the court of the people, the Versailles government had not shrunk from the greatest crime of all: civil war.

Citoyennes of Paris, descendants of the women of the Great Revolution, the women who, in the name of the people and justice, marched upon Versailles and carried Louis XVI off as a captive—we, the mothers, wives, and sisters of the French people, will we go on allowing poverty and ignorance to make enemies of our children? Allowing them to kill each other—father against son, brother against brother—under our very eyes, for the whim of our oppressors, who want Paris handed over to foreigners and annihilated?

The cause of Paris was the cause of all Europe, and the Commune's revolution had a universal importance. Germany was trembling in the wind of revolution; Russia was seeing the defenders of liberty perish, but another generation was arising in its turn, 'ready to fight and die for the Republic and for social change.' Ireland and Poland, Spain and Italy, were recovering their strength to join in the international struggle of the people. England was feeling the effects of a revolutionary movement; Austria was obliged to crush the revolts of the Slavic population that she held in bondage. '*Citoyennes*, the gauntlet is down. We must win, or die.' Those who said, 'What do I care about the triumph of our cause, if I must lose my loved ones?' had to realize that the only means of saving those they loved was to fight, for this fight could finish only in the victory of the people. Besides, as far as their husbands and brothers were concerned, their lives were already at stake; it was the children who would pay for their defeat; for 'neither we nor our enemies will hear of mercy.' Let the women prepare, then, to defend and avenge their brothers: 'And if we have neither rifles nor bayonets, there will still be paving stones to crush the traitors with.'

This passage, clearly expressing the ideas of the International about the class struggle, was signed by 'a group of *citoyennes*.' It was the first official act of the *Union des Femmes Pour la Défense de Paris et les Soins aux Blessés*. An announcement followed: all women were urged to attend a meeting on the 11th of April, at 8 p.m., at the Salle Larched, Grand Café des Nations, 74 rue du Temple, there to constitute arrondissement committees. Summing up the appeal, the announcement addressed itself to *citoyennes* 'who know that the present social order bears within itself the seeds of poverty and of the death of all liberty and justice . . . who welcome the rule of work and equality, and who are ready to die for the triumph of the Revolution.'

Following this meeting on the 11th of April, the Central Committee of the *Union des Femmes* was provisionally appointed. With no time wasted, Elizabeth Dmitrieff and seven women workers—Adélaîde Valentin, Noémie Colleville, Marquant, Sophie Graix, Joséphine Prat, Céline and Aimée Delvainquier —told the Executive Commission of the Commune: 'At this hour, when danger is imminent and the enemy is at the gates of Paris, the entire population must unite to defend the Commune,' which stood for 'the annihilation of all privilege and all inequality,' and which was to take account of all just demands,

without distinction as to sex. This distinction had been maintained by the 'necessities of the antagonism upon which the
privilege of the governing classes had rested.' Social reform,
which was to ensure 'the rule of work and of justice,' thus
possessed an equal importance for all citizens, male and female.
Consequently, a great number of women had resolved that 'in
the event that the enemy should come through the gates of
Paris,' they 'would fight, and win, or else die for the defence of
our common rights.' But this organization could succeed only if
the Commune backed its action. It therefore requested that the
Commune give it a hall in every *mairie* in which its committees
could establish centres permanently open to the public, and
that it take on the printing costs of the circulars and posters that
were needed for publicity. There had to be collaboration
between the *Union des Femmes* and all the official organisms of
the Commune: 'The government commission would need only
to turn to the Central Committee of *citoyennes*, in order to have
the necessary number of women ready to serve in the medical
centres or, if need be, at the barricades.'[33]

But the revolutionary current that the *Union* stood for was far
from expressing all the leanings of the women of Paris, even
among those who had rallied around the Commune. Actually,
the women were as much divided by their social origin as were
the men. On the 3rd of May, a poster pasted up in the streets
demanded peace in the name of 'a group of *citoyennes*.' 'The
women of Paris, in the name of the Nation, in the name of
honour, in the name of humanity itself, ask for an armistice.'
They believed that the courage and resignation they had displayed that winter during the Siege gave them the right to be
listened to by the various parties, and they hoped that 'their
capacity as wives and mothers will soften hearts in Paris, as well
as in Versailles.' This vocabulary is obviously vastly different
from that of the militant women of the International. Tired of
suffering, terrified by the unheroic misfortunes that threatened
them, they appealed to the generosity of Versailles and Paris,
begging both sides to lay down their arms and to try to find a
peaceful solution. All women, they said—those who feared for

their children's lives, those whose husbands were fighting either from conviction or to 'earn their daily bread at the ramparts,' the calmest women and the most 'exalted'—all demanded peace.[34]

This was by no means the opinion of the *Union des Femmes* which, on the 6th of May, replied with an indignant manifesto:

In the name of the Social Revolution that we acclaim, in the name of the demand for working rights, for equality, and for justice, the *Union des Femmes Pour la Défense de Paris et les Soins aux Blessés* protests with all its might against the shameful proclamation to the *citoyennes* which appeared the day before yesterday, and which issued from an anonymous group of reactionaries. . . .

How could anyone appeal to the generosity of Versailles, the generosity of 'villainous murderers'? There was no possible conciliation 'between liberty and despotism, between the People and its oppressors.' Conciliation would be treason, the negation of all the hopes of the working class—hopes for total social reform, abolition of all privilege, the substitution of the rule of work for the rule of capital, the worker's liberation by the worker. This struggle could end only in the victory of the people, and Paris ought not to flinch from it, for

it bears the banner of the future. . . . United and resolute, ennobled and enlightened by the suffering that social crisis always draws in its wake, profoundly convinced that the Commune, representing the international and revolutionary principles of the people, carries in itself the seeds of social revolution, the Women of Paris will prove to France and to the world that they too, at the moment of supreme danger—at the barricades and at the ramparts of Paris, if the reactionary powers should force her gates—they too know how, like their brothers, to give their blood and their life for the defence and the triumph of the Commune, that is, the People. And then victorious, at one in uniting and agreeing upon their common interests, working men and working women, in full solidarity, with an ultimate effort, will annihilate forever every vestige of exploitation and exploiters. Long live the social and universal Republic! Long live Labour! Long live the Commune![35]

5

THE *UNION DES FEMMES*

THE UNION DES FEMMES *Pour la Défense de Paris et les Soins aux Blessés* was in fact the women's section of the French International. Its contemporaries[1] were not unaware of its affiliation and its importance, both of which were made much of during the parliamentary inquiry into the 18th of March insurrection. Barral de Montaud did not hesitate to attribute to the *Union* every initiative taken by women during the Commune[2]—no doubt an exaggeration.

The *Union des Femmes* was organized—we do not know when —by a friend of Karl Marx, Elizabeth Dmitrieff, who was already helping to administer the *Comité des Femmes* created by Jules Allix. She was a strange person, whose importance would never have been suspected from the almost empty dossier the Council of War kept on her[3]—which indicates the extent of the negligence with which these military men conducted the inquiry. 'It has not been possible to ascertain what the Dmitrieff woman was doing before the 18th of March,' we read there. They would have had only to refer to one document—also preserved in the War Archives[4]—to see that she had already participated in the *Comité des Femmes*. Not one witness was called. As far as the officers of the Council of War were concerned, Elizabeth Dmitrieff, born somewhere in Russia, came out of the blue on the 18th of March. They recall only her elegance, comparable to that of Théroigne de Méricourt:* she always wore a riding habit, a felt hat trimmed with red feathers, and a silk scarf of the same colour fringed with gold, which 'crossed her bodice from right to left,' as the insignia of her rank. For the rest, there are a few copies of articles under her name, and a

* A heroine of the 1789 Revolution who ran a *salon* and later helped to storm the Bastille; she was nicknamed 'the Amazon of Liberty.'—*Trans.*

certificate of citizenship taken out in the name of the *citoyen* Henri Colleville—not much to go on.

Today, however, we are much better informed. The young woman known in Paris during the Commune as Elizabeth Dmitrieff was born in 1851, in the province of Pskov. She was the daughter of a former hussar officer, Louka Kouchelev, and a young nurse, Nathalie Troskevitch. In his will, her father acknowledged her only as his 'ward.' Like Louise Michel, Elizabeth Dmitrieff was of irregular birth. This common origin may have predisposed them to a keener resentment of social injustice. But the harshness with which the former officer treated his serfs was, perhaps, also not without influence on his daughter's revolt. However that may be, Elizabeth received an excellent education and, as was customary in the higher ranks of Russian society, learned several languages. In her father's library at Saint Petersburg she found works in French, German, English, and Italian, and read them avidly, as she did the most modern Russian periodicals to which her mother subscribed. These were the years of the sixties, when the young Russian intelligentsia was 'going out to the people' and passionately discussing 'new ideas'; the emancipation of the serfs and of women, the reform of education and of justice, the theories of art for art and art for society, materialism and spiritualism, the value of science, and many other questions—we find them echoed in the works of Dostoyevsky. Besides Tolstoy, Turgenev, and Dostoyevsky, who were at the height of their talents, a new, more 'radical' type of writer was appearing: the poet Nekrasov, the dramatist Ostrovsky, the critic Dobroliubov, and especially the philosopher Chernyshevsky, who was then in Siberia paying for the boldness of his social ideas. In Saint Petersburg, Elizabeth participated in all these discussions. But in Russia, as in France, women were forbidden to study in the universities. Thus Elizabeth decided to leave Russia and, like many girls of the Russian intelligentsia, study in Switzerland. To that end, she agreed to a *mariage blanc* with Colonel Tomanovsky; he was much older than she, and tubercular, but he was in favour of women's emancipation. This model husband thus gave her a social position, a rank among the nobility, and freedom. In Geneva, Elizabeth met a group of young Russian revolutionaries, who gave their allegiance to the First International. She was the person whom they selected to go to London to contact Karl Marx. 'Dear citizen,' they wrote to him, 'allow us to present to you our best friend, Elizabeth Tomanovskaya, who is sincerely and profoundly devoted to the revolutionary cause of Russia. We should be happy if, through her, we might know you better, and if, at the same time, we could acquaint you in more detail with the circumstances of our activity, of which she will be able to speak to you extensively. . . .' Elizabeth arrived in London during the summer of 1870. She rapidly formed a friendship with Karl Marx and his daughters. In a letter (the 7th of January 1871) to Karl Marx, she wrote: 'I thank you for your kindness and for the interest you show in my health. Naturally, I do not want to take up your time, but if you had a few free hours on Sunday night, I am convinced that your daughters would be as happy as I to see you at our house.' At the same time, she informed him about the agrarian situation in Russia:

Regarding the alternative that you foresee in the problem of how communal property will fare in Russia, unfortunately it is very probable that it will be transformed into small individual properties. I venture to send you a copy of the *Narodnoye Dielo* (*The Cause of the People*), in which this problem is examined. Certainly you know the study by Hoksthausen, which appeared in 1847, describing the communal system in Russia. If by any chance you do not have it, let me know; I own a copy and could send it to you immediately. In the articles on landed property which you are reading at present, you will see that Chernyshevsky mentions it often, and quotes passages from it. . . .

This is a valuable letter, indicating not only the friendly nature of the relations between Elizabeth and Marx, but also their intellectual affinities. This very young woman—twenty years old—showed herself to be perfectly aware of Russian social problems, and gave relevant information to the man who was already considered, along with Mikhail Bakunin, the leader of the international revolutionary movement. Karl Marx was deeply impressed by the personality of Elizabeth Tomanovskaya: it was she whom in 1871 he entrusted with a mission to Paris, doubtless a mission of inquiry, but also one of organization; for we meet her again leading the *Union des Femmes Pour la Défense de Paris et les Soins aux Blessés*.[5]

Under her stimulus, the *Union des Femmes* was formed on the 11th of April. From then on meetings were held regularly in different quarters of Paris. On the 13th of April, the second meeting took place in the *mairie* of the 3rd arrondissement, in the rue du Temple; the third, in the *mairie* of the 4th arrondissement;[6] and so forth. In the *Union*, there were several women who had belonged to Jules Allix's group. But it is impossible to compare the social origin of the supporters of these two associations, for only in the second case, and then incompletely, do we know their professions. André Léo, who belonged to a committee of the former, did not figure in the second group. Nathalie Lemel's case was the opposite. In the 11th arrondissement, ten members of the committee of Jules Allix went over to Elizabeth Dmitrieff's union; six went over in the 8th arrondissement, five in the 17th, four in the 5th, six in the 7th. But these were exceptions. Elizabeth Dmitrieff was recruiting women who were new to militancy, and who came from a distinctly proletarian background. In the 13th arrondissement, for example, we find one maker-up of men's clothing, one linen-draper, three seamstresses, two bootstitchers, and one woman whose profession is not indicated. In the 16th arrondissement, there are one maker-up, four seamstresses, one linen-draper, and one bookstitcher. Out of 128 members, we know the professions of 60. All women's trades are represented there: fifteen seamstresses, nine waistcoat-makers, six sewing-machine operators, five dress-makers, five linen-drapers, three makers-up of men's clothing, two bootstitchers, two hat-makers, two laundresses, two cardboard-makers, one embroiderer of military decorations, one braid-maker, one tie-maker, one schoolteacher, one perfume-maker, one maker of jewellery, one gold-polisher, one bookstitcher, and one bookbinder. The Central

Committee, which in principle was made up of twenty members representing the twenty arrondissements of Paris, accurately reflected this social composition. The list that has come into our hands does not indicate who had the responsibility in the 2nd and the 15th arrondissements. But for the rest, we come across the seamstress Anna Mallet (1st arrondissement); the sewing-machine operator Marquant (3rd); the hat-maker Angelina Sabatier (4th); the embroiderer of military decorations Victorine Piesvaux (5th); the bookbinder Nathalie Lemel (6th); the linen-draper Octavie Vataire (7th); Marie Picot (8th), whose profession, if any, is unknown; the seamstress Bessaiche (9th); the dressmaker Blanche Lefebvre (10th); the seamstress Marie Leloup (11th); the seamstress Forêt (12th); Mme Chantraile (13th), who had no profession; the waistcoat-maker Rivières(14th); the bookstitcher Aline Jacquier (16th); Aglaé Jarry, without profession (17th); the gold-polisher Blondeau (18th); the seamstress Jeanne Musset (19th); and the cardboard-maker Gauvain (20th). And finally, Elizabeth Dmitrieff.

The general staff of the *Union des Femmes*, its Executive Committee, was composed of four workers—Nathalie Lemel, Aline Jacquier, Blanche Lefebvre, and Marie Leloup—and three members who had no occupation—Aglaé Jarry, Elizabeth Dmitrieff, and a Mme Collin, whose arrondissement is unknown (unless it be the 2nd or the 15th, which had no representatives).[7]

The *Union*'s organization is detailed in statutes that were published in the press:[8] 'A responsible organization of Paris *citoyennes* who are resolved to support and defend the cause of the people, the Revolution, and the Commune, has just been founded to give assistance in the work of the government's commissions, and to serve at ambulance stations, at field kitchens, and at the barricades.' In each arrondissement there were created committees responsible for recruiting women who wanted to participate in these services; for the administration of funds coming from voluntary subscriptions; for summoning the women of the *Union* 'at any hour of the day or night,' on the orders of its Central Committee and at the request of the Commune commissions; and for giving tasks to its members.

In short, the arrondissement committees were charged with the mobilization of women: they had to send in to the Central Committee a daily report of their activities.

These arrondissement committees were composed of eleven members. They had to be open day and night, and hold a plenary meeting at least daily. The president was designated by rotation. She was aided by a board, subject to dismissal, consisting of a general secretary, two assistant secretaries, and a treasurer. Every other day, a financial report had to be sent to the Central Committee, as did all funds in excess of what was essential to the functioning of the arrondissement committee. Every member of the *Union* had to give a contribution of 10 centimes (the same dues as those of the International) and to acknowledge the authority of the Central Committee.

As we have seen, the Central Committee was made up of delegates from each arrondissement. It, too, had to be open twenty-four hours a day. The plenary sittings took place twice a day. The board was composed of a general secretary, three assistant secretaries, and a treasurer. A seven-member executive committee was entrusted with maintaining liaison with governmental commissions. The members of the executive committee wielded a card stamped with a seal and signed by the members of the Central Committee. They wore a red rosette in their buttonholes as an insignia.

The money that remained in the coffers, after the administration costs had been met, was to be used in the following manner: for supporting impoverished or ill members of the *Union*; for paying the committee members who had not the means to devote their full time to the *Union*; and finally for 'buying petroleum and weapons for the *citoyennes* who will fight; should the occasion arise, weapons will be distributed according to the drawing of lots.' Not much is heard about this Article 14; yet it seems very important. It would be absurd to think that this petroleum was bought to light lamps; the petroleum and the weapons go together in the same category. They are both means of combat. The *Union des Femmes*, then, foresaw the eventuality of incendiarism as a defensive measure.

1. "This naïve Manicheism." Pure heroes or grotesque vandals—two retrospective attitudes to the men and women of the Commune.

2(a) "The sacred revolt of the poor, the exploited and the oppressed." A club meeting in the parish of Montrouge, April 28th 1871, by an unidentified amateur artist, "C.A." or "A.C.", whose sketchbook of the Commune is now in the Archives Nationales.

2(b) "A woman wearing trousers—there's a scandal in itself!" Cantinières of the "Lascars" and the "Vengeurs de la République" seen by "C.A." and a girl-soldier drawn by the Spanish artist Daniel Vierge for his employers on Le Monde Illustré.

There is no way of escaping this conclusion: any other interpretation would be dishonest. But it would be equally
dishonest to become more indignant about the incendiary
petroleum of the Commune than about the incendiary shells
of Thiers.

At the Ministry of War, I came across the minutes of the 7th
arrondissement committee; these allow us some slight grasp of
the committee's everyday life.[9] It was not, perhaps, too
significant a committee. Of its ten members, who do not
correspond entirely to the general report drawn up by Elizabeth
Dmitrieff, we find a linen-draper, Octavie Vataire, and nine
other women whose professions we do not know. Six came from
Jules Allix's committee—a very high ratio, which we do not
find elsewhere. As the *Union's* statues prescribed for them, these
women worked out a set of rules for procedure. Every course of
action had to be approved by two members, and everybody had
to be present at the 'office' from eight in the morning to seven at
night. The office was to remain open until nine o'clock. Each
member was to receive 3 fr 50 per day, which seems a lot (in the
9th and 12th arrondissements, the *mairie* paid 2 francs).[10] If one
confines oneself to the account book, whose entries run from
the 24th of April to the 17th of May, the income of the *Union*
in the 7th arrondissement was minimal. On the 25th of April
there were 2 fr 20 in the till, and in the evening the Central
Committee was sent what remained after the day's expenses:
1 fr 20. On the 27th of April, a *citoyen* gave them 50 centimes,
but on the 3rd of May, 30 centimes had to be given to the
delegate to the Central Committee so that she could take the
bus. As for asking the members for the 10 centimes membership
fee, this seems to have been entirely omitted. As one member of
the municipality observed, how can one ask for 10 centimes from
women 'who have not even the wherewithal to buy bread'?
Since the Central Committee did not reply, the 7th arrondissement committee decided against collecting this membership
fee. On the 15th of May, the treasurer concluded that she had
no more funds to keep. Indeed, all she had left, on the 17th of
May was 5 centimes.

But this penury did not hamper the committee's activity. It sent to the Central Committee a nurse from the 106th Battalion, who had no more medicaments and wanted to know where she could obtain some more. It summoned women to the twentieth meeting of the *Union*, which was to be held in the *mairie* on the 8th of May. It made a list of the working women in the district, and asked for the concession for the sandbags being sewn for the barricades, in order to distribute work to the women of the arrondissement. On the 17th of May, the Gros-Caillou gun-powder factory exploded, and the *Union* attended to giving clothing to the victims, and finding them new lodgings.[11]

In the other arrondissements we find similar activities. The members of the 2nd, 10th, and 11th arrondissements went to search among the debris for the inhabitants of Neuilly, who had been bombarded by the Versailles army.[12] In the 5th arrondissement, they reminded a colonel of the elementary rules of military discipline: 'It is urgent that you refuse passes to all Guards' wives.' These visits provoked disorder, and hindered defence; and 'this causes much unpleasantness for our nurses who are on duty devoting themselves to tending our wounded.'[13]

But if the defence of Paris and first aid for the wounded appeared as the primary objectives of the *Union des Femmes*, its organization of labour was even more important, for this carried within itself the seeds of that social reform which gives the Commune its historical significance. As a consequence of the war, the Siege, and then the events of the 18th of March, a great number of shops had closed down. Their owners had preferred to leave Paris for safer places, Versailles or the provinces. Although most of the men were mobilized in the National Guard, unemployment was rampant. In the besieged city, the manufacture of cartridges, sandbags for the barricades, and military equipment provided the women with some means of sustenance. Women came to the military supply office and the Ministry of Labour, asking to be given work. Three thousand women seem to have been employed making cartridges.[14] Vuillaume, in *Mes Cahiers Rouges*, tells us that he supervised a workroom of five hundred to six hundred pretty girls who were assembling fulminate cartridge caps.[15] And Lissagaray describes the workroom in the Corps Législatif building where fifteen hundred women were sewing sandbags for the barricades: 'A tall and beautiful girl, Martha, distributed the work; she wore a red, silver-fringed scarf that her friends had given her. Happy songs alleviated their tasks. Every evening, the wages were paid out, and the workers received full payment for their work, 8 centimes per bag. The middleman of former days would have left them 2 centimes at the most.'[16] Saint-Pierre-de-Montmartre had been changed into a workroom which employed fifty women making military uniforms.[17] But these were only stop-gap measures.

Since the 18th of March the contractors remaining in Paris had lowered wages. Perhaps this was an attempt to create a current of hostility against the new government, by aggravating the economic situation. A report on contracts for military clothing negotiated with the firm of Monteaux-Bernard points out that at a payment of 3 fr 75 for a tunic and 2 fr 50 for trousers, it was impossible for the women working for this firm to live. The working-women's associations gave 6 francs for the same thing. If the Commune accepted this competition between capitalist work and co-operative work it 'would lose its dignity,' and the women would again see their piece-rates decrease. Never again should the Commune have recourse to buying from intermediaries: 'This would mean that the enslavement of the workers would continue, through centralization in the hands of the exploiters. . . .' Léo Frankel concludes that the Commission for Labour and Exchange should demand that the contracts that could be passed directly with the co-operatives be entrusted to them.[18]

Indeed, numerous demands were addressed to the Commission for Labour and Exchange. On the 3rd of May, Octavie Tardif, one of the directors of the *Union des Femmes*, who was at the same time responsible for the International in her arrondissement, presented the Commission with a petition bearing eighty-five signatures: 'We have to have work, for our brothers, our husbands, and our sons cannot provide for the needs of our

families.' But this work had to be distributed in each arrondissement to avoid travelling, waste of time, and 'the much greater
inconvenience of neglecting our children.' The fitting out of the
National Guard could provide immediate work.[19]

During the course of a discussion by the Commune about the
articles deposited at the Mont-de-Piété, Frankel adopted
Octavie Tardif's suggestion. The women of Paris had no work;
the National Guardsmen had only 30 sous a day to live on.
Poverty was widespread among the workers of Paris. Workshops had to be organized, but not 'National Workshops,' like
those of 1848. 'These would be workshops that would hand out
work; the women would be given work to do at home. For,
while we are creating work, we think that it is important, at the
same time, to bring about reforms in the work women do.'[20]
These reforms have a Proudhonian ring to them, even though
Frankel belonged to the Marxist group of the First International: if women must work, they should at least be able to
remain at their own fireside.

We have a plan for the organization of women's work which
reflects the ideas Frankel expounded before the Commune.
This plan is neither signed nor dated, but the printing order for
200 copies is in the hand of Benoît Malon.[21] This is one of the
most important documents for understanding the Commune's
deeper meaning, beyond its mistakes and shortcomings.

The 18th of March Revolution, that spontaneous achievement by
the people amid circumstances unique in history, is a great victory
for the Law of the People, in the implacable struggle that they carry
on against all tyrannies—a struggle begun by the slaves, continued
by the serfs; a struggle that the proletariat will have the glory of
ending in the achievement of social equality. The movement that
has just been born was so unexpected, so decisive, that professional
politicians have understood nothing of it and have seen in this great
movement only an insignificant and aimless revolt. Others have
insisted on limiting the very idea of this Revolution by reducing it
to the simple demand for what they call municipal franchise.

But the people are not mistaken. What they see in the Commune is indeed communal autonomy, but also 'the creation of

the new order, that of equality, solidarity, and liberty, which shall be the crowning of the communal revolution that Paris has the honour of having initiated.' Therefore Paris must not only think of defending itself, but must also enter vigorously upon the path of social reform. The Commune has an imperative duty toward the workers from whom it has sprung: to take decisive measures on their behalf. While the men are fighting, the Commune should concern itself with their wives and children, should give them support and work. But charity workshops are not to be trusted. 'The crisis we are passing through is a terrible one. We must act, and act quickly, all the time refraining from resorting to expedients, to attempts which sometimes may fulfil the exigencies of an unusual situation, but which create for the future dreadful difficulties like those that followed upon the closing of the National Workshops in 1848.' Therefore, the stop-gap of charity has to be rejected. 'Assistance, in the strict sense, presents dangers of another order. It tends to encourage laziness, and to debase character. The Commune should therefore abandon the old mistaken procedures, be inspired by the very difficulties of the situation, and put into practice means which will outlive the circumstances that gave them birth.'

How is this goal to be attained? There will have to be special workshops for women's work, and sales outlets for the finished products. Each arrondissement will provide receiving centres for raw materials, which will be allocated to the women individually or in groups, and places to store and sell the products. A committee of women will be called upon in each arrondissement to put this plan into effect. The delegate to the Financial Commission of the Commune will open a credit account with the municipal councils for the realization of the plan. . . .

This organization of work was to be taken in hand by the *Union des Femmes*. Elizabeth Dmitrieff, representing the *Union*, sent a very detailed report to the Commission for Labour and Exchange. She emphasized the significance of the socialistic, not charitable, nature of this plan:

Any reorganization of labour tending to assure the producer of the proceeds can be effectuated only by means of free productive associations making advantageous use of the various industries to their collective profit. In taking work away from the bondage of capitalistic exploitation, the formation of these organizations would eventually allow the workers to run their own business.

It would modify not only the social relations of production, but also the forms of work, which were inhuman. It was absolutely necessary that there be variety, for 'the continual repetition of the same manual movement has a deadly influence upon the organism and the brain.' The shortening of the working day should also be taken into consideration, for 'the exhaustion of physical strength inevitably brings about the extinction of moral strength.' Finally, it would be a good idea to abolish 'any competition between workers of different sexes,' since, in the struggle they were waging against capitalism, their interests were identical. Wages ought to be equal for equal work.

If these associations were to develop, each of their members had to belong to the International, and the State had to grant them a social loan, at 5 per cent interest, repayable by annuities.

Elizabeth Dmitrieff had few illusions about the profundity and duration of the women's enthusiasm for the Commune. The organization of work was urgent, for 'it is to be feared that the feminine element of the Parisian population, revolutionary for the moment, will return, because of continual privation, to the passive and more or less reactionary state to which it belonged in the past.'

Therefore, the Central Committee of the *Union des Femmes* asked that the Commission for Labour and Exchange give it the task of fitting out the military, and that it put at the disposal of the *Associations Productives Fédérées* the money necessary to exploit factories and workshops which had employed women, and which had been abandoned by their owners. Next came an enumeration of feminine professions, ranging from typographers to glassblowers and illustrators, and naturally including all the clothing trades.[22]

Certain statutes make it clear that all the working women's productive associations were to be federated, and be responsible to the arrondissement committees of the *Union des Femmes*. The Central Committee was to maintain liaison with similar foreign organizations, to facilitate exportation and exchange of products. The framework of the *Union des Femmes*—the Central Committee, the Executive Committee and the arrondissement committees set up to participate in the defence of Paris—could also serve to organize labour upon a socialist basis. The arrondissement committees were to keep registers in which women of various occupations would come to enroll, in order to form federated productive associations, and also keep a record of women working at home.[23] Each arrondissement committee was to nominate five members to constitute the Federation of Women's Associations. Aided by the Central Committee of the *Union des Femmes*, a commission was to draw up final statutes, which would be submitted to the arrondissement committees and approved by the general assembly. A purchasing committee, in agreement with the Commune Commission for Labour and Exchange, would decide what expenses to incur. A member of the Central Committee would have a permanent seat on the former Ministry of Public Works (a woman in a ministry: what a bold innovation!). A committee would choose which samples to manufacture; another, composed of cashiers and accountants, would establish the cost price. Yet another would keep a record of the buildings abandoned by their owners.

Military outfitting would furnish the women with immediate work, but the future had to be provided for. Linens were of prime importance for Parisian commerce. 'If convents and prison enterprises were done away with, it would be possible to raise wages.' Feathers and artificial flowers were luxury items, true, but 'it is important to prepare a new future for this industry.' Besides, seasonal unemployment was considerable in this type of work, and the women of this group would have to be associated to other tasks. The ideal was still for women to do their work at home. 'Sewing-machine operators would be able to work at home, if society helped them to own the instruments of their work.'[24] Thus, in these revolutionary plans it was not a question of collectivizing the means of production, but of furnishing the producers with their working implements.

But the state of a society is not altered in a few weeks. Despite the willingness of the Commune and the *Union des Femmes* to make a radical change in working conditions, the situation of working women remained precarious, and worsened from day to day. There were too few co-operative workshops to prevent factory managers from bringing wages even lower, or to force them to set more equitable prices. Promises were not kept. 'They said that military trousers would be paid for at 2 francs, and jackets at 4 francs.' But 'just as in the good old days,' the prices had gone down to 1 fr 40 for trousers and 2 fr 50 for jackets. 'This shameful exploitation must cease. We must have the women with us at any cost.'[25] The women who sewed National Guard Uniforms wrote in *Le Vengeur*, on the 14th of May: 'The intelligent, hard-working woman must cease being the victim, slave, and dupe of the owners, who enrich themselves by her suffering and at her expense.' They asked that the previous prices be re-established, or else that they be given full power to make use, for their own profit, of the enterprise in which they were working.[26]

In any event, the men and women of the Commune, in an isolated city in the heart of a hostile country, entered into a merciless struggle against a government that had both army and money on its side. As if they had the future before them, these men and women were getting ready for a basic transformation of production, and seeking to blaze a path of social justice. It is on account of this faith that the Commune and its supporters are admirable, and, to a certain extent, exemplary; the efforts of the Paris Commune in 1871 inspired the social reorganization of Communist Yugoslavia.

Moreover, the *Union des Femmes* did not limit itself to these projects. On the 10th of May, it invited working women 'with substantial practical and theoretical knowledge' to meet in the *mairie* of the 10th arrondissement in order to reach an understanding with the Central Committee about the measures to be taken for the reorganization of labour. And on the 15th of May, it informed all women that this reorganization had been delegated to the *Union* and advised them to register at their *mairie*.[27]

Poor women who did not even have the 10 centimes to pay for their membership in the *Union des Femmes* immediately responded to this census being undertaken by the arrondissement committees. We have, for the 5th, 7th, 10th, and 11th arrondissements, lists of women ready to participate in the new workshops.[28] These lists accurately reflect the distribution of feminine occupations. Out of 71 women registered at the 10th arrondissement, we note 26 seamstresses, 9 laundresses, 3 burnishers, one gilder; all the others are connected with the clothing trades. In the 11th arrondissement, 140 out of 238 women list themselves as seamstresses; then there are one sewing-machine operator, one bootstitcher, one gold-hammerer, and one gold-polisher. Among the non-proletarian professions, there are three schoolteachers, one trained nurse, one accountant, one salesgirl, one pianist, one cellist, and one chorus-singer. The others—linen-drapers, dressmakers, corset-makers—all have to do with sewing. Throughout there are few industrial workers.

In accordance with the Commission for Labour and Exchange, Elizabeth Dmitrieff, Nathalie Lemel, Aline Jacquier, Blanche Lefebvre, and the other members of the Executive Committee of the *Union des Femmes* called a meeting of all working women on the 18th of May, at the Bourse; three delegates for each trade corporation were elected, thus constituting the syndical chambers. Each chamber was to elect two delegates, who would make up the Federal Chamber of Working Women.[29] On Sunday, the 21st of May, the working women were convoked again, this time to the Hôtel de Ville, for the definitive constitution of the syndical and federal chambers.[30]

But on the same Sunday the Versailles troops entered Paris. It was no longer a time to build the future, but a time to fight.

6

THE CLUBS

HOWEVER GREAT THE IMPORTANCE of the *Union des Femmes*, it would be wrong to attribute to it all women's demonstrations and activities during the Commune. Just as the International was not the sole power behind the Commune, the *Union des Femmes* accounted for only a part of feminine action. The women who spoke in the Clubs, cared for the wounded, brought provisions—and the soldier-women who elicited the sympathy and enthusiasm of some, and the criticism and sarcasm of others —were not, for the most part, affiliated to the *Union*. Louise Michel did not take part in it, although she was a member of the International. André Léo's membership is open to conjecture. The Montmartre Women's Vigilance Committee, which was already in existence during the Siege, continued to function independently. Sophie Poirier, Béatrix Excoffon, and Anna Jaclard were active in the Vigilance Committee, and none of them belonged to the *Union*.

Anna Jaclard had been a member of Jules Allix's committee. Like Elizabeth Dmitrieff, she was born in Russia, the elder daughter of an artillery general, Vassily Korvine Krukovsky, who believed that he was descended from the kings of Hungary. On her mother's side, she was the grand-daughter of General Schubert, a member of the Academy of Sciences. This doubly aristocratic origin did not prevent the secretary of the Russian Embassy in Paris, in 1871, from referring to her as a 'harpy' and a '*pétroleuse*.' From the estate at Palibino, where she spent her youth in luxury, Anna Vassilievna Korvina Krukovskaya had travelled a long road to the streets of Paris.

Sophie and Anna, General Korvine Krukovsky's two daughters, had been brought up with the greatest care. But like Elizabeth Dmitrieff, they were infected by the great wind of

revolution which, during the sixties, were blowing over the
young generation of the intelligentsia. Sophie, who became a
very distinguished mathematician and held a chair at the
University of Stockholm, has left us some memorabilia of this
revolution. 'It can be said that at this time, between 1860 and
1870, one single problem preoccupied the educated classes of
Russian society: the conflict between the young and the old. A
sort of epidemic spread among children, and especially among
young girls: the desire to flee from the paternal house. . . .'
It was learned that a girl from the district had escaped abroad,
and that another had left for Saint Petersburg to join the
'nihilists.' At Palibino, a student, the son of the local Orthodox
pope, was the one who spread this news. Under his influence,
Anna began to read philosophy and sociology, and to write.
A Dream, signed with the masculine pseudonym of Yuri
Orbelov, was published by Dostoyevsky in the magazine
Epoch, which he ran, in 1864. A correspondence ensued between
the writer and the general's daughter. They met at Saint
Petersburg, and excitedly discussed literature and politics,
about which they did not agree. Consequently, with his own
brand of logic, Dostoyevsky asked for Anna's hand in marriage.
She refused. 'Sometimes I am astonished myself,' she explained
to her sister, 'that I am unable to love him. He is so good, so
intelligent, so kind. But he needs a woman who would devote
herself to him fully. I cannot do that.' However, the two sisters
had to find a way of escaping from the General, the estate, and
the family. Like Elizabeth Dmitrieff, Sophie entered into a
mariage blanc with a young scholar, Vladimir Kovalevsky, and,
thanks to this chaperon, crossed the frontier, taking her sister
Anna with her. The trio parted immediately. Vladimir remained at Vienna to study geology and paleontology, Sophie
went to Heidelberg to follow the lectures in physics, and Anna
went to Paris to devote herself to social problems. The separation angered the general, who refused to send Anna money. To
earn a living, she started work as a bookbinder in a printing
shop. This girl of the high aristocracy simultaneously discovered
poverty, the necessity for work, and the workers' revolution.

'When I left for France,' she wrote in 1869, 'I did not suspect that a dream of the overthrow of the bourgeois regime was so close to being realized.' It was during a Blanquist meeting that she met Victor Jaclard, a medical student, whom she married. But pursued by the police of the Empire, Victor Jaclard sought refuge with his wife in Switzerland. They followed political events closely. She wrote to her sister:

Jaclard is impatiently awaiting information about the state of mind in Paris. The news of the French defeats and the disturbances in Paris keep us on the alert. We have decided to go there despite the danger—a danger which, for Jaclard, is even greater, since he has been sentenced to deportation. But in the face of the present circumstances, one cannot remain idle. The lack of resolute men, men who have heads on their shoulders, is too self-evident for thoughts of saving one's own skin.[1]

The Empire fell; Victor Jaclard and his wife went back to France. Jaclard took part in the battle of the 31st of October, and was then appointed deputy-mayor of the 13th arrondissement, colonel of the 17th Legion, and member of the Central Committee of the National Guards. As for Anna, she took part in Jules Allix's *Comité des Femmes* in the 18th arrondissement[2] and, with André Léo, in the Montmartre Vigilance Committee. Since she seems to have met Elizabeth Dmitrieff in Switzerland, in the Russian section of the International, it is odd that Anna did not join the *Union des Femmes*.

The relations between the Montmartre Vigilance Committee and the *Union des Femmes* do not seem always to have been of the best. On the 22nd of April, Anna Jaclard, André Léo, and Sophie Poirier issued an appeal to the women of Montmartre to form ambulance stations.[3] The *Union des Femmes* took umbrage at seeing André Léo's name at the bottom of the poster, and published a protest in the newspapers.

The Central Committee of the *Union des Femmes pour la Défense de Paris et les Soins aux Blessés* deems it necessary to inform all members of the *Union* that the *citoyenne* André Léo, while giving an explanation of her motives in lending her name to a committee alien to our union, has declared that she has no official connection with the afore-mentioned Vigilance Committee, and attested to her desire to remain a member of the 10th arrondissement committee of the *Union des Femmes pour la Défense de Paris et les Soins aux Blessés*.[4]

Thus, from the very beginning of its existence, the *Union des Femmes* assumed all the characteristics of a 'monolithic' party which intended to rule all activities of its members and to retain a monopoly over their initiatives. Moreover, we do not know how André Léo followed up this affair. The only certain fact is that her name does not figure in the list of members of the *Union des Femmes* which is preserved in the War Archives.

The Montmartre Vigilance Committee, like the *Union des Femmes*, ran workshops, recruited ambulance nurses, aided the impoverished wives of the Fédérés, sent women speakers to the Clubs, and went hunting for defaulters from conscription.[5] Its activity, therefore, exactly duplicated that of the *Union des Femmes*, but it had eluded the *Union*'s control—whence, no doubt, the latter's annoyance. The certitude of being in the right, and the resulting intolerance, are characteristic of every revolutionary party. But the 18th of March was not a day for any one party. The Commune was the expression of various tendencies—Jacobin, Blanquist, Internationalist—whose vague outlines we find repeated among the women's movements. But the women who spoke out in the Clubs, with varying degrees of cogency, more often than not represent nobody but themselves, or else a spontaneous expression of popular opinion: their role was that of the chorus in Greek tragedy.

The Clubs, which had already exerted great influence during the Siege, regained all their importance during the Commune. Many women participated in them; some Clubs were even exclusively for women. 'We intend to give them a major share of our space,' we read in the newspaper *Le Révolution politique et sociale*.

Yet the greatest space will be reserved for reports of the meetings of the *citoyennes*' clubs. It is time for us to halt the injustices and prejudices of which women are victims. When we have placed every *citoyenne* in a position where she can earn a living, when strong men no longer steal from them the work that is theirs by right, our daughters will no longer sell their honour to the vilest counter-jumper. . . . I shall never cease to protest against the unfortunate lot that the egoism of modern society has imposed upon them.[6]

Here again, the opinions of contemporaries were utterly opposed, and are worth quoting next. Maxime du Camp: 'On the 3rd of May, out of curiosity, I went to the opening of the *Club de la Révolution Sociale*, in the church of Saint-Michel des Batignolles. Seldom have I seen a sillier spectacle. A lot of women were there; a few men self-consciously keeping their hats on; babies squealing; Commune members girt with their red sashes, lording it in the churchwarden's pew.' The organ intoned the *Marseillaise*. 'Screeching sopranos, rumbling bassi-profondi, yapping trebles. . . . The organ played the *Chant du Départ*, and the assembly began to bray louder than ever.' Naturally, the speeches could be nothing but stupid: ' "Our oppressors have kept the people, without whom they would be nothing, in darkness for long enough. . . ." Tomorrow they are to expound upon a weighty question which merits the medita-tion of all patriots: "Woman in the Church and Woman in the Revolution." ' In the eyes of Maxime du Camp this question was utterly ridiculous.[7] The *Journal Officiel* of the Commune depicts the same meeting in these terms: 'The church was packed full, and women were in the majority. One had the feeling that the husbands going off to fight for the Commune had left a hardy seed of revolutionary ideas behind them at home. . . .' Here there is no mention of braying: 'The organ opened the meeting with the *Marseillaise*, sung all the way through by the club's *citoyens* and *citoyennes* with admirable enthusiasm. This patriotic song, reverberating in the vaulted ceiling, produced a majestic effect. . . .' After several 'very interesting' revolutionary speeches, people left to the *Chant du Départ*, having settled the agenda on the subject 'Woman in the Church and Woman in the Revolution.'[8] It would be impossible to find two passages that were at once more in agreement, and more contradictory. The whole difference is in the tone, in the mind of the narrator. Benoît Malon and Lissagaray also emphasized the importance of the Clubs. In them the 'holy revolt of the poor, the exploited, the oppressed, against the exploiters, against the tyrants'[9] was preached. If few precise ideas could be extracted from these discussions, at least they were 'stockpiles of fire and courage.'[10]

So let us walk through Paris, touring the Clubs of the Commune; but let us be wary of the eye-witnesses who guide us. Fontoulieu, the Abbé Amodru, the Abbé Delmas, and the Abbé Ravailhe are, understandably, somewhat horrified by this occupation of the churches by henchmen of the antichrist. A correspondent of *The Times*, in his turn, escorts us into a women's meeting in which the bourgeois feels himself to be in very evil surroundings.

Several 'Red' newspapers had alerted him that meetings would soon be organized at which *citoyennes* 'might congregate' and give vent to their enthusiasm. He is dubious whether a man can attend without personal danger, but he hearkens only to his courage and his professional conscience; thanks to the protection of 'a news-woman who occupies one of the kiosks on the Boulevards,' he and a friend slipped into one of these assemblies of ill repute. It was held on the Boulevard d'Italie, in a dilapidated outbuilding over which a red flag was flying. The room was glutted with women and children, women of 'the lowest order of society,' naturally, wearing 'loose untidy jackets' and 'white frilled caps upon their heads.' At the end of the room, there was a table 'littered' with papers and books, behind which stood *citoyennes* wearing red sashes. One of these, young and pretty (curious that this reporter did not *see* her as old and ugly—we have here a proof of 'objectivity'), spoke—held forth, I should say—upon the rights of women. She spoke in a foreign accent that shocked our Anglo-Saxon (this may have been Elizabeth Dmitrieff); what she was saying, moreover, seemed to him utterly idiotic. It was a diatribe against the stupidity and cowardice of men, and an appeal to the women of Paris to defend the barricades. The words of the lady orator were, essentially, of little importance to the reporter. What struck him more was her beauty. 'She seemed very handsome, and might have sat for the portrait of one of the heroines of the first Revolution.' However, this man was unhappy about the look in her eye. He would 'not like to have been her husband.' The second orator, however, 'seemed tolerably respectable,' with her black dress and her bonnet. But her speech, still according to this reporter, was as 'rambling and inconsistent' as the preceding one. Perhaps it would not be necessary to defend the barricades, but there remained for the women the imperative duty of gathering the wounded up from the battlefield, and thus of saving countless lives. It was also necessary to take care of the field kitchens. The woman speaker recalled the example of Jeanne Hachette and the women in the Revolution of 1789, and hurled a few harsh words at the clergy. As for the third speaker, she attacked society's exploitation of the poor and defended the Republic. 'A vague and unnecessarily repetitious speech.' Thereupon, professional duty done, our reporter and his friend prudently made themselves scarce, for, he said, their presence had been noticed and God only knew what might have happened to them. As they left, a lady 'held out a bag and solicited a trifle on behalf of the new society.'[11] Such was a Women's Club during the Commune, as seen by an English bourgeois.

Let us continue our stroll. At Saint-Jacques-du-Haut-Pas and at Saint-Séverin there were Clubs for both men and women. Fornarina de Fonseca often spoke at Saint-Séverin.[12] She was an Italian, whose family had a strong revolutionary tradition. Her grandmother, Eléonora de Fonseca, who was a lady-in-waiting to Marie Caroline, Queen of Naples, had espoused the ideas of the French Revolution and had founded a newspaper, *Il Monitore Repubblicano*. Arrested by order of the king, she had been freed by the French in 1799. But upon the restoration of Ferdinand IV she was condemned to death and executed.[13] Her grand-daughter proudly revived this heritage, and never failed to invoke her grandmother's memory whenever she spoke in a Commune Club.

The church of Saint-Sulpice was defended by its parishioners, and the Club did not move in there until the 14th of May.[14] Women were in the majority, and made up the Club's clerical staff. Paule Minck and Lodoyska Kawecka often gave speeches there. The latter, too, was of Polish origin. Her husband, the doctor Constantin Kawecki, had studied at Strasbourg and had been appointed Commandant of the 202nd Battalion of the Fédérés, then Lieutenant Colonel of the Turcos of the Commune. Lodoyska contributed to *Le Journal des Citoyennes de la Commune*, and was soon to fight for the defence of the Gare Montparnasse. Both of them were ultimately to seek refuge in London.[15] In the 15th arrondissement, the *citoyens* and *citoyennes* of the *Cercle des Jacobins* met in the basement of the church of Saint-Lambert de Vaugirard.[16] The *Union des Femmes* held a meeting there on the 26th of April, presided over by an Austrian, Mme Reidenreth, who, it was said, exerted a great influence on the women living in Vaugirard. 'She was a woman in her forties, tall, strong, of very high colour, and wearing a Zouave uniform. Her hair fell over her shoulders in long coils wound around with red ribbons. At her belt hung two very richly worked American revolvers.' Two women attended her: Julie Burroit, a seamstress, and Anna Lavigne, a *cantinière*. At this meeting, only women were admitted. They discussed the influence of religion.[17]

At Sainte-Elisabeth-du-Temple, the offices of Mary's month went on being celebrated in the Lady Chapel, while to the right the local Women's Club was holding a meeting.[18]

On the 27th of April, the church of Saint-Nicolas-des-Champs was occupied by the Club which had formerly held its meetings in the Salle Molière.[19] At that first meeting they considered prostitution and the means of wiping it out. The parish priests were outraged to hear 'the most scabrous subjects treated without circumspection before an audience composed for the most part of women and children,' and would not permit any religious exercises to be held in a church that had been thus desecrated.[20] The Club took little heed of these protestations. The red flag was raised over the church and the president, Landeck, declared in the name of the Commune that these

monuments belonged to the nation: 'let the priests say Mass
there when they will but we shall also use them for the job we
have got to do.'[21] Not many women were there at the outset.
An identity card, countersigned by the Club's secretaries, had
to be shown at the entrance. But this measure was not enforced,
and the 'lost women' of the quarter flowed in.[22] And certainly,
in the 3rd arrondissement, there must have been many prostitutes in the audience. It was all the more understandable that
the prostitutes—despised by everyone, even though people
showed only amused indulgence for the men who used and
exploited them—often viewed the revolutionary government of
the Commune as a possibility of bettering themselves in the new
society. Prostitution considered as an economic consequence of
low wages and of poverty was part of the order of the day, and
means were sought of making it disappear.

Landeck, the chairman, was assisted on the committee by a
jewellery-maker, Marie-Jeanne Bouquet, *femme* Lucas. She was
a friend of Félix Pyat and of several officers in the Fédérés.[23]
In the audience, one could find a bootstitcher, Clotilde Vallet,
the widow of a certain Legros, and 'companion' of a delegate to
the Central Committee, Gandon, by whom she had two
children, in accordance with the Parisian people's custom of
not getting married either in church or at the *mairie*, but of
practicing faithful *unions libres*.[24] There was also the wife of a
savings-bank employee, Jeanne-Marie Jobst.[25] A woman,
Pauline Mengue (Paule Minck?), arriving from the provinces
came to declare that the communal movement was making
great progress there, and that sympathy and admiration for
Paris were increasing[26]—words of hope that warmed people's
hearts.

On the 4th of May, the curé of Saint-Eustache received
orders to put the church at the disposition of the Club. On the
5th, the crowd moved in. 'It really must be said,' notes Abbé
Coullié in horror, 'that women form the bulk of this terrifying
mob.' But, in compensation, it was the ladies of La Halle who
brought a threatening petition before the Commune, demanding that 'their venerable curé be set free.'[27] Besides, even though

'under those holy vaults, evil doctrines and more than one impiety' had been heard, the curé acknowledged that the church had not been subjected to any looting, and that the sanctuary had never been occupied.[28] Seen from the other side, the 'impieties' become 'an admirable sermon.' One witness noted a speech worthy of the Gospel According to St. John, to which liberty and equality had been added. 'The people were as devout as at Divine Worship. What more religious, indeed, than the Revolution? Numerous women were present, and were listening attentively to what was being said. . . .'[29] In this Club, they were listening to a *cantinière* of the 84th Battalion, Mme Brossut, Joséphine Dulimbert, (who in 1870 had edited *Le Moniteur des Citoyennes*), Elizabeth Deguy, and Marie Menans, whom we shall meet later upon the barricades.[30]

The *Club des Libres Penseurs* met at Saint-Germain-l'Auxerrois. There too, the Club was of mixed sexes, and we re-encounter Lodoyska Kawecka, dressed in Turco trousers and a crimson velvet hussar's vest adorned with embroidery. She had gold-tasselled boots and a hat with a red cockade. From her blue sash hung two revolvers. She came to the Club when she was not out with the Fédérés, shooting.[31] Nathalie Lemel, too, was there.[32]

Before an audience of men and of women 'who smoked'—which was particularly horrible—were expounded the 'impious' doctrines of the liberation of women. A resolution favouring divorce was voted for by acclamation. 'We must admit,' remarked a leader-writer in *Le Cri du Peuple*, 'that the supporting arguments, developed with a veritable eloquence, seemed to us irrefutable.'[33]

The *Club des Prolétaires* met at Saint-Ambroise. There, too, many women were present. Mme André, a laundress, was its secretary. We have fairly complete information on this Club, thanks to the minutes of its meetings preserved in the War Archives.[34] *Citoyenne* Thiourt (or Thyou), who spoke many times, displayed great violence and zeal. In the Place de la Bourse, she had asked directions of a *citoyen*; he had answered that, in that quarter, there lived no citizens, but ladies and gentlemen. Consequently, on the 13th of May, she demanded

that cannons be placed on that square to silence all the reactionaries. On the 16th of May, she called for the arrest of all
priests until the end of the war. On the 18th, she announced the
presence of twelve chassepot rifles hidden in the rue Neuve-des-
Boulets, and undertook to search for defaulters. *Citoyenne* Madré,
on the other hand, thought that women should not take up arms
to look for hidden traitors, but should form groups to work on
the barricades (18th of May). On the 20th of May, *citoyenne*
Valentin urged women to 'guard the gates of Paris, while the
men go to battle.' Then she demanded that the clothing left in
the religious communities be sold or distributed 'to dress poor
children,' and that 'the flowers upon the altars, in the chapels,
and all around the madonnas, be given to schoolchildren as
prizes, to decorate the garrets of the poor.' The proposition was
unanimously adopted. Perhaps I am wrong in lingering over
this detail, unworthy of a 'serious' historian. But I find it admirable that in the midst of fighting, in the midst of poverty, in the
feverish atmosphere of the Clubs, a woman should think of
giving flowers to children. This seems to me quite indicative of a
deep sensibility which rarely appears in revolutionary movements, which, because they must confront the most urgent
situations, have to be schematic.

At the church of Saint-Eloi, we see *citoyenne* Valentin again,[35]
as well as a seamstress, Marie-Catherine Rogissart, who
belonged to the 12th arrondissement women's group responsible for seeking out defaulters.[36]

On the 12th of May, about thirty women led by Lodoyska
Kawecka, who indeed seems to have played an important part
in the Clubs, went to ask the beadle of the church of the Trinité
to turn over the keys of 'that communal edifice' to the *Club de la
Délivrance*. They were accompanied by several unarmed
Fédérés. That evening, the meeting opened at eight o'clock,
before an audience composed mostly of women. The president
seems to have been twenty-five years old. Lodoyska Kawecka
preferred the role of adviser, so that she might take part in the
discussion. Women gave speeches about possible means of
regenerating society. André Léo gave a reasoned exposé of the

tenets of socialism; an old woman, known locally as '*la mère Duchêne*,' was particularly violent. A hundred defaulters ought to be executed as an example: 'What are the lives of a few bad citizens, when we are concerned with founding liberty?' Nathalie Lemel urged women to take up arms for the defence of the Commune: 'We have come to the supreme moment, when we must be able to die for the Patrie. No more weakness. No more uncertainty. All women to arms. All women to duty. Versailles must be crushed. . . .'[37]

Let us move on to Notre-Dame-de-la-Croix, in Ménilmont-ant. Paule Minck had gone to ask the curé for permission to hold meetings in his church. The *cantinière* Lachaise was among its most ardent members.[38]

At Saint-Christophe-de-la-Villette, an old woman urged those present to sing the *Marseillaise* instead of hymns, for 'there is no God any more.'[39] And Sidonie Herbelin summoned women to meet 'in the Black Crows' barn.'[40]*

Louise Michel often presided over the *Club de la Révolution*, which met at the church of Saint-Bernard-de-la-Chapelle. On the 13th of May, they voted to do away with the magistracy and the statutes then in force, and to substitute a 'legal com-mittee entrusted with working out a legal plan which would have some relevance to the new institutions and to the people's aspirations.' They also voted for the abolition of religious wor-ship, the arrest of priests in league with the 'monarchist dogs' (*monarchiens*) and the execution of one hostage every twenty-four hours until Blanqui, who was imprisoned by the Versailles government, was returned to Paris. Then there were social measures: the articles deposited at the Mont-de-Piété were to be remitted without charge to the defenders of the city and to citizens in need, the licensed houses of prostitution were to be abolished, and the Commune was to consign the public works it undertook to 'corporations of working men and women.'[41]

On the 3rd of May, the *Club de la Révolution Sociale* was opened in the church of Saint-Michel des Batignolles.[42] There,

---

* '*à la grange aux Corbeaux*'—*corbeau* being, of course, an anticlericalist's word for a priest.—*Trans.*

too, women were in the majority. The dressmaker Blanche Lefebvre, of the *Union des Femmes*, played an important role. Wearing a red sash and carrying a revolver at her waist, she took the floor almost every night. Tall, thin, and sunburnt, she loved the Commune 'as others love a man'; she was to die for it on the barricades. She reported young men who were obtaining from the Commune passes which enabled them to leave Paris: 'If these abuses continue, we, *citoyennes*—we shall be obliged to climb up on the ramparts to avenge our brothers who have been abandoned by cowards.' She asked that women's movements also be watched: 'Let a woman be placed at every gate with a secret password, so as to know if the *citoyenne* may or may not leave the city.' She also demanded that counter-revolutionary newspapers be banned.[43] A laundress, Victorine Gorget, demanded 'a strong organization that would allow us to use all the vital energy of the population for resistance; without which we shall have to open the gates to the army of Versailles.'[44] The seamstress Marie Ségaud, *femme* Orlowsky, 'who also goes in for literature,' was an habituée of the *Club Saint-Michel*.[45] The rumour went around that the Bishop of Paris and the Abbé Deguerry had been freed. The Club delegated *citoyennes* Lescluze and Efligier, and *citoyen* Franklin, to make sure that these men were still in prison; they felt that it was important to keep these hostages, since Blanqui had not yet been freed.[46] But the invasion of the church by these infidels aroused the indignation of the damsels of the parish. These pious young ladies, whom we know only by their first names—Marie, Cécile, Félicité, Angèle—decided to blow up the Club, and the church along with it. Fortunately, the curate cooled their worthy ardour.[47]

Let us end our stroll with the *Club de la Boule Noire*, where we recognize our old friends of the 18th arrondissement Vigilance Committee. Sophie Poirier was its president, Béatrix Excoffon its vice-president. The latter seems to have exerted a moderating influence on the members of this club; this, at least, is what she told the Council of War. She intervened, once to defend nuns against a woman who demanded their execution, and at other times concerning the abolition of prostitution and the organization of work. 'At the next-to-last meeting of the *Boule Noire*,' stated Béatrix Excoffon before the Council of War,

a *citoyen* named Barois proposed a motion whose objective was to demand the exchange of Blanqui for the Archbishop of Paris, and the execution of that prelate if the proposition was not accepted. In my role as vice-president, since Mme Poirier was unable to attend, I submitted the proposition to the assembly, which accepted it unanimously; it was decided that the report of the meeting be sent immediately to the Commune. At the last meeting, on the 20th of May, the same *citoyen* asked if the assembly wanted the Archbishop to be shot. Everyone's reply was negative.[48]

The question of pulling down the Vendôme column was also brought up: 'I once said that the Vendôme column had cost four million men, and it would have been better to have the soldiers that the victims of the First Empire could have fathered to fight against the Prussians, than to possess a pile of bronze.'[49]

7

OPINION AND ACTION

OUR TOUR OF the Clubs will have enabled us to make out what subjects were being discussed there, with such passion and violence.

No doubt the women in the Clubs had only very vague ideas about socialism. But what they did know, what they did feel in a confused and visceral fashion, was that they had worked all their lives for ridiculous wages, and that, if nothing were to change, their children would be like themselves: poverty-stricken and exploited. To a young man who was expounding the goals of the Commune, an old working woman in a blue apron, with a checked kerchief on her head, got up and answered:

He tells us that the Commune is going to do something so that the people won't starve as they work. And about time too! Here I've been a washerwoman for forty years, I've been working every blessed day of the week, without ever having anything to put in my mouth or to pay the rent. The price food costs! And so why is it that some can rest from one New Year's Day to the next, while we are always at work? Is that fair? It seems to me that if I were the government, I'd manage things so that working people could be given their turn to rest. If the people had holidays like the rich do, *citoyens*, they wouldn't complain so much.[1]

Women like André Léo, Louise Michel, and Nathalie Lemel came along to speak and explain the way in which society was to be transformed: capitalistic exploitation would be abolished, and tools and workshops handed over to the people.

To this claim for justice for the working class was added the claim of women, who were doubly exploited. At the *Club de la Révolution Sociale*, they discussed woman's situation 'according to the Church and according to the Revolution.'[2] A motion in

favour of divorce was approved at the *Club des Libres Penseurs*.[3]
At Sainte-Elisabeth-du-Temple, they demanded that women
having a specified number of children receive a pension. This
proposition seemed grotesque to the reactionary onlooker who
reported it; but is it not the origin of family allowances?[4] The
Clubs, depicted by the adversaries of the Commune as lairs of
bandits, drunkards, and prostitutes, were demanding measures
whose morality was entirely puritanical. The Vigilance Committee of the republican *citoyennes* of the 18th arrondissement
voted for a motion which would tend to make the prostitution
that had been increasing for some time disappear from the
streets. The motion was signed by the president, Sophie Poirier,
the secretary, Anna Jaclard, and two assistants, Mmes Barois
and Tesson. Four hundred signatures followed.[5] The *Club de
l'Ecole de Médecine* demanded 'that all women of suspect morality
plying their shameful trade on the public thoroughfares' be
immediately arrested, and likewise 'the drunkards who have
forgotten their self-respect'; that the cafés be closed at 11 o'clock
at night; that smoking concerts be forbidden. This document
was approved unanimously.[6] The residents of the 1st and 2nd
arrondissements congratulated the municipal council of the
11th for having taken measures concerning prostitutes and
drunkards, and asked that a decree of the same sort be applied
to their neighbourhoods. Nobody could take a step without
being scandalously accosted by women of ill repute, especially
in the rue du Petit-Carreau, rue de Montorgueil, rue Saint-
Honoré, etc. It does not appear that this expansion of prostitution, which a century later exists in the same streets, can be
attributed to the circumstances created by the Commune.[7]
In response to this appeal, the municipal council of the 2nd
arrondissement closed down the licensed brothels.[8] The members of the Commune in the 15th arrondissement had prostitutes
and drunkards arrested: 'Any intoxicated member of the
National Guard will be deprived of his pay for four days; his
pay will be distributed to the neediest children in his company.'[9] Staff officers who had been banqueting with tarts at
Peters' restaurant were sent to Bicêtre, with pick and shovel, to

dig trenches; the girls were sent to Saint-Lazare to make sand-bags.[10] Edouard Moreau, Civil Commissioner to the Delegate for War, proposed that every drinking establishment from which a drunken man was seen to leave be closed, and that no woman not possessing a regular pass be permitted to enter forts or entrenchments.[11] The ideal Commune would have been Savonarola's Florence.

What was to become of these prostitutes who could no longer ply their trade? Some of them turned up at the Hôtel de Ville asking to be allowed to care for the injured. They were refused this honour, for, Louise Michel noted, the men of the Commune wanted pure hands tending the Fédérés. But for Louise Michel, these women, the victims of poverty and of society, had their right to a place in the new world which was being born, and which ought to reject any moral condemnation. 'Who had more of a right than they, the saddest victims of the old world, to give their life for the new one?' Therefore she directed them to a committee of women (the 18th arrondissement Vigilance Committee? the *Union des Femmes*?) 'whose spirits were generous enough to let these women be welcomed.' 'We shall never bring shame down upon the Commune,' these prostitutes said. Many, indeed, died courageously on the barricades during the Bloody Week in May, as did that 'Henriette-Tout-le-Monde' whose story has been told by Maurice Dommanget.[12]

The Clubs were also interested in everyday life, organizing soup kitchens,[13] and helping the poor. At the *Club des Prolétaires*, *citoyenne* Mayer was outraged that assistance had been refused a mother of nine, ostensibly because she had been employed in a convent.[14]

In this Paris, besieged anew, people lived in terror of informers and policemen. It was the gendarmes who were accused of bombarding Paris, when the commandant of the Mont-Valérien refused to carry out this task.[15] The agents of Versailles were suspected of having blown up the cartridge factory on Avenue Rapp. Thus all Thiers' toadies, their families, all those whose sympathies were with the Versailles government, were distrusted. Demands were made for all able-bodied men to be conscripted into the ranks of the Fédérés. Louise Leroy, Octavie Tardif, Antoinette Decroix, and others whose husbands were fighting for the Commune, protested against 'the cowards who . . . not content with merely hiding while their brothers are avenging our desecrated Paris, still dare to scoff at good citizens doing their duty and risking their lives.' If they refused to sign up, the women demanded that they be put under house arrest and publicly called to shame.[16] *Citoyenne* Gérard, of 159 rue Amelot, wrote: 'The primary duty of a government is that of enforcing its decrees. If it does not possess that firmness, its enemies will not fail to exploit its weakness, and even its most ardent supporters will be demoralized.' While all republicans were fighting and dying for the Commune, able-bodied men were calmly going about their business and making fun of the fighters. This situation could not go on.

My husband belongs to the 7th Marching Company of the 141st Battalion. He has been at the fortress of Issy since Sunday, the 30th of April. There he is fighting to defend our rights. I am not sorry for it for I myself encouraged him to go; it was his duty. But my heart bleeds when I see that absolutely no men but those who feel like it are fighting. The cowardice of the defaulters remains unpunished.

There were Fédérés who had abandoned their posts, and yet were continuing to draw their pay. She did not want to make any denunciations, but she feared that the Commune's weakness would frustrate all its plans for the future. 'The feeling of the fighting men is that the Commune should, as quickly as possible, proceed to a general census of the population, and the immediate induction of all able-bodied male citizens.'[17]

Under the pressure of public opinion and of the Clubs, General Cluseret decided that every man from nineteen to forty years of age be obliged to serve in the National Guard: a useless measure, since it provided only a very weak contingent of men who were really eager to fight (the partisans of the Commune had long since been at the ramparts and the forts). A clumsy measure, too, since it gave the Commune the appearance of being dictatorial (which it rarely was), inquisitorial, and insufferable—while remaining ineffective.[18]

However that may have been, the women were given the responsibility for this policing of the people. In the 12th arrondissement a 'battalion of women' was formed, in which the seamstress Marie-Catherine Rogissart, whom we have already encountered at the *Club Eloi*, played an important part. According to a witness whom she had accused of being a Versailles spy, she had said: 'I'll make you all go and fight, you're nothing but a bunch of layabouts. Me, I'm a woman, and I have more courage than any of you. Like it or not, you're going to fight the Versailles murderers.'[19] Joséphine Taveau, *femme* Semblat, led the search for sailors for the Commune.[20] A charwoman, Marie Audrain, *femme* Vincent, appears to have been a sort of recruiting agent. She tried to enlist all the men in her neighbourhood, and even talked about giving the women weapons 'to go and avenge their murdered husbands and brothers.'[21] The textile-carder Françoise André, *femme* Humbert, sought out two defaulters.[22]

For lack of policemen, most of whom had left for Versailles, the Commune women attacked their wives and families who had remained in Paris. The cook Mélanie Jacques, *femme* Gauthier, denounced a policeman's wife: 'Assuming that the government of the Commune was a legal one, she believed that she was doing a patriotic deed by denouncing this woman.'[23] At the head of twenty Fédérés, Claudine Lemaître, *femme* Garde, had a policeman's widow arrested and had all his uniforms, symbols of a loathed domination, thrown out of the window.[24] Louise Arzelier, *femme* Jumelle, called 'The General of the Commune' in the neighbourhood, denounced a policeman's niece as a Versailles agent.[25] The laundress Suzanne Preu, *femme* Dutour, denounced a wine merchant for his remarks. He was said to have declared that 'the Versailles government really ought to send all the *Communards* to Cayenne.'[26]

One could give example after example, taken from the reprieve dossiers or the archives of the Councils of War. Most of these women were acting out of political conviction. The writs accusing them noted the 'fanaticism' of their opinions, that is, their devotion to the Commune, and stated with aston-

ishment that they 'had no previous criminal record.' Out of all
these denunciations, however, one may assume that a few
sprang from private vengeance.

Moreover, the Clubs found that the women entrusted with
hunting out defaulters and Versailles agents did not put into
their task all the zeal that could be desired. The *Club Saint-
Ambroise* complained that the women did not put placards up
on the defaulters' doors, as they had been told to.[27]

Women, then, sounded the call to armed struggle, to the
preparation of the barricades, not only in the 18th arrondissement Vigilance Committee and the *Union des Femmes*, but
individually, during conversations at the Clubs and in the
streets. At the *Club Révolutionnaire*, *citoyenne* Frenozi demanded
that 'if the Versailles government has not returned *citoyen*
Blanqui to us within two days, the hostages we have in our
hands be shot. It's been almost a month now that we have been
negotiating,' she added, 'let him be returned to us! This is the
simplest means of forcing them to hurry up and return him.'[28]
The softness of the Commune was criticized, but its activity was
passionately supported. At the National Circus, in the Boulevard des Filles-du-Calvaire, before six or seven thousand people,
a woman, *citoyenne* Baule, back from the provinces, demanded
that the Commune establish a programme that would combine
the claims of Paris with the aspirations of 'our friends beyond the
Seine.' This was, she asserted, the only way of getting the
support of the provinces. 'The provinces love us, love the Commune. But they do not understand us yet. They do not quite
know where we are going, and what they would involve themselves in by following us.' Millière, who presided at the meeting,
congratulated the speaker. They decided to designate sections
by *départements*; in these, men and women would group themselves according to the province they had come from, and study
the possibilities of Commune activity in the *départements*.[29]

This picture of public opinion would be incomplete if one
passed silently over the deeply anticlerical nature of the Clubs.
This anticlericalism had strong and far-reaching roots: in the
novels of George Sand, Eugène Sue, and Victor Hugo, who had

been the intellectual leaders of the people throughout the nineteenth century. For Victor Hugo, the abbey, and the convent in particular, was 'one of the dankest secretions of the Middle Ages.' It was 'a congregation of owls trying to face daylight.'[30] For George Sand, it was a place 'of lies and imposters.'[31] Tales circulated about the corpses in the Eglise Saint-Laurent, or about the instruments of torture in the Picpus convent—tales which seemed to issue from the novels of Eugène Sue, and which found a naïve credence in the audience of the Clubs. People were outraged. They demanded that the nuns in hospitals and schools be replaced by *citoyennes*[32] and that priests and nuns be arrested until the end of the fighting. All of this did not take place without excess and violence, usually verbal, of which the detracters of the Commune have compiled many a florilegium. In the eyes of the people of Paris, the Church was closely allied to bourgeois interests: the one was rejected along with the other.

8

EDUCATION

TO ESTABLISH the future society of which it dreamed, the Commune had to mould men and women who were free of the stamp of clericalism. It was necessary to organize a secular system of education, and to make provisions for new schools for girls, whose schooling had always been so badly neglected— especially technical schools, which would prepare them to earn a living.

As early as the 26th of March, the Society for New Education named delegates who were to present a project for educational reform to the Commune. This committee consisted of three men—Menier, Rama, and Rheims—and three women, Henriette Garoste, Louise Laffitte and Maria Verdure (daughter of the schoolteacher Augustin Verdure, a member of the Commune). Without wasting any time, the delegates brought before the Commune, on the 1st of April, an educational plan reminiscent of the one drafted in 1849 by the *Association des Instituteurs, Institutrices et Professeurs Socialistes*, under the direction of Pauline Roland.

It was necessary for a republic to 'make young people ready for self-government through a republican education.' This problem took precedence over all others; if it were not solved, serious and lasting social reforms could never be envisaged. Therefore, all the educational establishments maintained by the Commune, the *départements*, and the State had to be opened to all children, regardless of their faith. In the name of freedom of conscience and of justice, religious or dogmatic instruction had to be abolished in State establishments: 'Let neither prayers, nor dogmas, nor anything that is reserved for the individual conscience be either taught or practised there.' Questions that were within the domain of religion, therefore, had to be removed from examinations. Teaching methods should always be 'experimental and scientific,' based upon 'the observation of facts'; therefore, religious teaching organizations could exist only as private or non-State establishments. In short, schooling had to be considered as a public service; it had to be free, complete, competitive insofar as professional specialities were concerned, and obligatory, whatever the social position of the parent. In response to the delegates of the Society for New Education, the Commune answered that it was in complete agreement with their plan, and that it considered this first step 'an incentive to set out on the path that it was determined to take.'[1]

The women's society *La Commune Sociale de Paris*, run by Jules Allix, and the Society for New Education joined forces to organize a meeting upon the theme 'Social Planning and Education.'[2] Twice a week, on Thursdays and Sundays, the Society for New Education brought teachers and parents together to discuss the reforms to be effected in the syllabuses and methods of instruction.[3] In a hall on the rue d'Arras, Edmond Dumay gave lectures every night about the new education, the family, and the rights and duties of children and parents. 'The husband and wife should be equal before the law and before morality; there can be only physical or intellectual inequalities, and different functions, in their association.' This association could be lasting only if it were based on 'a community of national elementary education.' On the other hand, families based on passion, self-interest, convenience, or the domination of 'the head of the house' were unstable. The dowry was an immoral custom: 'The true dowry is the worth of the fiancée.'[4] For her part, Louise Michel sent the Commune a summary of an educational method that she had been thinking about for a long time. It was necessary to teach as many elementary ideas as possible with 'the fewest, simplest, and most comprehensible words possible.' She attached great importance to the moral training of her pupils. Their awareness ought to be developed to such an extent that 'no reward or punishment can exist apart from the feeling of having done one's duty, or having

3(b) "Anonymous, or not much more than a name." A page from the sketchbook of "C.A."

3(a) "She seemed the very incarnation of Revolution." Louise Michel, from a contemporary caricature.

4. "Chimerical beings, analogous to salamanders and elves." Pétroleuses in action.

acted badly.' As for the religious problem, that should be left to the parents' wishes.[5] With her friends in the Montmartre Vigilance Committee—Sophie Poirier, Marie Cartier (née Lemonnier), and Mme Dauguet—Louise Michel demanded secular professional schools and orphanages to replace 'the schools and orphanages of the ignoramuses.'[6]

Maria Verdure, and Félix and Elie Ducoudray, representing the *Société des Amis de l'Enseignement*, proposed a plan for the reorganization of day nurseries. The problem of very young children was difficult for working women to solve. The ideal would be to excuse mothers from all work during the nursing period 'by means of the social reforms we are planning.' But, in the meantime, the day nurseries could do considerable service. They should not merely be considered as places to keep children of the poor off the streets; they should give them a start in education in pleasant surroundings. First of all, boredom, 'the greatest malady' of little children, ought to be avoided. Therefore the nurseries would include gardens, aviaries full of birds, and painted or carved toys representing animals, trees, and real objects. Bright colours everywhere. There should be ten women for the care of a hundred children—gay young women. Medical supervision would be provided for.[7] This dream of the *Communards*, which then seemed a demagogic utopia, is what people today are trying to attain within a variety of social structures.

But they were not content with vows and plans. As if the political part were already won, they put themselves courageously to work. At 40 Boulevard Victor-Hugo, they established a National Guard orphanage for the children of Fédérés and of working women who made military clothing or were ambulance nurses and thus were unable to take care of their children. 'The Republic will open its arms to them, offer them a bed, clothing, and food. It will teach them to be decent, hardworking, and brave.'[8] In the 8th arrondissement, the mayor, Jules Allix, took a census of the children. Out of 6,251, only 2,730 attended schools. The others were simply not enrolled, althought some of them received instruction at home. The private schools did little. Two Congregation schools had shut down. They had to be reopened. 'All children between the ages of five and twelve should be placed in school immediately, or, at least, it should be proven that someone is teaching them or having them taught.'[9] The girls' school on the rue de la Bienfaisance was turned into a pilot school, as we would say today, under the guidance of Geneviève Vivien. Children as young as three were admitted to it. Between five and seven, they were to get some conception of reading, writing, arithmetic, and spelling.[10] Paule Minck opened a school at Saint-Pierre de Montmartre.[11]

But they were also struggling against the religious communities, whose teaching went against the social goals of the Commune. In the 4th arrondissement, the priests and nuns were thrown out of the public schools. 'The Commune has no intention of offending any religious faith, but it has a strict duty to be on the watch lest the child, in his turn, be done violence by assertions which his ignorance does not allow him to judge or to accept freely.' Schoolteachers from that time on had to inculcate the children with a secular ethic: 'Teach the child to love and respect his fellows, inspire him with love and justice, and also teach him that he must learn for the good of the common interest.'[12]

This battle for secularization needed volunteers. The Commune urged citizens of both sexes who hoped to obtain jobs in elementary schools to bring proof of their qualifications and offer themselves as candidates at the Commission for Education at the Hôtel de Ville. For having accepted a teaching post in a nuns' school, a young bookseller from the rue Monge, Anne Denis, would be summoned to appear before a Council of War.[13]

This was indeed a direct participation in the Commune struggle, for the priests and nuns did not allow themselves to be ousted without a fight. Marguerite Tinayre, appointed inspector of girls' schools in the 12th arrondissement, went to visit the religious school on the Passage Corbes, in Bercy, and informed the Mother Superior that from then on the latter would have to address all her requests to her. Two weeks later, the mayor of the arrondissement, accompanied by a dozen women, expelled the nuns, who took refuge at Charenton.[14] The woman who ran the school on the rue Saint-Dominique complained that before the nuns closed their establishment, they had allowed a certain number of children to leave. People had come to demand the return of two of them. 'I count upon your good will,' she wrote in a panic to Raoul Rigault, the delegate to the Prefecture of Police, 'to have them brought back home.'[15] At the school on the rue des Bernardins, 'harpies'—a Commune supporter is speaking: to each his own harpies— harpies, then, had flogged the new schoolteachers; whereas at the school of the Marché aux Carmes, tradeswomen had thrown the newly-appointed headmistress down the stairs.[16] Faced with this resistance, the delegate to the Commune Commission for Education, Edouard Vaillant, decided to have all diehards arrested.[17]

But the problem was not only that of secularizing elementary education. Edouard Vaillant asked the municipalities to estab- lish professional schools. People were particularly concerned with women's technical instruction, which would eventually enable girls to earn a living. Mme Manière, a schoolteacher, organized a temporary workshop-school in the rue de Turenne. She submitted to the Hôtel de Ville an organizational plan for professional schools which would supplant the convent work- rooms. From their twelfth year onwards, girls would receive a responsible general and professional education, under the guidance of teachers or specialized craftswomen. 'The various disciplines would provide a favourable environment for a progressive education.' When the pupils were skilful enough, they would be paid for their work.[18] In the 8th arrondissement, Jules Allix organized a workshop which was to be both a school and a Home for young girls without either family or occupa- tion.[19] The art-school on the rue Dupuytren was reopened; under the direction of Mme Parpalet, it became a professional school of industrial art for young girls, giving instruction in drawing, sculpture, wood- and ivory-carving and all the fields in which the art of design can be applied to industry. Also,

literary and scientific instruction was to be carried on at the
same time as the practical courses.[20]

The evening before the troops of the Versailles government
entered Paris, the Commune Commission for Education had
decided to raise teachers' salaries: 1,500 francs for assistant
teachers; 2,000 francs for headmasters and headmistresses. For
the first time the equality of men's and women's salaries was
declared, 'seeing that the necessities of life are as numerous and
imperative for women as for men, and, as far as education is
concerned, women's work is equal to that of men.'[21] This
revolutionary, anti-Proudhonian decision is far from being
universally applied even today. At the same time, a committee
composed of André Léo, Anna Jaclard, and Mmes Périer,
Reclus, and Sapia was given the responsibility of organizing
and superintending all girls' schools.[22]

It is quite certain that in two months, petitioned on all sides
by claims as urgent as they were various, the Commune could
not successfully have carried through its educational reform. But
guide-lines had been drawn which the bourgeois Republic was
to follow in its efforts to secularize and organize the education
of girls. Women took an important part in formulating and
partially implementing these plans—which were much less
utopian than they were said to be.

9

A GREAT JOURNALIST

THE GOALS OF THE COMMUNE, the coherent thought which quickened the best of the *Communards*, are both expressed by André Léo's excellent articles. And one might wonder through what injustice of history a woman whose novels are above average, and who played an important role in the Commune, has nowhere found her rightful place. Benoît Malon—who, one must admit, became her husband—paid her this tribute: 'This woman, whose name is among those of the greatest writers of our time, and whom Rossel, who knew what he was talking about, called *citoyen* André Léo, was equally devoted to the cause of the people and to serving it with her writings, her speeches, and her total support.'[1] Yet literary historians who set third-rate writers up in the eyes of posterity never even mention her name, and the historians of the Commune scarcely notice her. No doubt there are several reasons for this. The first is that André Léo was a woman, and women need much more talent than do men in order to be recognized. Second, André Léo was implicated in the Commune, and literary historians generally tend to be very traditionalistic. Third, however devoted André Léo may have been to the Commune—a devotion that she retained all her life—she did not figure among its extremists, and did not hesitate to criticize the mistakes and violence of its partisans. Tending toward Bakunin rather than Marx, she thus cannot be ranked among the prophets and saints of the First International. In the eyes of orthodox Marxists, André Léo is an 'individual,' someone smacking of anarchism, and vaguely disturbing. In the eyes of anarchistic revolutionaries, she is much too reasonable. In the eyes of the bourgeoisie, she is a revolutionary. In short, there is no category for her; she is among those people who could not be annexed by any single cause.

In the newspaper *La Sociale*, André Léo became the zealous
but lucid promoter of the Commune. As early as the 9th
of April, she recorded the isolation of Paris, the mutual lack
of understanding between the capital and the provinces. 'Both
are in the wrong, and for Paris, the more intelligent, the fault is
perhaps greater.' Thus it was necessary for Paris to enlighten
the countryside and the provinces, and explain that they all had
the same oppressors. It was right for Paris not to imitate the
violence its enemies had done to thought and liberty, not to
transgress the principles that were the very bases of its demands.
In this, André Léo implicitly poses the eternal question of means
and ends. How can just policies be enacted by unjust means,
when the end is always contained in the means which are used
to achieve it, and which determine it? 'We must uphold our
faith in a worthy manner; we must show the idea which we have
the honour of representing in all its brilliance; we must not let
it be obscured by error or anger, so troubling the consciences of
those who see ideas only through men.' Therefore, one should
not proclaim a Commune and then act as if it were a Constituent Assembly. As a Commune, Paris owed allegiance to the
assembly elected by the provinces. By fighting against this
assembly, Paris was no longer Commune but Revolution.
Therefore Paris should make a frank avowal of the social,
revolutionary idea it represented. 'There are no susceptibilities
left to be spared. We have nothing to lose and all to gain' by
making such an avowal. It was not a fight to the death between
Revolution and Monarchy, between poor and privileged,
between worker and parasite, between the people and its
exploiters. The peasant was also the victim of the exploiters;
but the truth of his condition was hidden from him by his
antiquated ideas. Thus he had to be shown where his interest
lay. Granted, it would have been preferable to appeal to his
intelligence. But whose fault was it if this was impossible? Who
had abolished freedom of the press? Who had refused the people
education, 'without which universal suffrage is nothing but a
trap in which democracy is caught, and perishes'? The responsibility devolved upon the men of lies and treason who had

wanted merciless, bloody battle.[2] Next came a manifesto,
drafted almost entirely by André Léo, addressed to the rural
workers. It was necessary to end the antagonism between
workers and peasants, between the city and the country (a
problem against which all the twentieth-century revolutions
would stumble). 'Brother, you have been deceived. Our interests
are the same. What I am asking for, you want too; the freedom
that I demand is your own. . . .' What did it matter whether
the oppressor was called landowner or manufacturer? Everywhere, the producers of wealth lacked the necessities of life.
Everywhere, they lacked 'liberty, leisure, the life of the mind,
and the life of the heart.' For centuries it had been said that
property was the fruit of labour. This was a lie. That house,
that land, on which the peasant worked all his life, did not
belong to him; or if they did belong to him, he was burdened
with debts, and he or his children would have to sell them.
'The rich are lazy; the workers are poor and will remain poor.'
Against this injustice Paris had risen and wanted to change the
laws. 'Paris wants the peasant's son to be as well educated as
the son of the man who is rich, *and rich for no reason*, for human
knowledge is the common good of all men.' Paris no longer
wanted a king or highly-paid ministers. The savings here would
make it possible to establish homes for the aged. Paris wanted
those responsible for the war to pay the 5 billion francs owed to
Prussia. Paris wanted justice to be free, and to be done by judges
chosen by the people. Finally, Paris wanted 'the peasant to have
his land, the worker to have his tool; work to be available for
everybody.' It was said that the Parisians were socialists,
'dividers.' But who said that? The thieves who cried 'Stop,
thief!' to put people on the wrong track. The real 'dividers'
were 'those who do nothing but get fat from the work of others.'
The cause that Paris was defending and the cause of the worker
were thus the same. The generals who that day were attacking
Paris were those who had betrayed France: the deputies appointed by the provinces wanted to restore Henri V. 'If Paris falls,
the yoke of poverty will remain on your neck, and will pass on
to your children.'[3]

On several other occasions André Léo came back to the necessity for making the countryside aware of the truth about Paris, for purging the provinces of the poisonous calumnies spread by the Versailles press. 'Can we let this infamous old man (Thiers) dishonour Paris? Do we want the provinces and Paris to end up as mutual strangers, more enemies to one another than are rival nations?' France was being sold to traitors, and nothing but Paris stood in the way; therefore Paris had to be crushed. Let Paris proclaim the truth. 'The truth is the religion of every honest heart. The only atheist is he who does not possess it.' Therefore it was a question, not of supporting or fighting the Commune, but of proclaiming truth: 'The men of the revolutionary government have their faults and errors; so be it. But it is nonetheless true that they are risking their lives to support the great, the true, the only genuine revolution of this century, the breaking of the monarchical sac in which the embryo revolution has been choked for more than seventy years.'

But since, as a rule, women are practical, André Léo did not stop at generalities, nor at vows. She proposed the founding of a newsletter which Paris, through the *Union Républicaine*, would send twice a week to all the papers in the *départements*, to give them accurate information on how things stood.[4]

If channels of information in Paris were free to operate, the indefatigable André Léo said again on the 16th of May, the urban and rural population would understand that they had to unite against their exploiters. For both of them hated war. That was why the peasants had voted 'for peace.' What people in the provinces condoned most in the Parisian Revolution was that it had killed some generals. 'A great cry must be raised, powerful and unanimous enough to reverberate in the very heart of the villages—the cry that never goes unheard: that of the martyr dying for his faith.' This was the faith in communal liberty, in the Republic, in Equality.[5]

Paule Minck went to the provinces to try to make the voice of the Paris Commune heard. But she was preaching in the desert.

In the midst of political passions, André Léo continued her

efforts at clarification and truth; moreover, whatever its errors
and faults, she was convinced that the Commune was on the
side of historical truth and justice. Thiers had promised to
apply 'the common right' to Paris. But what, then, was 'the
common right'? 'We live in an age when words have to be
defined. The common right of Thiers and of the Assembly is the
liberty of ignorance and the slavery of thought.' While villages
had the right to choose their mayor, cities of more than six
thousand inhabitants had the right to nothing but a mayor
appointed by the government. Why this difference of rule?
Either

the countryfolk, farmhands, masons, shepherds, and so on are all
philosophers, who in solitude weigh the strong and the weak of things
human, from Seneca to Montaigne, in the shadow of the oaks of
Saint Louis and the beech trees of Virgil; while on the other hand,
the towns are populated by loathsome, faithless, lawless bandits, all,
as is well known, habitual criminals, who in this turbulent century
have come out of their traditional caves into the daylight of Belleville, Montmartre, and Les Batignolles

—or else the villages were illiterate, 'reduced to the sermon and
the almanac,' while the towns knew more or less how to read,
write, make judgments, form opinions, as Thiers himself had
done, through study and discussion. Intelligence was precisely
what Thiers and his 'men of order'—those legitimist notables,
Orléanist bourgeois, financiers, landowners, manufacturers—
did not trust. It was all too clear why.[6]

The municipal law of Paris, just passed by the Versailles
Assembly, furnished yet another proof of the notables' great
fear. Passy, an aristocratic district with 42,000 residents, was to
have the same number of deputies as Popincourt, inhabited by
183,000 workers. And one had to have lived at least three years
in the same place in order to vote. 'For this assembly of stick-in-
the-muds, immobility is a sign of virtue. The oyster is the
symbol of sagacity.' Furthermore, municipal officials would be
unpaid. 'They have thought it all out. Workers, my friends, be
advised that you will appoint one of yourselves to administer

your interests. You may do it; nobody has forbidden you. Just one thing: the men you elect will have to have an independent income, or learn to live without food.' You want 'the common right': here it is. Equality? Take it. 'The strong-box is God, and the Assembly is its prophet.'[7]

But although André Léo ceaselessly attacked the Versailles government, she did not shrink from criticizing the actions of the Commune. She was outraged at the suppression of reactionary newspapers, and dissented from the editors of *La Sociale*, who had approved of this measure. 'On this point I must disclaim any responsibility, out of respect for the principles which constitute all the power and reason of democracy. In my opinion, to deny these principles is to deny our mission. If we act as our enemies do, how will the world choose between them and us?' (the thorny problem of means and ends, which poses itself to every revolutionary conscience). Let lies and calumny, when necessary, be attacked with justice, but 'let freedom of thought be inviolable.'[8]

She was equally indignant when the Commune was silent, particularly in the serious cases like that of Rossel, delegate to the Ministry of War. Exasperated by the anarchy and weakness he saw in the Commune, Rossel threw in its face an arrogant and magnificent letter of resignation: 'Provisionally appointed by you to the Ministry of War, I find that I am no longer able to bear the responsibility for a command in which everyone deliberates and no one obeys. I cannot remove the obstacles, for the obstacle is you, and your weakness; I do not want to make an attempt on public sovereignty. I resign and have the honour of requesting a cell in Mazas.'[9] André Léo energetically took Rossel's part: his letter was 'the cry of a conscience,' she wrote. If he was wrong, let it be proven; if he was right, let justice be done, not to citizen Rossel, but to the abuses that were ruining the Commune, which he was not alone in noting. 'Why these reticences? Why this winnowing of facts? Why these closed doors? Are there still some things that are good to tell the public, and others that are to be hidden from them? But by what right? Do we not know that this is the denial of popular sovereignty and of the rights of Truth?' The conflict that was rife among the leaders of the Commune jeopardized not the ideas it was defending, but the men who represented and temporarily personified them. Men could be replaced; they could always be found. The real saviour was Truth. What was there to hide? Why were the Commune meetings secret? Did not the Commune have to account to the people? 'The people who are dying for this cause have a right to know who is serving them, and who betraying them. A true democracy is not distrustful of truth, for it is made of truth. It comes from truth, it moves toward truth; it dies only for want of light.'[10] The next day, André Léo returned bravely into battle, defending Rossel against the Commune and the Central Committee that had accused him of conspiracy. It was an indictment of the Central Committee. She accused certain of its members of being at the bottom of a monarchical conspiracy; it was against their will that the 18th of March had become a social revolution. This accusation compels the historian's belief no more than does the charge brought against Rossel, which it so neatly countered. But André Léo was right in declaring, along with Edouard Vaillant, Jourde, Delescluze and many others, that the Central Committee had augmented anarchy and indiscipline, undermined the Commune and greatly contributed to its incapacitation and impotence.

What has the Central Committee done since the election of the Commune? It had announced in noble words that it was stepping down without ulterior motives, but its actions have contradicted its words. It has set itself up as a rival of the elected power. It has sown disorder and division in the ranks of the National Guard. It has stirred up the soldiers against the commanders, and the commanders against each other. . . . It has insisted on taking over the administration of the military, and this administration is in a deplorable condition. . . .

In short, the Central Committee was following only one principle of organization, 'that of disorder.' 'When an heroic people are fighting for a great idea, they have the right to ask their representatives for a little clear-sightedness, courage, and

common sense,' she continued. But she was not content with
defence and accusations. Ever practical and positive, she asked
the Commune to appoint immediately a commission of inquiry
to seek out the truth. But let them make haste, for the provinces,
which were coming round to the Commune, were disgusted by
all these disputes. The Versailles government was taking advantage of their internal discord to secure its position.[11]

Unlike most of the men of the Commune, who so often went
astray into useless discussions, devoting themselves to details
and neglecting what was essential, André Léo never lost sight
of the two objectives that, if the Commune were to triumph,
were the most urgent: the indispensable support of the provinces, and the armed struggle against Versailles. In a very fine
article, she extols the soldiers of the Commune, those sixty
thousand men who, for more than three weeks, had held their
own against a hardened army of experienced soldiers, policemen, and gendarmes. Who were they, those dead men whose
names and professions were listed every day? A shoemaker, a
stonecutter, a carpenter, a blacksmith.

The soldier of the present Revolution is of the people. Only yesterday, he was in his little shop, his chest bent down to his knees, plying
his awl or his needle, or hammering iron. How many people passed
by without knowing, without believing, that a *man* was there?
Today, this stonecutter, this shoemaker, this carpenter, this smith
suddenly straightens up and, putting aside his tools and his apron,
heads for the battlefield. He does the greatest thing that a human
being can do: he dedicates himself to his faith, he fights for an idea
whose victory he may not be there to see. This poor man gives the
most precious of all human possessions—his life—to humanity.

There was an abyss between the imposed discipline of the
soldier and the 'free resolve' of the revolutionary fighter—the
man who took his rifle and renounced all his attachments,
renounced his very life, for his idea. Where did this devotion,
this heroism come from? Not from 'advanced classical studies
and from that worship of virtue which do such a good job of
inspiring the young bourgeois.' What these men of the people
made one realize was that 'humanity has not degenerated,

France is not dissolute.'[12] André Léo upbraids the neutrals and the cowards, the people who went about their own insignificant business while others were fighting. If they were against the Commune, let them go to Versailles, where people were plotting 'against justice and liberty,' where people were fighting to defend the 'exploitation of man.' But if they were 'for communal liberty, for the idea that is not written, but lived,' for liberty in equality, let them join the ranks of the defenders of the Commune. Doubtless the men representing the Commune were not above criticism. But they were, for the most part, men of good faith; moreover, they could be changed by election. Others were marred by 'certain intemperances.' Certainly, action had to be taken, although fatigue and the lack of healthy food had much to do with these abuses. These were not, in any case, adequate reasons to excuse oneself from serving the Commune.[13]

Finally, she appeals to all women to join the struggle. If democracy had been vanquished until that time, it was because the democrats had never taken women into account. At that moment, it was a question not only of national defence, but of the defence of justice and liberty. At that time, Paris was far from having too many fighters. Women like Louise Michel and Mme de Rochebrune had given an example 'and were the pride and the admiration of their brothers-in-arms.' Let women fight, therefore, alongside their sons, their husbands, their brothers; then the Versailles soldiers, who had been duped by slanderous lies, would understand that they were not facing a group of sedition-mongers, but the people united. All women could not fight, but all could care for the injured or organize the feeding of the troops. 'Therefore I suggest that General Cluseret immediately start three enlistment registers, one for armed activity, one for aid to the wounded, and one for mobile kitchens.' The women would come in droves to sign up.

But when in fact women attempted to answer the appeal of the Commune, they came up against the incomprehension of battalion commanders and doctors. André Léo looked for the causes of this, and patiently resumed the discussion, as we shall see later.[14]

Thus, in all her articles, André Léo displayed lucidity and

practicality. She clearly distinguished urgent necessities from illusory reforms which could be really applied only after victory; in this she showed herself to be infinitely more realistic than most of the men of the Commune. First it was necessary to win, and this meant that Paris must obtain the support of the provinces; hence her explanations to the peasants. It was necessary to fight; hence her praise of those volunteers who had chosen to give their lives for the Commune, and her appeal to women. But André Léo never lost sight of the fact that the end did not justify the means, that truth had to be the people's weapon against reaction, whose domination could rest only upon a network of lies. It is a pity that being a woman, André Léo was not able to sit among the members of the Commune. In the midst of all the chattering, she might have been able to make them listen to words of common sense, reason, and intellectual integrity.

Artists also put their talent at the service of the Commune. At the Tuileries, concerts and popular performances were organized in aid of the widows and orphans of the Republic. The people took possession of the royal apartments, in which they had not set foot since 1848. They crowded in, peaceful and joyous. Many spectators were not able to enter, but they refused to take back the price of their seat, 1 fr 50 or 3 francs. They were given, as a souvenir, a red cockade and a copper medal in the shape of a Phrygian cap.[15] Rosalie Bordas, who had become famous in Paris by singing *La Canaille* the day after the assassina- of Victor Noir, and then *La Marseillaise* at La Scala after the declaration of war, appeared dressed in a short white skirt and a huge red sash, which trailed behind her. Once again she sang *La Canaille* and the refrain was picked up and chorused by the crowd:

> In the old French city
> There's a race of iron men,
> The furnace of their fiery soul
> Has forged to bronze their skin,
> Their sons are born on straw,
> Their palace is a slum.
> That's *La Canaille*—
> Well, I'm one of 'em.[16]

At a sign from Rosalie Bordas, a Fédéré came out of the wings and handed her a red banner; she slowly unfurled it and wrapped it around herself. She went on singing. 'It was a thrilling sight,' Vuillaume tells us. 'The red of the gold-fringed banner was like a bloodstain on the white skirt: her hair spreading out on her bare shoulders, her broad chest, her solid, muscular arms, her gaze fixed on high, as if in a brutal ecstasy— she symbolized the heroic *canaille* who were fighting on the ramparts.'[17]

Agar (Mme Charvin), of the Comédie Française, also contributed to the popular performances at the Tuileries. In each drawing room, she declaimed Auguste Barbier's *Lyre d'Airain*, and *L'Hiver*, by the destitute and consumptive poet Hégésippe Moreau.[18] This participation in the Commune festivities won her, from Versailles, the insults of *Le Figaro*. 'Once upon a time there was a princess who prided herself on protecting the arts, since she was an artist herself. For some reason, she became infatuated with a mediocre tragedienne, with a bleating and doughy delivery,' and forced her upon the Comédie Française as a *sociétaire*. After the fall of the Empire, this ingrate began to recite Hugo's *Les Châtiments* against her benefactors. 'At the present time, rolling upon this slope of cowardice, flattering the sovereign *canaille*, as she used to flatter the Empire and its entourage, the exprotégée returns to the Tuileries, with red ribbons on her bodice, to gabble socialist verses and to slobber insults upon a society which found an undeservedly high place for her.' And, the editor promised her, she would be deported to Cayenne, along with the '*citoyenne*' Duguerret, who had dared to give performances at the Vaudeville for the benefit of the Fédérés. To these threats Agar replied with dignity. Yes, she had recited *La Lyre d'Airain* and *L'Hiver* at the Tuileries, for the benefit of widows, orphans, and the wounded. 'I often recited these poems during the Empire, before the Emperor, and often at the *salons* of Princess Mathilde. I have never recited *Les Châtiments*, and the entire Théâtre Français will bear witness that I have refused to recite it.' As for her gratitude and esteem, these belonged for all time to Princess Mathilde. This declaration of fidelity toward a member of the imperial family is not without elegance, after the fall of the Empire and in the full sway of the Commune. She added, moreover, 'I am ready to go to Cayenne. For that, I await a new denunciation from you. I do not fear your attacks at Versailles any more than I fear the Commune in Paris.' She would continue, therefore, to give assistance to those who were suffering, from whatever cause.[19] Agar was not to go to Cayenne: but, black-listed after the fall of the Commune, she left with a touring company for Switzerland, and had to leave the Comédie Française in 1872.[20]

But let us leave these very Parisian anecdotes.

IO

WOMEN UNDER FIRE

FOR THE PURPOSE of logical exposition we shall separate the three fields of women's activity under fire: as nurses at the first-aid posts, as *cantinières* and as soldiers. But life is not logical, least of all during a period of revolution. During the Commune struggle, the boundaries among such manifestly diverse activities were not well established. On the battlefield, Louise Michel both tended the wounded and took part in the shooting; she was part of the 61st Battalion, the army corps commanded by Eudes. After having taken Les Moulineaux, they entered the fortress of Issy.

Two or three days afterwards, red flag unfurled, about twenty women came to see us—Béatrix Excoffon, Malvina Poulain, Mariani Fernandez, and Mmes Gaullé, Dauguet, and Quartier. They were answering the appeal that had appeared in the newspapers; they tended the wounded, but they also took up the rifles of the dead. . . . There were also several canteen workers there, Marie Schmitt, Mme Lachaise, Victorine Rouchy . . . many others, whose names could fill a book.[1]

Men and women touched with the fire of revolutionary passion commit themselves utterly to the multiple tasks Revolution demands of them. We are dealing here, not with functionaries, but with living people who have freely chosen the total fulfilment of their destiny. This is why, throughout this study, we re-encounter the same women—at the Clubs, the committees, the first-aid posts, and even, rifle in hand, at the last barricades. And behind every name, behind all the anonymities that make up the 'masses' and supply material for statistics, there is a living person, unique and irreplaceable in his own special features.

On the 13th of April, the Commune had passed a decree for

the organization of a medical corps. Each company was to be composed of twenty doctors and orderlies, ten vehicles, and a hundred and twenty stretcher-bearers. In each arrondissement, two, three, or four sections had to be ready day and night. To each section were to be added two women attendants who would serve with the stretcher-bearers. They would be given the pay of 1 fr 50, and the rations allotted to non-commissioned officers and National Guardsmen.[2] Anna Jaclard, André Léo, and Sophie Poirier responded to the summons of the Commune by the following appeal:

The *citoyennes* of Montmartre, at a meeting held on the 22nd of April, have decided to put themselves at the disposal of the Commune to form first-aid companies which will follow the corps that are fighting the enemy, and carry our heroic defenders from the battlefield. The women of Montmartre, inspired by the revolutionary spirit, wish to attest by their actions to their devotion to the Revolution.[3]

In the name of the 18th arrondissement Vigilance Committee, Anna Jaclard, Sophie Poirier, and Béatrix Excoffon organized a meeting at the *Club de la Boule Noire*, 'for all *citoyennes* who want to lend their active support to the demand for all our rights, to go and help the wounded on the battlefield, or to care for them in the hospitals.'[4]

For in effect, in addition to caring for the wounded, changes were proposed in the organization of the public assistance system. The 18th arrondissement Vigilance Committee again, in a petition with two hundred signatures, protested against the presence of nuns in hospitals and prisons, and demanded that they be replaced 'by devoted and courageous mothers of families, who would do their duty better than the nuns.'[5] These measures for secularization were demanded by all the Clubs. In the arrondissements, the Catholic boards of charity gave way to communally sponsored relief committees: 'The idea of alms-giving must be replaced by the spirit of solidarity which binds republicans together and imposes assistance upon them as a duty.'[6] The poorhouses on the rues Thouin, Boutebrie, Saint-Jacques, and the rue de l'Epée-de-bois were taken over by women loyal to the Commune.[7] In the Saint-Lazare prison, as in the Beaujon hospital, nuns were replaced by women of the people.[8]

Thus, in the realm of public assistance, the Commune acted as a revolutionary power. It shattered the pre-existing apparatus, and attempted to substitute another system conforming more to its own viewpoint: in this case, the secular viewpoint. Insofar as it was a revolutionary power, the Commune would have done better to take over the Banque de France than to carry out measures on a secondary level, which disorganized the hospital services and contributed to futile and inextricable disorder. But the men of the Commune did not discern the hierarchies of urgency. Their debates, like their decisions, were often marked by revolutionary childishness.

The ambulance-nurses of the Commune, for their part, published a very urgent appeal. They declared that they

do not belong to any society whatever. They live only for the Revolution; their duty is to tend, on the very field of battle, the wounds made by the poisonous bullets of Versailles, and when the hour demands, to take up their rifles like everyone else. In the event of reaction triumphing somewhere, as it might, they will not neglect their right to fire the powder-magazines; for wherever it may be, the Revolution must not be vanquished. Long live the Commune! Long live the Universal Republic!

This document is signed by Louise Michel, who must have drafted it (her style is recognizable), and by her friends Mariani Fernandez, Malvina Poulain, and Mmes Gaullé, Quartier, and Dauguet.[9]

The *Union des Femmes pour la Défense de Paris et les Soins aux Blessés* recruited women both for work at the dressing-posts and as *cantinières* and soldiers. The 4th arrondissement Women's Committee urged all 'devoted and patriotic' *citoyennes* to meet at the *mairie* 'to organize and come to the aid of the wounded.'[10]

All these appeals did not remain theoretical. The women of the 18th arrondissement organized a permanent aid-post at l'Elysée-Montmartre.[11] Louise Michel and her friends organized a mobile ambulance station at Neuilly; Béatrix Excoffon and eighteen other women formed another one at Issy.[12] The *Union des Femmes* ran a station with eight nurses at Petit-Vanves.[13] Béatrix Excoffon has preserved for us, in a vivid account, the impromptu character of these ambulance stations. 'Off we went to the Porte de Neuilly. Along the way, many people gave us lint and bandages; I bought what medicaments we needed at a chemist's. And there we were, turning Neuilly upside down to see if there were any wounded left, not suspecting that we were right in the middle of the Versailles army.' A lieutenant of the Fédérés asked them what they were going to do, with their red banner. 'I replied that we were going to tend the wounded, and that we wanted to cross the bridge to get nearer to the noise of cannon-fire.' Even though they did not have passes from the Commune, the lieutenant authorized them to continue on their way, since they were not armed. Having crossed the bridge, they heard the cannons toward Issy. A young woman advised them that if they wanted to go farther they should call the ferryman 'on the island.' But, she added, 'you must say that you are women from the Commune. Otherwise he will not let you cross in his boat.'[14] The ferryman let them into the cabin, cut a long branch from a tree and fastened to it the red flag that Béatrix Excoffon portrays herself as holding. From the bank, the gendarmes fired, without hitting them. Finally, they reached the fortress of Issy, where they met Louise Michel and the 61st Battalion. Béatrix Excoffon remained at Issy for about two weeks, as ambulance-nurse to the Enfants Perdus.[15]

Others continued to tend the wounded of the Commune, as they had tended the wounded during the Siege. Such was that 'distinguished' old lady of whom Vuillaume tells us, who 'was guilty of no other crime,'[16] or Victorine Brochon, who was wanted as a *pétroleuse*, and who has left us valuable memoirs about the Siege and the Commune. We also find her at Issy in the heat of battle, tending, with ridiculously inadequate equipment, the men who had been incurably maimed by the 'nicked bullets' of Versailles.

Unfortunately, we lacked everything. We had no bandages for dressings. We had to give those wretched men little cartridge boxes to drink from. In spite of everything, the disabled did not voice a single complaint or regret. They were in pain, but they seemed happy to have retaken the fort, happy to be giving their lives to establish a more just and fair society. For all of us, the Republic was a magic word.

The medications that were so sorely lacking were rediscovered too late in an abandoned military van. The wounded died during the night. 'If I were to live a hundred years, I should never be able to forget that terrible slaughter.'[17] Another nurse, Alix Payen, gives us a concurring statement in a letter to her mother. She came from the Milliets, a family of Fouriérist republicans, and obtained a nursing diploma that allowed her to follow her husband on to the battlefields of Issy, Vanves, Clamart, Levallois-Perret, and Neuilly. She observed the men's discontent, because of 'bad administration, excessive fatigue, and especially because the trenches were badly defended; there were only a quarter of the men necessary.' But she also observed the courage, the nobility, and the thoughtfulness of 'these children of Paris.'[18] A Fédéré, Alphonse Freye, asked the editors of *Le Cri du Peuple*, 3rd of May, to be so kind as to give him 'a corner in the paper' to thank an ambulance-nurse of the 169th Battalion of the National Guard, who had been caring for the wounded on the battlefield and had saved his life.

But, in this struggle to the death, Versailles had no more mercy for nurses than it had for prisoners: both were shot. Lieutenant Butin, sent with truce flags to gather up the injured at the fortress of Vanves, was greeted with rifle fire by the Versailles soldiers despite his white flag and the flag of the Geneva Convention; he had to return in haste to his own lines. An ambulance-nurse who was going to the aid of a wounded man was raped and killed by five Versailles men.[19] The matter was laid before the Commune, which considered applying the decree on hostages which had been passed on the 5th of April, after the massacre of Flourens, Duval, and prisoners taken by Versailles. This decree aroused the indignation of all right-

minded people, but was merely a response to the murders
committed by order of Thiers. Moreover, the debate revealed
that the men of the Commune were much more respectful of
their enemies' lives than were their adversaries. Urbain, under
the influence of his mistress Marie Leroy (herself influenced by
a Versailles agent, Barral de Montaud), asked that ten hostages
be shot within twenty-four hours, in reprisal for the murder of
the ambulance-nurse; but the Public Prosecutor of the Commune, Rigault, declared that as far as he was concerned, he
would rather let ten guilty men escape than strike down a single
man who was innocent. Consequently he asked that a grand
jury be formed.[20] The decree on hostages was not actually
applied in reprisal for the murder of the ambulance-nurse. It
would take the mass murders of Fédérés by the Versailles army,
during the Bloody Week in May, for the exasperated crowds to
abandon themselves to violence against the hostages.

Despite their good intentions, the volunteer nurses were often
not well regarded by the officers. In *La Sociale*, André Léo
recounted the mishaps of the nurses from the 17th arrondissement. Bearing an order from the municipality and a Red Cross
armband, they appeared at the Porte de Clichy to offer their
services. The commandant of the 34th Battalion accepted four
of them. The others went on to Levallois; from there they were
sent to the staff headquarters of General Dombrowski, at
Neuilly. There the officers bombarded them with equivocal
jokes. 'Why all these obstacles?' asked their spokesman. 'Do
Paris and the Revolution have an excess of devotion at their
service?' They met Louise Michel who, with two friends, was
cooling her heels in an anteroom. She had left the fortress of
Issy for Neuilly, where the fighting was the most fierce. But they
refused to put her to work. 'Ah,' she said, 'if they would merely
let me tend our wounded! But you would never believe how
many obstacles, how much teasing and hostility, there have
been!'

Everywhere along the outposts, André Léo noticed a dual
attitude toward the ambulance-nurses. The officers and surgeons were clearly hostile to them; the troops were in favour of

them. Similarly, in 1849, Jeanne Deroin, standing for election (illegally, as it happened), had encountered only sarcasm in the bourgeois districts, whereas those who heard her in the Faubourg Saint-Antoine greeted her sympathetically.

Alongside that bourgeois, authoritarian mentality, so narrow and so petty, which unfortunately exists in so many of our commanders, there blazes in our *citoyen* soldiers the keen, exalted, profound sentiment of the new life. It is they who believe in the great forces that save the world; they acclaim these forces, they do not proscribe them. They know that the right of all is implied in their right. Whereas most of the commanders are still only military men, the soldiers are real citizens. . . .[21]

Rossel—a student at the Ecole Polytechnique who became Minister of War under the Commune and who was without doubt one of the strangest and most attractive figures of the Revolution—expressed his regrets at the situation André Léo pointed out to him, and asked her to tell him 'through the public press' (a consistent revolutionary, Rossel was a foe of secrecy) how to set it right.[22] 'The noble and frank tone of your recent proclamations,' answered André Léo, 'made me sense a man who was incapable of common bias. You know better than I what you can do to make use of the devotion of republican women, for that is inherent in your power. . . .' Women were running up against masculine prejudices and the surgeons' *esprit de corps* at a time when, on the contrary, it was necessary to move toward 'that responsible brotherhood of men and women, that unity of feelings and ideas, which alone can form, in honour, equality, and peace, the Commune of the future.' The Republic could be established only upon such a recognition of equality. André Léo submitted to Rossel an idea of Dr Jaclard's, the head of the 17th Legion (as we have seen, his wife Anna played an important role in the organization of the ambulance stations). Doctors without antifeminine prejudices, and the three or four young women who had passed their examinations at the Ecole de Médecine, were to be placed in charge of several ambulance stations. 'These women had the courage to

force the doors of science; they will certainly not fail to serve
Humanity and the Revolution.'[23] But, the opposite to Rossel,
General Dombrowski displayed an eminently reactionary
attitude toward women. André Léo sharply reminded him that
without the participation of women, the 18th of March would
have ended in failure: 'You would never have been a General of
the Commune, *citoyen* Dombrowski.' She asked the general to do
a little reasoning. Could the Revolution have been accom-
plished without women? That had been the mistake of the First
Revolution: women had been excluded from freedom and
equality; then, returning to Catholicism, they had strengthened
the forces of reaction. The republicans were full of inconsistencies: they did not want women to be under the sway of the
priests, but they were upset when women were free-thinkers
and wanted to act like free, equal human beings. The republicans had dethroned the Emperor and God, only to put themselves in the place of both. The republicans needed subjects—
or, at least, subjected women. They did not want to admit, then
as before, that woman was responsible to herself. 'She should
remain neutral and passive, under the guidance of man. She
will have done nothing but change her confessor.' But God
possessed one enormous advantage over man: he remained
unknown, which enabled him to be an ideal. Religion condemned reason and knowledge. The Revolution, on the other
hand, postulated that reason and liberty be exercised in the
search for Truth and Justice. 'The Revolution is the liberty and
the responsibility of every human being, limited only by the
rights of all, without privilege of race or of sex.' Therefore
women could not but be concerned; yet people talked about the
freeing of man, but not of woman. Women were rejected and
discouraged when they wanted to serve the Revolution. Consequently they were thrown into the ranks of the reactionaries.
A history of the period since 1789 could be written under the
title 'A History of the Inconsistencies of the Revolutionary
Party.'[24]

But this attitude of many Commune officers toward women
corresponded to an age-old feeling that was too deep and too

widespread for it to be easily changed, despite various interventions. Thus the *Club de la Révolution Sociale* in its turn asked
the 17th arrondissement municipal authorities to intervene on
behalf of ambulance-nurses with the surgeons and battalion
commanders.[25]

Armed women, whether *cantinières* or soldiers—often they
were both at the same time—drew the attention of the admirers,
as well as of the detracters, of the Commune. With their
chassepot rifles, their revolvers, their cartridge cases, their red
sashes, and their fantastic Zouave, naval, or infantry uniforms,
they were the target of caricaturists; a woman wearing trousers
was a scandal in itself. With astonishment, Mme Blanchecotte
described 'those women's faces, sinister, fate-ridden, almost all
of them very young, and some very beautiful.'[26]

We find them scattered in the midst of the troops. In principle, there were four *cantinières* per battalion, but often there
were many more—accompanying their husbands or lovers,
fighting and firing beside them. Often groups of them could be
seen marching in line, with their red banner, before the astonished onlookers in the street. 'A band of women armed with
chassepots today passed by the Place de la Concorde. They were
going to join the Commune fighters,' noted *La Sociale* on the
5th of April. A women's company, under the command of
Colonel Adélaïde Valentin and Captain Louise Neckebecker,
was incorporated into the 12th Legion.[27] On the 14th of May, a
hundred or so women went to the Hôtel de Ville to ask for
weapons. Gambon, a member of the Committee of Public
Safety, had some distributed to them.[28] The reactionary newspaper *La Justice* adds, with an irony that is at once scornful and
uneasy, 'One would like to smile. Might we be returning to the
Vésuviennes of 1848, and might the laurels of *citoyen* Bormes be
disturbing *citoyen* Gambon's sleep?'*[29]

---

* The Vésuviennes was a women's political club formed during the
Revolution of 1848. Bormes, a distinguished chemist and a devoted Versailles
partisan, was hired by the Scientific Delegation of the Commune to make
successful explosive compound. He was arrested on the 18th of May, suspected of manipulating the compounds—which, indeed, he probably did—so
that no explosive could be made. He was freed on the 24th of May—*Trans.*

These *cantinières* and fighting women were involved in all military engagements. Insofar as they were women—those 'females,' as Dumas *fils* said—they were doubly insulted and maltreated by Versailles.

On the 3rd of April, on the occasion of a sortie during which Flourens and General Duval were murdered by Versailles soldiers, the geographer Elisée Reclus, taken prisoner, gives us the following account of a *cantinière*. 'The poor woman was in the row in front of mine, at the side of her husband. She was not at all pretty, nor was she young: rather, a poor, middle-aged proletarian, small, marching with difficulty. Insults rained down upon her, all from officers prancing on horseback along the road.' A very young hussar officer said: 'You know what we're going to do with her? We're going to screw her with a red-hot iron.' A vast, horrified silence fell among the soldiers.[30]

Often these women were heroic. Even the most ardent antifeminists have rarely denied that women have courage. At Neuilly, a *cantinière* with a head wound had the wound dressed and then returned to combat. Another, chased by a gendarme, suddenly turned around and killed him point-blank. Her comrades and the crowd cheered her when she got back within the Paris walls.[31] On the Châtillon Plain, a *cantinière* was the last to retreat, with a group of National Guards, and kept on turning round to shoot.[32] In the 137th Battalion, a young *cantinière*—almost a child—never stopped firing the cannon despite the shells, coming from Châtillon, which were falling all around her.[33] When the Fédérés had succeeded in evacuating the fortress of Vanves, by means of the catacombs and quarries undermining the region, the newspapers noted that 'it was women who, in this situation, showed the most calmness, presence of mind, and courage. The ambulance-nurses attempted to carry off the wounded. The *cantinières* were distributing stimulants, and keeping watch over the torches.'[34]

The *cantinière* of the 68th Battalion was killed by an exploding shell.[35] Among the Fédérés killed in a battle at Neuilly, *The Times* correspondent noticed three women's bodies. One of them was still holding the broken stub of a sabre. 'She was a beautiful girl, with her black hair braided around her head.'[36]

Most of these women remained anonymous. Others, killed in battle or lost in the defeat, are not much more than a name: Mme Oudot of the 208th Ménilmontant Battalion;[37] Honorine Siméon, cited, at Clamart for having stayed constantly in the trenches, and having 'done cartridge duty under enemy fire, when the National Guards themselves were hestitating to go and fetch cartridges.'[38] *Citoyenne* Lens, of the 261st Battalion, mother of three, 'an honourable woman, respected by all,' was killed at the fortress of Issy.[39] Victorine Rouchy, of the Commune Turcos, was congratulated by her comrades for 'the courage that she showed in following the battalion into fire, and the humanity she had for the wounded during the battles on the 29th and 30th of April.'[40]

Marguerite Guinder, *femme* Lachaise, was, like Victorine Rouchy and many others, at once a *cantinière* and a nurse. But we are a little better acquainted with her than with most. Born in Salins in the Jura in 1832, she was a clothier by profession. She had been married to someone named Prévost, and had had a child by him; but she was separated from her husband, and for eleven years had been living with a bronze-setter, Lachaise, whose name she bore. This is another example of those unions which could not be legitimized because of the ban on divorce, but which were as faithful and durable as legitimate marriages. The officers of the Councils of War always seemed to consider this 'concubinage' as an indication of immorality, and one further charge against the women brought before them; yet at this time, adultery in polite society was regarded with the greatest indulgence. Never has 'class' morality been so flagrantly displayed. Both Lachaises went with the 66th Battalion to Issy and Meudon.[41] The Fédérés of the 66th requested that the Commune extend recognition to the heroism of their *cantinière*:

In the fighting of the third *inst.* (April), before Meudon, she displayed conduct beyond all praise, conduct of the greatest virility, remaining all day long upon the battlefield despite the harvest of shots falling around her, busy caring for and bandaging up the numerous wounded, in the absence of the services of any surgeon. In testimony of which, citizen members of the Commune, we are come to draw your attention to these acts, in order that the most perfect courage and unselfishness of this republican *citoyenne* be done justice to.[42]

Certainly the style of this citation leaves much to be desired, but the defenders of the Commune were humble, and often illiterate, people.

Rifle in hand, Mme de Rochebrune avenged the death of her husband.[43] Victorine Louvet, General Eudes' wife—his 'companion,' as was the expression among the Blanquists to whom Eudes belonged during the Empire—is as frequently cited for her courage. She was a life-long friend of Louise Michel. In 1865, they spent their holidays together; Victorine was then preparing for her 'exams.'[44] She was courageous and, furthermore, combined civil courage with military courage (the two are not quite the same thing); she displayed both when her husband was arrested, after the raid on La Villette in August, 1870. The examining magistrate knew that Eudes was hiding Blanqui. He urged Victorine Louvet to disclose the revolutionary's hiding place. But no threat (true, they did not talk in terms of torture, in those days) could make her break her silence.[45] Naturally, Maxime du Camp and others have heaped mud, abuse, and slander upon this woman. In their eyes, a physical blemish was a sign of moral decadence: 'With her wide eyes illuminating a delicately-coloured face, framed by lavish, light-chestnut hair, Mme Eudes could have passed for a perfect beauty, were it not for the nasty strawberry-mark which, spreading down between her eyebrows, made this madonna-like face horribly crude.' Maxime du Camp considered her vulgar, pretentious, and coarse. He was outraged at seeing her fence with Raoul Rigault, the young Public Prosecutor of the Commune: 'I imagine that she has given up being a woman, or, at least, that she would have liked to be a woman with a beard.'[46] Such is their tone. Louise Michel points out that 'Mme Eudes did not shoot badly, either,' at the fortress of Issy.[47] And *The Times* correspondent saw her as another

Jeanne Hachette, 'carrying, not a hatchet, but a real rifle, which she used with remarkable coolness, always picking out her man and taking her own good time to aim accurately.'[48]

But among all these women who soldiered for the Commune, a place apart must be given to Louise Michel; her great figure dominated them all. She was everywhere at once: soldier, ambulance-nurse, orator. She was to be found in the Clubs and on the battlefields, in the Montmartre Vigilance Committee and in the ambulance stations she helped to organize. She also proposed to undertake a strange mission: that of going in person to Versailles to assassinate Thiers, whom she believed to be the most responsible for the situation. Ferré and Rigault, to whom she disclosed this plan, succeeded in dissuading her from it; the murders of Generals Clément Thomas and Lecomte had already aroused public opinion against the Commune. Besides, they added, 'you won't be able to get as far as Versailles.' Louise Michel wanted to prove to them that this plan, although perhaps absurd, was feasible. She got so dressed up that 'I did not recognize myself,' reached Versailles without interference, and made her way into the park in which the army was camped; there she propagandized for the 18th of March Revolution, and left as tranquilly as she had come. Then she bought newspapers in a large bookshop. Since she did not lack a sense of humour, she enjoyed reading the greatest ill of the bloodthirsty Louise Michel. Finally she came back to Paris, bearing the Versailles newspapers as trophies.[49] But her courage and audacity were not satisfied with these dangerous pranks. She was everywhere —at Neuilly, at Les Moulineaux, at the fortress of Issy—with her rifle in her hand. 'Thus I had, as comrades-in-arms, the Enfants Perdus in the Hautes-Bruyères, the artillerymen at Issy, and at Neuilly, the scouts of Montmartre'[50]—and, especially, the Fédérés of the 61st Battalion, to which she belonged. 'An energetic woman fought in the ranks of the 61st Battalion; she has killed several policemen and gendarmes.'[51] They gave her a Remington rifle instead of her old one. 'For the first time, I have a good weapon.' She has left us several vignettes of that war, at once workmanlike and murderous: 'Now we are fighting. This is battle. There is a rise, where I run ahead crying "To Versailles! to Versailles!" Razoua throws me his sabre, to rally the men. We clasp hands on high, under a rain of shells. The sky is on fire.' She opposed the timorous and shamed the hesitant. A panic-stricken Fédéré wanted to surrender the Clamart station: 'Go ahead if you want to,' she said, 'but I will stay here, and I'll blow up the station if you surrender it.' And she sat herself down with a lighted candle, at the doorway of a room where ammunition was stored.[52]

She also went out into the field to tend and bring back the wounded. As in the early days at Vroncourt, her pity extended even to animals: she went out under fire to rescue a cat. But she was also an intellectual who was introspective in the midst of action. One night, when she was on guard duty at the Clamart station, with a former Swiss Guard who had joined the Commune, we overhear this strange dialogue: 'What effect is the life you lead having upon you?' 'Why, the effect of seeing before us a shore that we must reach,' replied Louise Michel. Under fire, she read Baudelaire with a student and played the harmonium in a Protestant church at Neuilly, near a barricade. She jotted down, during a march, the impressions of a poet: 'We are going to the fortress of Issy by way of a little rise among some hedges. The path is strewn with violets that are being crushed by the shells. . . .' Or again, on guard at the Montmartre cemetery: 'Some shells came over at regular intervals. One would have said a clock was striking—the clock of death. In this clear evening, balmy with the fragrance of flowers, the marble seemed to come alive. . . .'

II

THE BLOODY WEEK

NEVER HAD THERE BEEN so many flowers as there were that
Spring.[1] On Sunday, the 21st of May, the weather was fine and
people felt much more like going for a stroll than like fighting.
Many Parisians attended the concert given at the Tuileries in
aid of the widows and orphans of the Commune. During its
session of the 19th of May, the Commune had closed down the
theatres, and the Versailles bombardment of Paris had stripped
the ramparts bare.

The Versailles troops entered the city that Sunday at three in
the afternoon. The Commune was not informed of this until
seven o'clock; the Parisians did not learn the news until
Monday morning, the 22nd.

Paris, which had seemed enfolded in the sweet sleep of May-
time, awakened. But in the streets there appeared clumsy
posters which, in the long run, disorganized the defence:
'Enough of militarism. No more staff officers with braid and
gilt along every seam . . .'[2] This appeal was directed to no one
but 'bare-armed fighters,' those who had revolutionary faith.
Thus the last vestiges of discipline—indispensable to any armed
combat, revolutionary or not—were destroyed. Thus Paris was
to fight district by district, street by street, house by house,
barricade by barricade, without an over-all plan, but with
savage, insane, desperate heroism.

The entire population was summoned to the barricades. 'Let
even the women join their brothers, their fathers, their husbands! Those who have no weapons can tend the wounded, and
can haul paving-stones up into their rooms to crush the invader.
Sound the tocsin; set all the bells ringing; fire all the cannons.'[3]

Everywhere the streets bristled with barricades, despite the
admirable plans of Haussmann, who had taken all possible

precautionary measures to prevent them. 'What could I have been thinking of,' wrote Jules Vallès; 'I believed that the city was going to appear dead before being killed. And here are all the women and children getting into the fight. A beautiful girl has just raised a brand new red banner, and above these grey stones it has the effect of a poppy on an old wall. Your paving-stone, citizen.'[4] Women in rags and women in silk dresses,[5] young girls and old ladies, were sewing and filling sandbags, were working with pickaxes and mattocks, all day and, by gaslight, all night. The ladies of La Halle erected, in half a day, a sixty-five-foot-long barricade, at the intersection of the Place Saint-Jacques and the Boulevard Sébastopol.[6] In the Place du Panthéon, a barricade was built by women and children singing the *Chant du Départ*. 'Federal' women, wearing long red scarves and red cockades on their black dresses, led the work.[7] And a regiment of women, led by a white-bearded officer, was seen crossing Paris. 'While we admire the courage of our modern heroines, we think wistfully of the time when people engraved on the tombstones of Roman matrons: "She stayed at home and spun wool," ' observed an editor of *La Vérité*, with a touch of nostalgic antifeminism.

Who were these women who were building barricades? Some of them can be identified by means of the proceedings of the Councils of War which have come down to us, and which condemn them 'for having made, or helped to make, barricades in order to oppose the action of the civil police.' There was the wine merchant Modeste Trochu, *femme* Mallet, born in 1829 in Bourg-des-Comptes (Ille-et-Vilaine): in order to construct a barricade in the rue Saint-Jacques, she distributed among the Fédérés some pickaxes which men from the Highway Department had stored with her; she gave them something to drink, planted a red flag on the barricade, and cried 'Long live the Commune'; and she reported her neighbour at 346 rue Saint-Jacques, because the latter had hidden her husband 'so that he would not march along with the others.'[8] And Joséphine Mimet, *femme* Bernard, stocking-mender, born in 1833 at Adilly (Deux-Sèvres): she brought coffee, night and day, to the fighters at the barricades, and was seen, rifle in hand, on the rue Saint-Antoine.[9] And Virginie Lenordez, *femme* Vathonne, dairywoman, who was born in 1823, at Saint-Pierre-Eglise (Manche): she had urged her son to fight for the Commune, had worked on the barricades at the rue des Charbonniers and the rue d'Aligre, and challenged passers-by: 'Your paving-stone, citizen!'[10] And the braidworker Rosalie Gaillard, born in 1836 in Saint-Gervais-les-Bains (Savoie): she had been seen, all the day of the 23rd and the night of the 23rd–24th, sewing sandbags in the garden of the Tour-Saint-Jacques.[11] And Elodie Duvert, *femme* Richoux, born in Toulouse in 1826, who kept a little restaurant on the rue Saint-Honoré-Chevalier. Elodie Richoux came from a bourgeois family. Her husband, a civil engineer, had been killed during the Italian campaign; her brother was an artist in Meudon. 'Courage, friends!' she cried to those who were building the barricade at the corner of her street and the rue Bonaparte, 'Courage, hurry up, we'll wipe out those Versailles swine!' And she went with the Fédérés to break down the door of the bookseller Repos, whose books were used as building materials. She brought food to the fighters, and a mattress on which they could rest.[12]

Then there was the feather-dealer, Eugénie Dupin, *veuve* Léger, born in 1836 in Bussy-Saint-Georges (Seine-et-Marne): she had urged her lover to serve the Commune, and had helped to build the barricade on the rue Ténier.[13] And Alphonsine Blanchard, called 'The Peasant,' journey-woman, born in 1844 in Saint-Jean-de-la-Ruelle (Loiret): with a rifle slung across her back, she worked at building the barricade on the rue de Lyon, and forced each passer-by to lay down a paving-stone upon it.[14] And Célina Chartrus, *veuve* Godefroy, born in 1832 in Agen, a professional nurse: armed with a revolver, she carried paving-stones for the barricade on the rue de Meaux.[15] And Joséphine Courtois, *veuve* Delettra, a seamstress who was no longer young, being born in 1820 in Laroche (Haute-Savoie): she had already fought at Lyon in 1848, where she had been called 'The Queen of the Barricades'; yet the years had taken away none of her revolutionary faith. She had been seen attending the *Club de la*

Boule Noire and the *Club de l'Eglise Saint-Bernard*; now, armed
with a rifle, a red sash over her dress, she was requisitioning
empty casks belonging to '*le sieur Gallier*' to build a barricade at
the corner of the rue Doudeauville and the rue Stephenson.
She handed out cartridges, and even sent her little girl to take
ammunition to the fighters.[16] Around her there were other
women, among them Marie Cartier, née Lemonnier, clothing
maker, born in 1833 in Rainfreville (Seine-Inférieure): we
have seen her before as a member of the 18th arrondissement
Vigilance Committee, signing, along with Louise Michel, a
petition to obtain professional schools and secular orphanages.
She, too, was rolling Gallier's casks along to build the barricade.[17] And then there was Jeanne-Marie Quérat, *femme* Jobst
born in Guignen (Ille-et-Vilaine) in 1824, married to a savings-
bank employee: she used to attend the *Club Saint-Nicolas-des-
Champs*, and had urged her son to fight in the ranks of the Commune.[18] And Madeleine Billault, *veuve* Brulé, born in 1820 in
Châtellerault, boot and shoe dealer: she handed out shovels and
and pickaxes to the Fédérés, got them to requisition a furniture-
remover's pantechnicons, and carried orders in the midst of the
firing.[19] And Marguerite Fayon, journeywoman, born in 1835
at Coren (Cantel), whose lover was a second lieutenant in the
Federal Guard and a member of the Vigilance Committee: in
the thickest of the fighting, she carried cartridges to the men
defending the barricades.[20] And Marie-Augustine Gaboriaud,
born in 1835 in Ardelay (Vendée), whom the neighbourhood
had named 'La Capitaine': she was the 'companion' of a stonecutter, Jules Chiffon, a captain in the 121st Federal Battalion.
Sashed in red, armed with a revolver, she led him to the
the barricades at the Pont d'Austerlitz and the Boulevard
Mazas, organized an ambulance post, and let the Fédérés into
a house to defend the barricade at the Avenue Daumesnil.[21]
And Eugénie Rousseau, *femme* Bruteau, a hairdresser born in
Warcq (Ardennes) in 1826: she called her neighbours to the
barricades, cleaned rifles, washed them to cool them off,
recharged them, and brought them to the fighters; she went
under fire to gather up the rifles of the dead. She had made a

banner out of a red rag, and started a barricade at the corner of
the rue Myrrha and the rue Poissonnière and remained there
until the end. When everyone else despaired, she was still crying
out her hope: 'See, Dombrowski has arrived! We're saved!
Long live Dombrowski! Long live the Commune!'[22]

A remark is called for here. A large proportion of these women
were born in the provinces. As for the men, the proportion was
less, but still quite considerable: the Parisian insurrection of
1871 was carried out by provincials. There are doubtless several
explanations for this paradox. These men and women who had
broken all ties with their villages and come to Paris, had given
proof in their private lives of a will to renewal, a spirit of
adventure, which also were what impelled them to join the
ranks of the Social Revolution. Doubtless, too, they were less
integrated into traditional urban life. Those who are settled
always compose the bulk of conservatives; peasants are
adequate proof of this. These hypotheses are certainly worthy
of further research.

The Versailles troops advanced slowly and cautiously. They
had learned at some cost, during the last two months, that these
ragamuffins fought bravely. They preferred to turn their flank
rather than give frontal attack. From the first, Thiers' soldiers
made it clear that the struggle would be ruthless: at the Baby-
lone barracks, sixteen Fédérés who had been taken prisoner
were immediately put to death, and the Versailles troops shelled
the Ministère des Finances. The firemen of the Commune
extinguished this first act of incendiarism.

The women fought shoulder to shoulder with their men:
mostly unorganized, they had come there either because their
husband or lover was involved in the battle, or because a barricade had been built at the end of their street. But a committee
of the *Union des Femmes pour la Défense de Paris*, for its part, had
met for the last time on the 21st of May, at the *mairie* of the 4th
arrondissement, presided over by Nathalie Lemel. On the orders
of the Commune, they left, red flag in the lead, to defend Les
Batignolles.[23] A hundred and twenty women held the barricade
at the Place Blanche, and halted the troops of General Clinchant

for several hours. Not until 11 o'clock, exhausted and without ammunition, did they withdraw; those who were taken were killed on the spot.[24] Among them fell the dressmaker Blanche Lefebvre, of the Organizing Committee of the *Union des Femmes*—she who had 'loved the Revolution as one loves a man.' The survivors doubled back on to the Place Pigalle, where they held out for three hours more; then the last of them retreated to the barricade on the Boulevard Magenta. 'Not one survived. This is one of the many episodes of this legendary barricade,' remarked Lissagaray.[25]

Nathalie Lemel doubled back from Les Batignolles to the Place Pigalle, where she had planted a red banner. She does not seem to have done any firing. She cared for the wounded, and urged the Fédérés to hold out. 'Her appearance impressed me,' says an eye-witness, 'for she was the only older woman amid a group of young girls, all armed with rifles and wearing ambulance nurses' armbands as well as red sashes.' Elizabeth Dmitrieff, for her part, flung a last order to the 11th arrondissement committee: 'Muster all the women, and the committee itself, and come here immediately to go to the barricades.'[26] We find her at Montmartre with Louise Michel; at the Faubourg Saint-Antoine with Frankel. Louise Michel held the Montmartre cemetery with about fifty men from the 61st Battalion. Soon they were no more than twenty, then fifteen; they retreated to the barricade on the Chausée Clignancourt. Suddenly the National Guards arrived. 'Come on, there are only three of us,' cried Louise Michel—but the National Guards turned out to be from Versailles. They seized her, and threw her back into the barricade trench. When she got up, half-dazed, her comrades had disappeared. The Versailles men were ransacking the houses. 'I saw only one means of stopping them, and I cried out at them, "Fire! Fire! Fire!"'[27]

At this point we must bring up the question of the fires for which eye-witnesses and bourgeois historians have ascribed full responsibility to the *Communards*. These fires actually had several causes: first, the incendiary shells and the petroleum bombs which the Army of Versailles had been using since the beginning of April. Many houses in Paris and the suburbs were thus burned, during the Second Siege of Paris, by the shells of the partisans of order and property. These were, no doubt, 'correct' fires—regrettable, certainly, but normal facts of war. Some of the fires during the last week of May were also attributable to Bonapartist agents, who were trying thus to eliminate any traces that were compromising for the personnel of the Empire. In fact, it is strange to note that the *Communards*, those 'dividers,' did not attack the houses of the rich; that the *Communards*, those anticlericals, did not burn down churches; but that what disappeared in the flames were buildings like the Cour des Comptes and the Conseil d'Etat, or the Ministère des Finances—buildings that contained the archives of the Empire's administration.[28] Perhaps, too, some people hoped to receive large indemnities for the loss of their property.

But, having made these reservations, it is certain that the Fédérés bore a great part of the responsibility for the Paris fires. 'Fever of the besieged,' 'the madness of despair,' 'revolutionary vandalism'—easily, but a little too hastily, said. Actually, the Versailles troops fired from the shelter of the houses until the insurgents had exhausted their last ammunition; then they rushed forward and shot down the defenders. It was to counter this tactic that the Fédérés set fire to the buildings near the barricades; thus they flushed the Versailles soldiers out into the open. Marx vindicated the Commune, which 'used fire strictly as a means of defence, to keep the Versailles troops from the avenues which Haussmann had opened out expressly for artillery fire.' For the Fédérés, it was a question of 'covering retreat, just as the Versailles troops opened their advance by shells which destroyed at least as many buildings as did the Commune.'[29] Moreover, the Fédérés resorted to incendiarism only when Versailles began its mass execution of prisoners—which was what invested the struggle with its final and inexpiable character.

But there was also another factor at work. If the defence of the rue Royale or the rue de Lille required that the buildings near the barricades be set afire, no rationale of a military nature

justified the burning of, for example, the Tuileries; we must
have recourse to another explanation. Benoît Malon is the one
who gives it to us: 'It was permissible for the people of Paris,
that magnanimous people who for a century had sacrified the
best of each of its generations for world progress, that people
which, at that very moment, was being slaughtered for its
republican faith—to burn the Palace of Kings.'[30] Lissagaray
goes further: 'The angry flames seemed to rise up against Versailles, and to tell the vanquisher returning to Paris that there
was no longer any place for him there; that those vast monuments of monarchy would shelter monarchy no more.' And he
adds the theory which makes archeologists wince, but which is
justifiable if one still believes in the power of symbols: 'The
sovereign—whatever it be, people or king—never forgives the
enemy his symbols. So it was that in the sixteenth century and
in '89, neither the royalty nor the bourgeoisie could rest until
the nests of stone of feudalism had been destroyed and razed to
the ground.'[31]

On the sites of the fires—the Légion d'Honneur, the rue
Royale, the Tuileries—women as well as Fédérés were arrested.
Did they play a part in setting the fires? Does the myth of the
pétroleuses correspond to any reality? We shall discuss this
question later.

In spite of bitter local defences, the Versailles troops advanced
little by little. At the corner of the rue Racine and the rue
de l'Ecole de Médecine, the barricade was held by women.[32]
Women fought on the rue du Pot-de-Fer. On the rue Mouffe-
tard women brought a fleeing sergeant back into the fighting.[33]
In the Place du Panthéon, women prepared rifles, while the
men fired.[34] The barricade on the Place du Château-d'Eau
exerted a sort of fascination. An English medical student, who
had set up a dressing-station alongside it, tells us: 'Just at the
moment when the National Guards began to retreat, a women's
battalion turned up; they rushed forward and began to fire,
crying "Vive la Commune!" They were armed with Snider
carbines, and shot admirably. They fought like devils. . . .'
Fifty-two were killed there. Among them, a girl in her twenties,

dressed in the uniform of the Fusiliers Marins, 'rosy and beautiful with her curly black hair,' fought all day long: Marie M.,
whose first name at least we know among all these dead, anonymous women who will never be counted.[35] The English
student goes on:

A poor woman was fighting in a cart, and sobbing bitterly. I offered
her a glass of wine and a piece of bread. She refused, saying 'For the
little time I have left to live, it isn't worth the trouble.' The woman
was taken by four soldiers, who undressed her. An officer interrogated her: 'You have killed two of my men.' The woman began to
laugh ironically and replied harshly: 'May God punish me for not
having killed more. I had two sons at Issy; they were both killed.
And two at Neuilly. My husband died at this barricade—and now
do what you want with me.' I did not hear any more; I crawled
away, but not soon enough to avoid hearing the command 'Fire,'
which told me that everything was over.[36]

There are hundreds of similar stories on record. An enemy of
the Commune, Arsène Houssaye, tells us that a girl, well-known
in the rue Richelieu and the Place du Palais-Royal, was
arrested, revolver in hand, in a house from which two shots had
issued. She denied it at first. And then, suddenly: 'All right, yes;
I did the shooting.' 'Until then,' says Arsène Houssaye, 'they
had taken her for a mere whore, dishevelled and full-bosomed,
trailing a faded silk dress, with cheap jewellery in her ears and
on her fingers. But that proud tone in which she replied after
so many days of humiliation was the beginning of her transformation. "Yes, it was me," she answered, "and I'd have liked
to kill all the Versailles people with one shot because they have
killed my lover. And I have only one regret: it's having killed
just one of them. And if I could start all over again, I would."
A few minutes later, they shot her against the iron bars of the
Louvre colonnade.'[37]

But repression struck not only the fighting men and women
taken with weapon in hand, or those who openly proclaimed
themselves responsible for their acts; it struck at random. Every
poor woman was suspect. Even more so if she carried a shopping
basket or a bottle: she was a *pétroleuse*, and was executed on the

spot to the furious cries of the mob. A woman recognized her
husband among some arrested Fédérés; she wanted to talk to
him. A blow from a rifle butt threw her on to the pavement.
Her child rolled in the gutter.[38] The husband of Marguerite
Tinayre, who had not been involved in the insurrection, was
shot without a trial. Any expression of grief alongside the
common graves in which the Fédérés were heaped up was proof
of complicity. Any weeping woman was a 'rebel's female.'[39]

As for the women who were executed, they were treated somewhat
like unfortunate Arabs belonging to insurgent tribes. After they were
shot, while they were still in their death throes, they were stripped of
some of their clothes, and sometimes the insult went further, as in the
Faubourg Montmartre or the Place Vendôme, where women were
left naked and sullied upon the pavements.[40]

Even partisans of Versailles were arrested, like that society
woman whom a deputy of the National Assembly found by
accident among the women arrested as '*pétroleuses*.'[41]

Prisoners, both men and women, who were being sent to
Versailles in a long column were subjected to the insults, jeers,
and blows of an unleashed mob. Some women dragged themselves along, exhausted, leaning upon their neighbours. But
others walked with head held high, like that girl mentioned by
The Times correspondent: 'The crowd heaped its outrages upon
her. She did not flinch, and shamed the men by her stoicism.'[42]
Society women beat the prisoners with their parasols. My great-
grandmother, caught up in the crowd, cried 'Those poor
people!' 'Be quiet, madam,' someone said to her, 'or they'll take
you too.' Even Maxime du Camp was outraged.[43] *Le Figaro* was
somewhat embarrassed; but it consoled itself by thinking that
these insurgent women were all prostitutes, and, as such, had
no right to any pity.[44]

Having got safely away from her barricade in the nick of time,
Louise Michel changed her bullet-rent skirt, borrowed a hooded
cape to look 'as bourgeois as possible,' and went back to her
school on the rue Oudot, where she lived with her mother. The
concierge told her that the Versailles people had come to look

for her, and had arrested her mother instead. Out of her mind with grief, she ran to the nearest police station. 'She is in Bastion 37,' the chief of police told her, 'but she must have been shot by now.' Louise rushed to the Bastion, saw her mother in the courtyard, and gave herself up to take her place. She saw members of the Montmartre Vigilance Committee, the *Club de la Révolution*, and Fédérés from the 61st Battalion. Nearby they were shooting an unidentified man who had been mistaken for Mégy. No matter, it was just one more dead man. General de Galliffet arrived. 'Galliffet, that's me,' he shouted. 'People of Montmartre, you think I am very cruel. I am even more so than you think.' Thereupon Louise Michel, who had lost none of her insolence, sang softly: '*C'est moi qui suis Lindor, berger de ce troupeau.*'* The prisoners burst into laughter. 'Fire into the mob,' cried the furious Galliffet. But, weary of killing, the soldiers did not fire.

The prisoners were herded into a group. Louise Michel, with her undeniably poetic temperament, has described their departure and the long march in the night. 'We marched, lulled by the regular pace of the horses, going off into the night lit occasionally by red fires. . . . It was really the unknown, a dream-fog wreathing round every detail.' The prisoners were made to go down into the La Muette ravine: 'Rays of moonlight slid between the horses' hooves on that narrow path we were descending.' 'What are you thinking about?' a soldier asked her. 'I am looking,' she answered.[45] Then it was Versailles, and Satory.†

There she recognized Malvina Poulain and Béatrix Excoffon, who had been called for execution three times, and who, for four days, had been sleeping on the cobblestones of the courtyard.[46] There, too, were an old nun who had given a wounded Fédéré a drink of water; an idiot woman who did not know

* "Tis I who am Lindor, shepherd of this flock.' Lindor (cf. the pseudonym of Almaviva in *Le Barbier de Séville*) was the popular name for any extravagantly romantic 'Latin Lover'.—*Trans.*

† The Satory Depot lay southwest of Versailles. It was a vast, fortified plateau and one of the four major prisons used by Versailles for incarcerating its *Communard* prisoners before shooting many of them.—*Trans.*

whether she had been arrested by the Commune or Versailles; a deaf-mute woman who, it was said, had cried 'Vive la Commune!' Each day, Louise Michel was told she would be shot the next morning. 'As you like,' she answered.

Those nights at Satory were like bad dreams. The women had been shut up in a sort of loft. 'On the floor were snaky, silvery little threads forming currents between veritable lakes, large as ant-hills, and filled, like rivulets, with a nacreous swarm. They were lice. . . .'[47] In the courtyard, prisoners were crammed together in the rain, lying in mud. From time to time, they were fired upon at random. Sometimes names were called out and men would get up. They would be given shovels with which they had to dig their own graves.

Béatrix Excoffon and Louise Michel appeared before a joint commission which interrogated them. Desperate to have news of her children and to exonerate her mother, Béatrix took responsibility for everything of which she was accused. 'Take care, you wretch,' a gendarme said to her, 'you are going to get yourself shot.'[48]

As for Louise Michel, she answered insolently. Yes, she had been involved in the La Villette affair; yes, she had been at the burial of Victor Noir; at the demonstration on the 31st of October, yes; at the demonstration on the 22nd of January, yes; and during the Commune, yes, she had been in the marching battalions. They picked out the 'ringleaders' Louise Michel, Eulalie Papavoine, Victorine Gorget, and about forty others, who were sent to the Chantiers prison, then to the Versailles house of correction. At the end of two weeks, they had the right to a pallet of straw for two, a tin of preserves for four. The recalcitrants were punished by being tied to a stake for several hours, as we are told by a schoolteacher, Mme Hardouin, who was arrested on hearsay evidence and then acquitted.[49]

All kinds of places were used as prisons. At the Gare de l'Ouest, there was a group of eight hundred women who had not been able to change their linen for weeks. The guards would strike them, usually in the breast. Some women had miscarriages; others went mad.[50] The forts and prison ships overflowed with prisoners. More than a thousand died of hunger and ill treatment.

It is officially acknowledged that thirty thousand Fédérés disappeared during the struggle. Others have said a hundred thousand. As with St. Bartholomew's Day, we shall never know the exact number of the victims of 'the week in May.'

12

WERE THERE ANY *PÉTROLEUSES*?

DID WOMEN PLAY a part in the Paris fires? *Were* there any
pétroleuses? Now that I have reached the heart of my subject
matter, I must admit that I do not know the answer; all I can
do is present the evidence and discuss it objectively.

The Enemies of the Commune accused women of having had
a part in setting Paris on fire. 'Everything was ready. The bottles
of petroleum were at hand, and men and women were stationed
to spread the oil and make a blazing mass out of the 2nd
arrondissement. The arrival of the Versailles troops had been so
sudden that it had upset this fine plan.' A reporter asserts that
he was given these details by a captain of the Vengeurs.[1] A little
girl, eight years old, arrested just as (so it was claimed) she
was about to throw some petroleum into a cellar, was supposed
to have said that there existed in Paris 8,000 *pétroleuses*, organized into a brigade by Ferré. In every quarter, they formed
squads commanded by female sergeants and corporals; their
responsibility was to fire buildings as fast as the Versailles
troops forced their way into Paris. The Versailles press gives
many other details: little placards bearing the notation B.P.B.
(*bon pour brûler*—good for burning) and a Bacchante's head,
were said to have been affixed to buildings that were to be set
afire. There was talk about petroleum eggs equipped with
nitroglycerine primers, and about balloons carrying incendiary
material. It was said that a *vivandière* had been arrested with a
keg containing two litres of petroleum. On the rue des Vinai-
griers, about thirty petroleum eggs had been found in the house
of two women. Soon acid was added to petroleum, *vitrioleuses* to
pétroleuses; these *vitrioleuses* were supposed to have been ordered
by the Commune to disfigure the officers and soldiers of
Versailles.[2]

By now, verisimilitude counted for little. *Le Figaro* stated that in Montmartre, a woman and a little girl had been arrested; *for an hour* they had been throwing petroleum into cellars; the proof of this was that their milk-can was still full of petroleum.[3] *La Patrie* reported that they had found, in the Faubourg Saint-Germain, the charred skeleton of a *pétroleuse*, with a pipe in her mouth; the proof was that her clothes were still soaked with petroleum. 'One assumes that it was the fire from the pipe which brought about this combustion,' the paper explained wisely. But what it did not explain is how petroleum-soaked clothing could remain on a charred skeleton.[4]

In this mass hysteria, *pétroleuses* were to be found everywhere. In the areas occupied by the Versailles army, it was enough that a woman be poor and ill-dressed, and that she be carrying a basket, box, or milk-can. At the corner of the rue de Rivoli and the rue Castiglione, a crowd gathered around a woman who had just been arrested by two artillery-men. She was accused of having thrown a bottle of petroleum at the Ministère des Finances, which had been burning for several days already. Two gendarmes beat her to death.[5]

Hundreds of women—who will ever know how many?—were thus summarily executed. Maxime du Camp himself made short work of these legends. He writes:

Since the morning of the 24th, Paris had been seized by madness. It was said that women were slipping into the quarters of the city already liberated by our troops, that they were throwing slow matches into the cellar vents, pouring petroleum on the shutters of shops, and lighting fires everywhere. This legend, excused and even justified by the horrible sights that people had before their eyes, was absolutely false. No house burned in the area occupied by the French army.

And he quotes the supporting statement of Colonel Hofmann, from the United States Legation, who on the 26th of May wrote: 'Petroleum is the madness of the hour. Peaceable housewives are closing the cellar openings that give on to the pavement, under the absurd pretext that gangs of women are roaming the streets and throwing petroleum into cellars, then setting fire to it.'⁶

On their side, the supporters of the Commune have flatly denied the existence of any *pétroleuses*. Louise Michel: 'The most insane tales have been going around about *pétroleuses*. There were no *pétroleuses*. The women were fighting like lionesses, but I saw no one but myself crying "Fire! Fire!" in front of those monsters.'⁷ Lissagaray, replying in 1897 to an inquiry in *La Revue Blanche* about the Commune (his ironic and disillusioned tone is very different from that of *L'Histoire* and the *Huit Journées*), nonetheless stated strongly: 'As for the *pétroleuses*, they were chimerical creatures, analogous to salamanders or elves. The Councils of War never succeeded in producing a single one.'⁸ And Karl Marx, in an interview for *The New York Herald* of the 3rd of August 1871, detailing the relations between the International and the Commune, declared that although the two had worked together, since they were fighting the same enemy, it was absurd to say that the leaders of the insurrection were acting upon orders received from the Central Committee of the International, in London. On the subject of the *pétroleuses*, he adds:

This story is one of the most abominable fabrications that has ever been invented in a civilized country. I am certain that not one woman, not one child, could be accused with the slightest semblance of proof of having laid petroleum in houses or of having tried to set anything on fire; and yet hundreds were shot for that, and thousands were deported to Cayenne. Anything that might have been burned was burned by men.

The New York Herald's reporter answered, 'I must say that I am equally convinced. I have never met a single person who really saw a woman or a child with petroleum.'⁹

What can we make of all of this? I believe that we must distinguish between two sets of circumstances: first, fire as a weapon of war, used as a means of defence by the Fédérés against the Versailles army, which was attacking with all the resources of a regular army, and ruthlessly murdering all insurgents taken prisoner; secondly, the incendiarism that was supposed to have been perpetrated in the quarters already occupied by the Versailles army. As for the latter, attributed specifically to the so-called *pétroleuses*, it would indeed seem that the whole thing was a myth, of which one of the most virulent slanderers of the Commune, Maxime du Camp, himself took little account. There is no question that what is involved here is one of those manifestations of collective fear, such as we occasionally encounter in history: the Great Fear of 1789, or even more recently, the fear that the world was coming to an end which impelled the masses of India toward their sanctuaries.

But the Paris fires, during the course of an armed struggle, present another problem. They were lit during the fighting, and lit by fighters. There is no reason to think that the women who were helping to build and defend the barricades did not also have a hand in these fires. In the statutes of the *Union des Femmes pour la Défense de Paris et les Soins aux Blessés*, we read the following brief sentence: 'Article 14: The money left over from the administrative costs will be used . . . for buying petroleum and weapons for the *citoyennes* who will fight at the barricades; should the occasion arise, weapons will be distributed according to the drawing of lots.'[10] It is difficult to allow, along with certain historians motivated by a kind of hypocritical daintiness, that the word 'petroleum' coupled with the word 'weapons' has, here, only a domestic meaning—harmless petroleum-oil to light the family lamps. It is more likely that petroleum had already been regarded as the ultimate means of defending the Commune.

The role of the *Union des Femmes* suggested by this document is confirmed by the testimony of Barral de Montaud, in *L'Enquête Parlementaire sur le 18 Mars*. I am well aware that Barral de Montaud was a sorry specimen. An agent of Versailles, he had succeeded in getting himself appointed leader of the 7th Legion of Fédérés, Through a very questionable woman, Marie Leroy, the mistress of the Commune member Raoul Urbain, he had engineered one of the most debatable measures of the Commune, the proposition that hostages be shot immediately in reprisal for the murder of an ambulance nurse.[11] But this loathsome side of the secret agent should not make us categorically reject his testimony when it corroborates the statutes of the *Union des Femmes*. According to Barral de Montaud, the International was not uninvolved in the Paris fires, 'since it was acting through the *Union des Femmes*. If it did not actually give the orders to fire buildings it furnished the means of doing so, for, I repeat, it was the Women's Committee, a subsidiary of the International, that did everything.'[12]

This is to give much too much importance to the International, which represented only one tendency of the Commune, and to the *Union des Femmes*, which was far from controlling the activity of all the women fighting. Very rarely do the court proceedings and the reprieve dossiers mention that the women accused belonged to the *Union des Femmes*. And with only a few exceptions—Nathalie Lemel and Elizabeth Dmitrieff—we do not find the names of the accused in the lists of members of the *Union* which have come down to us. And one has the impression that the Councils of War took a great deal of trouble to turn up '*pétroleuses*,' without much success.

Let us at the outset eliminate an affair of civil law that people attempted to turn into a political case, according to a well known process of amalgamation. This was the case of a certain Marie-Jeanne Moussu, *femme* Gourier; she was a laundress, born the 4th of August 1829 in Bourg (Haute-Marne).[13] 'The Moussu woman is the most perfect type one could imagine of these unspeakable creatures from the slums who, it is known, provided the Commune with powerful auxiliaries for the purpose of burning Paris,' we read in *La Gazette des Tribunaux* for the 23rd of September 1871. But the writer immediately adds: 'What is curious about this Moussu case is that she was guilty of the act of which she was accused, not at the time when the troops entered Paris, but long afterwards, on the 19th of June, when everything was over.' Curious indeed. This *pétroleuse*-come-lately must have been either very stubborn, or very fanatical, or very strange. Now she stated that she had tried to set fire to the house where she believed her lover to be living, to get even with him. We can well believe her. In any event, it is impossible to detect any hint of political intent in what she did. It is an affair of civil law, having no relation to the Commune; but it got Marie-Jeanne Moussu sentenced to death.

With the fire set in the Magasins du Tapis Rouge on the 25th of May, we find ourselves once more with acts of war. The Fédérés had sworn that they would die rather than surrender, and their commander, Brunel, had given the order to destroy the arsenal, whose flames were to erect a barrier before the enemy. Two women were accused as accomplices: a concierge, Louise-Frédérique Noël, *femme* Bonnefoy, born in Paris in 1827, and a parasol maker, Jeanne-Victorine Laymet, also born in Paris, in 1840. Jeanne Laymet was separated from her husband, a certain Roubert, and for ten years had been living with a mercantile agent, Ernest Levieux, by whom she had had a child. The two women, who got along very well, had shown great devotion to the Commune, worked at building the barricades, and had offered their windows to the Fédérés so that they might fire under shelter. They were also accused of having helped to set fire to the 'Tapis Rouge,' but the Fourth Council of War did not sustain this charge. They were sentenced to transportation to a penal settlement and deprival of civic rights, for having 'incited to massacre, pillage, and destruction of property, and for having participated in the construction of the barricades.'[14]

A cook, Eugénie Chilly, *femme* Desjardins—called 'La Picarde'—was accused of having carried petroleum, under her skirts and in her pockets, to her lover, an earthwork labourer named François Bufferne, a National Guard in the 6th Company of the 184th Federal Battalion, in order to set the Prefecture of Police on fire. She was sentenced to twenty years' hard labour.[15]

All these are small fry. There remain two much more important cases, which Maxime du Camp and other pen-pushers have bedecked with all their insults and embroidered with lyrical slander. These women were drunken Bacchantes, hysterical Messalinas dancing around a Spahi,* 'the black devil'—a round of infernal witches.

After the trials of the Commune members and those of the Central Committee, that of the *'pétroleuses'* took place on the 3rd of September 1871. On Tuesday, the 22nd of May, Eudes and Mégy, with the 135th Belleville Battalion and the Enfants Perdus, had occupied the rue de Lille, the rue Solférino, the Légion d'Honneur, and the Cour des Comptes. The battle with Versailles began, and as a means of defence, the Fédérés set fire to the Légion d'Honneur and to some of the houses on the rue de Lille. Among the fighters were seen several women, who were later arrested: Elizabeth Rétiffe, Joséphine Marchais, Eugénie Suétens, Eulalie Papavoine, and Lucie Maris, *femme* Bocquin. Two others escaped, a certain Mme Masson, who seems to have played an important role, and a very young girl who was gathering up the wounded.[16]

These women were coming and going, serving food and drink to the insurgents. Most of them were armed and wore red sashes, or were wearing the National Guard uniform. One, very tall, fired from the barricade on the rue de Bellechasse. Another was seen to roll a cask of petroleum against the door of the hotel at 6 rue de Bellechasse. These women, said witnesses, made 'horrifying remarks,' and forced the Fédérés to remain at the barricades.

None of these women (added the indictment) was ignorant of the plans of the insurgents, for they were crying at the top of their voices, 'Paris must be blown up.' In vain did they deny any participation in rioting and fire-setting, trying to give themselves a sublime role filled with charity and dedication. What they could not deny was that they had knowingly abetted the villains of the Enfants Perdus, and of the 135th Federal Battalion, and had assisted them in their criminal exploits.[17]

The women who appeared before this military tribunal were uneducated and quite incapable of defending themselves.

* Member of Moslem cavalry corps under the Ottoman Empire; in the French army, the Spahis were a cavalry corps of native Algerians and Senegalese, famous for their exotic dress uniforms.—*Trans.*

Elizabeth Rétiffe, a thirty-nine-year-old cardboard maker, was born in Vézelise (Meurthe).[18] For seven years she had lived faithfully with a Parisian ganger, whom she left because he used to beat her. During a period of poverty, she had taken her clothing to the Mont-de-Piété. From then on, she lived alone on her meagre wages. During the Siege, cardboard makers found work scarce. Elizabeth Rétiffe had to accept the relief furnished to paupers by the city of Paris: a pound of bread and sixty centimes. However, despite her poverty, she found the means to pay her rent regularly.[19] Even though she had been sentenced to twenty days in prison in 1853 for having got into a fight with a woman, and fined sixteen francs in 1855 for having insulted a policeman, she was liked in her neighbourhood of the rue du Temple 'for her gentleness, her honesty, and her good relations with everyone,' the police commissioner stated. Early in May, a neighbour, Eulalie Papavoine, urged her to accompany the 135th Federal Battalion of Belleville as a *cantinière*. She accepted, because she had nothing to live on. But she quickly became an ambulance nurse, because 'it grieved her so much to see those unfortunate wounded men.' Before the military tribunal, she asserted: 'I would have aided a Versailles soldier just as willingly as a National Guard.'[20] At the Palais de la Légion d'Honneur she had been seen dressed in a white tunic, wearing a red sash and carrying a rifle slung over her shoulder; but no one had seen her fire it. 'She was busy carrying round food, bringing drink to the barricades,' said a witness, 'and taking up the wounded.' 'I gave first aid before sending them to La Charité,' she confirmed.

'Did you not roll any petroleum casks?' the presiding judge asked her.

'No.'

And indeed, the witnesses, who recognized her, 'had never seen her do anything extraordinary.'[21]

The seamstress Eulalie Papavoine was born in Auxerre in 1846. She had 'no previous criminal record.' For two years she had lived with a journeyman engraver, Ernest Balthazar, by whom she had a child. Ernest Balthazar was a member of the

National Guard in the 135th Battalion, and she had followed him as an ambulance nurse to Neuilly, Issy, Vanves, Levallois-Perret, then to the Légion d'Honneur—everywhere that the battalion fought. Out of conviction? We do not know. Perhaps simply because a woman ought to follow her man, because that is an elementary rule of morality. An ambulance station had been organized in the rue Solférino, where there were still some victims left from the Avenue Rapp explosion. Eulalie Papavoine gathered up the injured, took them to the ambulance station for first aid, then accompanied them to the Charité Hospital. 'When the Légion d'Honneur started to burn, I was at La Charité,' she said. 'I was staggered at this news. I had indeed seen the petroleum casks, but I did not have anything to do with them.'[22]

'You certainly must have suspected that they were going to burn some buildings,' said the presiding judge. 'Why did you not leave the wretched people?'

'I wanted to share my lover's fate.'

'Why,' the presiding judge asked again, 'did you stay behind when the battalion fled?'

And poor Eulalie Papavoine, seamstress, gave this utterly simple and sublime statement:

'We had dead and wounded men.'[23]

There was nothing that predisposed Lucie Maris, *femme* Bocquin, born in Choisel (Seine-et-Oise) in 1843, journeywoman, to serve the Commune. The judges of the Council of War did not understand it at all: she was a 'quiet' woman, who had married a 'decent and hard-working' labourer; they had a child. Her behaviour was of the most 'regular' sort; in her district, she was thought of as an industrious worker, 'whose character was gentle and obliging toward her neighbours.'[24] Respectful of law and morality, she seemed, therefore, more like a candidate for a good-conduct award than a militant working to subvert society. But her husband left her to join the Army. She became acquainted with one Marcelin Dubois, a guardsman of the 135th Federal Battalion. For her, crime began with adultery. It was thus that Lucie Bocquin found herself at the

Légion d'Honneur on the 22nd and 23rd of May; there, on the barricade, she gathered up the body of her lover.

With Joséphine Marchais and Eugénie Suétens, we find figures that conform more to the stereotypes imagined by reactionaries, who expect all political rebels to be habitual criminals, out-and-out jailbirds who pose no problem to the pillars of a well-made social order.

Joséphine Marchais, journeywoman, did not leave a good reputation behind her in Blois, where she was born; no more so in Charonne where she was living. She had been sentenced to six months in prison for theft; her mother, to five years' imprisonment and ten years' police supervision for incitement to debauchery; her sister Madeleine was put in a house of correction until she was twenty, then sentenced to three months in prison for theft.[25] With a family like that, we know well what to expect: these reprobates could but join the Commune. Since the month of March, Joséphine Marchais had been a *vivandière* attached to the Enfants Perdus Battalion, to which her lover, a butcher's boy named Jean Guy, belonged. 'The rank of *vivandière* with the Enfants Perdus indicates right away of what the said Marchais is capable . . .' the indictment declares. She was accused of having participated in the looting of the town house of the Comte de Béthune, wearing a Tyrolian hat and armed with a rifle; of having said horrifying things to incite the National Guardsmen to battle ('Pack of traitors, go on and fight,' she cried to them, 'if I am killed, I want to kill first!'); of having led her lover Jean Guy, who wanted to desert, to the barricades. A witness stated that she seemed to him more dangerous than the Enfants Perdus themselves. But no one saw her laying any petroleum anywhere. Joséphine Marchais denied everything: she was merely going along the rue de Lille to return some linen that she had washed for the Fédérés.[26]

We are rather well informed about Eugénie Suétens, laundress, born in Beauvais in 1846. Her mother belonged to a family of 'decent and quiet' workers. But her father, a tailor, evinced 'advanced' ideas; in 1848 he had left Beauvais to settle in Paris. With such a father, it was not surprising that Eugénie

Suétens was sentenced, in 1867, to a year in prison for theft. Moreover, she had been living (true, for six years) in concubinage with a stonemason, Aubert, a quartermaster sergeant in the 135th Battalion. In the early days of the Commune she had joined the regiment as *cantinière*; she had taken part in all the fighting, at Neuilly, Issy, Vanves, and Levallois-Perret, where she had been wounded twice.[27] Armed with a chassepot rifle and wearing a red sash, she had been seen in the courtyard of the Légion d'Honneur. She was bringing drink to the fighters, taking up the wounded, and was said to have taken part in the building of the barricades.

She admitted having received provisions: three bottles of wine, candles, sugar, butter, sardines—which was merely, after all, the normal rations of fighting troops. But petroleum?

'I never touched any petroleum.'

'Were you given any money?'

'I was given ten francs to pay the ambulance nurses.'

But the presiding judge had another idea in mind:

'On the contrary, we believe that it was to encourage you to do what you were ordered to do: that is, to fire buildings.'[28]

This hypothesis was not confirmed.

One woman was not in the prisoners' dock: Mme Masson, who seems to have played an important role. A Mme Masson figures among the members of Jules Allix's committee, but not of the *Union des Femmes*. She was a blonde woman of about twenty-five, who had a German (?) accent and wore the silver-fringed red sash of the Commune and an armband. She was armed with a carbine and a revolver. It was to her that a Federal commandant had given sixty francs to pay the ambulance nurses, and she—she alone—had been seen firing.[29] We might perhaps have learned more from the interrogation of Mme Masson, since the other women who were accused were evidently nothing but accomplices.

What can we make of all this? The witnesses for the prosecution were categorical: the accused had not been seen to roll any barrels of petroleum. They limited themselves to cooking and caring for the wounded. 'After administering first aid,' said a

wine merchant, 'they came to my house and I gave them something to eat.' Yet it was he who had had Elizabeth Rétiffe
arrested. Did he, then, believe that she was guilty?

'If so, of what?'

'Of insurrection.'

'And of the fires too?'

'Certainly not.'

'Who lit the fires?' the presiding judge insisted.

'I don't know. To me, they're not guilty of that.'

'I'm aware that you didn't see these women with torches in
their hands. But I am asking for your impression. Did you not
see any petroleum?'

'No.'[30]

A dressmaker recognized the five accused women. She had
seen them passing with rifles slung over their shoulders. But
they had done nothing 'unusual.' They had been cooking and
tending the wounded.[31]

All of this greatly displeased the presiding judge. 'It is extraordinary that it should be so difficult to make the witnesses talk,'
he declared. Well, no matter. It was necessary to set examples:
he would set examples.

Captain Jouenne began his indictment, immediately elevat-
ing the proceedings to dizzying heights. Civilization itself was
at stake.

The horrible campaign against civilization begun on last 18th
March, by people who believe in neither God nor Country, as Jules
Allix, one of them, proclaimed, must bring before you not only men
forgetful of their most sacred duties, but also—and, alas, in great
number—unworthy creatures who seem to have taken it on themselves to become an opprobrium to their sex, and to repudiate the
great and magnificent role of woman in society.

And what, then, was this magnificent role? A 'legitimate'
wife, the object of our affection and respect, entirely devoted to
her family whom she serves as guide and protectress, must
exercise her influence over man, to maintain his respect for his
social duties.

'But if, deserting this sacred mission, the nature of her influence changes, and serves none but the spirit of evil, she becomes a moral monstrosity; then woman is more dangerous than the most dangerous man.'

Even though these seamstresses, journeywomen and laundresses could scarcely be mistaken for victims of culture, what Captain Jouenne was putting on trial was the idea of education for women.

If they were illiterate, one might perhaps grieve as one damned them; but, among these women—and I blush to give them the name of women—we find some who are unable to summon to their aid even the paltry resource of ignorance. . . . While lofty minds (and we must heartily second them) call for that important benefit of education for the people, what a bitter deception is this for them and for us! Among the accused, we shall see schoolteachers. These women cannot pretend that the notion of good and evil was unknown to them.

All this was the fault of the emancipation of women.

'And look where we are led by all these dangerous utopias,' continued Captain Jouenne. 'The emancipation of women, preached by scholars who did not know what power it was ordained they should exercise, and who, at the moments of uprising and revolution, wanted to recruit powerful auxiliaries for themselves.'

Indeed, what ridiculous fantasies had not been proposed to them?

'Have they not held out to all these wretched creatures bright prospects, incredible chimeras: women judges, women as members of the bar! Yes, women lawyers; deputies, perhaps, and—for all we know—generals? Generals of the Army? Certainly, faced with these miserable aberrations, we must believe that we are dreaming!'

After having appropriately stigmatized these pernicious doctrines and unlikely prognostications, the Captain called all the women of the Commune to account: the speakers of the Clubs ('those heroines of immorality, theft, and arson, who from the pulpits of our churches, have substituted criminal propaganda for the word of the Gospel'); the secular school-teachers ('who, desecrating the purity of childhood, have, in the schools, usurped the venerated functions of the Sisters of Charity'), and particularly that 'Michel woman,' who replaced hymns by the *Marseillaise* and the *Chant du Départ*, and whose trial would be of extreme importance.

But let us leave these generalities to return to the facts, to those unfortunate women who have been somewhat forgotten in their dock, and who could scarcely be said to have been contaminated by the principles of women's emancipation or by an excess of education. In all the testimony he heard, Captain Jouenne found the proof of their having been present among the insurgents (which was true), of the active part they took in the insurrection (which was probable), of their participation in looting (of butter and sardines), and in the fires (which was not at all proven).

The lawyer Thiroux pleaded for Elizabeth Rétiffe:

I look for an insurgent, I find a woman covered by the neutrality of Geneva. I look for a thief, I find a woman who pays her rent, even during the Siege: a small proof of a great honesty. . . . I look for an accomplice in murder, I find an ambulance nurse leading away the wounded. I look for a *pétroleuse*, and I see in her hands neither fire nor petroleum.

As for Eugénie Suétens, Sergeant Bordelais, who replaced the defaulting lawyer, 'relied upon the wisdom of the Council.' Joséphine Marchais was also defended by a military man, Lieutenant Guinez, who took 'the place deserted by the members of the bar.' They had refused to 'extend their hand to these outcasts of society,' he declared. Lieutenant Guinez was really an honourable man, and did what he could to save the accused woman whose defence he had undertaken: poverty was the cause of everything.

'I wonder, in our corrupt times, where a poor woman goes when she has no more bread?' What jobs, what work could she find? 'Young men not strong enough to carry a musket, men whom I accuse and scorn, hold a lot of jobs which might advantageously be filled by women, and do not hesitate to wrest from them their daily bread.' It was poverty, then, that impelled women to join the insurgents. 'Have pity, gentlemen,' he concluded, 'these are women. . . . Hearken to my plea: it is the plea of a soldier.'

These few words 'spoken with a simplicity and warmth that were entirely military, aroused murmurs of approval among the audience,' noted the reporter from the *Gazette des Tribunaux*.

Haussmann, who pleaded for Eulalie Papavoine, held against his client only her presence at the barricades and her filching of three handkerchiefs. In her case, he found no proof that she had participated in arson. For Lucie Bocquin, whose absent lawyer he was replacing, he simply asked for acquittal.

But this was not the opinion of the Council of War. The judgment was a terrible one: Elizabeth Rétiffe was condemned to death; Joséphine Marchais, to death; Eugénie Suétens, to death; Eulalie Papavoine, to transportation to a penal settlement; Lucie Bocquin, to ten years in solitary confinement.

Eugénie Suétens and Joséphine Marchais wept. Elizabeth Rétiffe remained impassive.[32]

Victor Hugo raised his great voice to defend the insurgents, whom he considered as revolutionary combatants and not as civil criminals.[33] Accordingly he asked for the lives of Rossel, Ferré, all the insurgents of the Commune and those three unfortunate women Marchais, Suétens, and Papavoine: 'One of them is a mother, and in the face of her death sentence, she said (Hugo is lending her his word): "So be it; but who is going to feed my child?" ' And the author of *Les Misérables*, who was not only a great writer but also a man of goodness and magnanimity (two substantives which are today found ridiculous and outmoded), went on: 'The entire social malady is in this statement. . . . Thus, here is a mother who is going to die, and there is a little baby who is also going to die in consequence. Our justice sometimes achieves such successes. Is the mother guilty? Answer yes or no. Is the child? Try and answer yes.'[34]

Was Hugo's intercession decisive? Either that, or the judges on the Commission for Pardons hesitated before the lack of evidence; at any rate, the death sentences were commuted to hard labour for life, and deportation to Guiana.[35]

A second '*pétroleuse*' affair attracted public attention on the 16th of April 1872, just as the public had begun to grow weary of the whole thing. This time it involved three women who were accused of having taken part in the fires at the rue Royale, the Place de la Concorde, and the Tuileries.

Once again, Maxime du Camp has left us fevered descriptions of Florence Wandeval, Anne-Marie Menand, and Aurore Machu. 'Three sinister females had been inspiring and inflaming the men, embracing the artillerymen, and displaying an immodesty unshamed by broad daylight.'[36] He accused them of having laid petroleum and of having indulged in obscene bacchanals in the midst of burning houses. 'Machu, Menand, and Wandeval, sweating, with their clothing undone, their bosoms almost bare, passed from man to man, sometimes screaming: "Drink!" ' ... etc. Such is his tone. To this, Brunel, commandant of the Fédérés, calmly replies:

The appearance in our ranks of shameless slatterns, half-naked women, *pétroleuse*-Messalinas who, like the mythological Furies, kindled courage and breathed life into arson, is an invention which, when all is said and done, can be accounted for. With such means, the picture is muddied, and the reader, beside himself, retains in his mind fantastic figures which nicely prepare him to welcome a monarchical restoration.[37]

Let us, however, try to see things a little more clearly. The dossiers of the Councils of War and of the Commission for Pardons, in their aridity, may perhaps permit us to do so.

On Monday, the 22nd of May 1871, the Federal Battalion led by Commandant Brunel attempted to join General Eudes at the Corps Législatif. With their cannons, they reinforced the barricades of the rue Royale and the Faubourg Saint-Honoré. The battle lasted until Tuesday noon. Then, fearing they would be surrounded, the Fédérés raised a barrier of flames between themselves and the Versailles army. There were women among the fighters. Some were dressed in naval or National Guard uniforms, and armed with rifles; others wore the armband of the Geneva Convention. They fought, or else gathered up the wounded. 'The women who followed the Fédérés must have helped them in all the crimes that were committed, for they were more fanatic than the men,' said a witness.[38] Three of them were arrested: Aurore Machu, Florence Wandeval, and Anne-Marie Menand. Had some *pétroleuses* finally been captured?

Let us dispense with Aurore Machu immediately. For her 'there was no alleged crime of arson.'[39] Dressed in a naval uniform, this woman aimed and fired a cannon in the Place de la Concorde. When she was not by her weapon, she was seen calmly seated under the dome of the Ministére de la Marine. It was said that her comrades bore her in triumph to the Hôtel de Ville, where she was commended for her skill and courage.[40]

In Florence Wandeval and Anne-Marie Menand, we find women who were, perhaps, more closely mixed up with the fires.

Florence Wandeval was born in Berchem, Belgium, in 1848. She came to France at a very early age, and first lived in Angers, which she left at seventeen to settle in Paris. She married someone named Baruteau, was separated from him, and lived with a lover, Bled, in the rue Boulard, under the name of Amélie Maison. A journeywoman, she had good references and had never been convicted of any crime. Then came the war and the Siege. Florence Wandeval joined the 107th Marching Battalion in which her lover was a sergeant, as an ambulance nurse. She remained there during the Commune. Before the Council of War, she stated that she tended the wounded, and had never had a part in any fires:

Lightly wounded in the leg, on Tuesday, the 23rd of May, I was awakened during the night when the remnants of Brunel's battalion were going to beat a retreat. We went back on to the embankments. At that time the Tuileries was burning, and columns of flame were rising from the Palace. I cannot tell you who set it on fire. I thought then, as I do now, that it had been started by the shells that were falling on every side.

She tried to exonerate not only herself, but her comrades as well: 'I swear in any case that nothing can make me suspect the Fédérés of being the cause of this calamity.' She told further how their little band got as far as Les Halles, and then dispersed. She went alone with a wounded man and looked for a doctor to care for him. Along the way, she was hit in the right breast by a bullet.[41] But the witnesses contradicted her, and their accounts were in agreement with each other. She was said to have been heard saying, 'I've just set the f . . . Tuileries on fire. Now a king can come; he'll find his palace in ashes.' And again: 'We've just set the Tuileries on fire, and from tonight on, many others will burn. No one but the people will rule.' She was said to have been injured leaving the Tuileries, as she went through the railings. 'You're a brave girl,' one of her comrades was supposed to have said to her. 'Ah,' she replied, 'there's worse to come.'[42] It must be conceded that these words have an unmistakably authentic ring. It does seem that Florence Wandeval was among the Fédérés who set the Tuileries on fire.

As for Anne-Marie Menand, called Jeanne-Marie (could it be Rimbaud's?*), she was known in the area around La Madeleine as 'the woman with the yellow dog.' She was a poor creature, an easy target for Maxime du Camp's ridicule: 'I have never seen such ugliness. Darkskinned, with staring eyes, dull and dirty hair, her face pocked and freckled, thin lips and a silly laugh, she had some wild quality about her, which reminded one of the panic of nocturnal birds suddenly put into the daylight. . . .'[43] We know the process: physical defects (including freckles) indicate a corresponding moral ugliness, and became a sign of predestination to evil. In the same way, but conversely, people like Vuillaume and Vallès never saw anything but beautiful, young, joyful, healthy girls among the Commune fighters—which is equally absurd.

But in any case, everything that we know of Anne-Marie Menand can hardly be said to confer upon her the ideal aspect of a revolutionary militant. She came from Brittany, and was born in 1837, in Saint-Séglin (Ille-et-Vilaine). She said that

* See p. 207.—*Trans.*

she was a cook, but she had left her last job in 1867 to go and sell newspapers in the kiosks along the rue Royale and the Place de la Madeleine. In October 1870, she went to Vincennes to sell brandy to the soldiers. But she was her own best customer, and was often seen drunk. She was also sentenced to six days in prison for having bought military clothing. After the armistice, she went on selling brandy, this time to the Prussians, and worked occasionally as a prostitute. A few days after the Commune, she returned to live in Paris, on the rue Saint-Honoré, and worked for her sister-in-law, who had a cheap eating-house on the Avenue de Wagram. Thus Anne-Marie Menand had nothing militant about her. She had been seen at neither the Clubs nor the *Union des Femmes*. And when she found herself mixed up in the battle, it was because they were fighting in her neighbourhood. She helped to tend the wounded who were being carried in makeshift ambulances, to 15 and 25 rue Royale. Accompanied by a Fédéré, she requisitioned linen, searched for food, and tried to find 'bourgeois-looking' clothes for the Fédérés so that they could escape. But she also had another role. She went into the houses that were to be burned.

'They've sent me to tell you to get out.'

'But why?'

'Because they're going to burn it.'

At the rue Boissy-d'Anglas: 'I've come to save you, because they're going to set this place on fire. Follow me.'

And to another witness who took refuge in the rue Saint-Florentin: 'Don't be afraid of anything; I'm with you.'[44]

All of this proved to the Council of War that Anne-Marie Menand knew the intentions of the Fédérés. From that to admitting that she herself had fired buildings was only one step, quickly taken. Especially since she had been heard to say: 'It's a good thing that this church (La Madeleine) is being looted. They deserved it.' And again, 'We're going to win, and we'll burn all the nobs' houses down.'

She was condemned to death, but her sentence was commuted to hard labour in Guiana. Florence Wandeval and Aurore Machu were sentenced to hard labour for life.[45]

Another woman, Marie-Jeanne Bouquet, *femme* Lucas, who was president of the *Club Saint-Nicolas-des-Champs*, was said to have shown the Fédérés how to make the Molotov cocktails of that day: a bottle of petroleum fitted with a wick. Twenty years hard labour.[46]

From prison, Anne-Marie Menand wrote to the curé of the Saint-Malo parish at Dinan, to clear herself of the accusations made against her: 'I was arrested like everyone, because they *were* arresting everyone, in the houses and everywhere. . . .' As for the governor of the Auberive prison, he did not see Aurore Machu as the Messalina that Maxime du Camp described. She was 'an indefatigable worker' and a good student at school; she had a timid disposition: 'Machu lets herself be led easily. Moreover, this unhappy woman bitterly deplores her weakness, which was the cause of her sentence.' As a result the Auberive governor interceded for her: she was a widow and the mother of two children without support; several times he asked that her sentence be reduced. But in vain.[47]

What, then, is there left to say about the '*pétroleuses*' women who, shoulder to shoulder with the Fédérés, struggled in the defence of the barricades, and took up the wounded? Among those whose names have been preserved by the judicial records, only Florence Wandeval and Anne-Marie Menand may have taken part in the fires. But certainly not Elizabeth Rétiffe, Eugénie Suétens, Joséphine Marchais, Eulalie Papavoine, or Aurore Machu—all of whom were, nonetheless, condemned as '*pétroleuses*,' because someone had to be guilty and no one could be found. But neither Florence Wandeval nor Anne-Marie Menand appear to be Commune militants. We find them neither in the Clubs nor in the *Union des Femmes*. They were individual women, involved in the battles by accident.

How, then, did the *Union des Femmes* participate in the Paris fires? Did it, indeed, play any role? Only the brief sentence in the statutes, putting weapons and petroleum on the same plane, might indicate so. But we have no evidence that the plan became fact. The women of the *Union* who died on the barricades of Les Batignolles or the Place Blanche have taken their secret with them.

13

THE EXECUTION OF HOSTAGES

ON THE 5TH OF APRIL as a counter to the execution, by the Versailles army, of Duval and Flourens, and as an attempt to stop the executions of prisoners, the Commune passed a degree concerning hostages, which resolved that any person accused of complicity with the Versailles government would be arrested, and that a grand jury would be formed and would pronounce judgment within forty-eight hours. Every accused person who was found guilty would be considered a hostage. Any executions of prisoners of war or supporters of the Commune would be answered by the execution of three times as many hostages.[1] This decree was not enforced, not even when the Commune learned, on the 17th of May, that Versailles had summarily shot an ambulance nurse under particularly revolting circumstances. However, a member of the Commune, Urbain—submitting unawares to the pressure of the Versailles agent Barral de Montaud, and his mistress Marie Leroy—had demanded that the April decree be immediately put into force. But nothing came of this: the Commune members were not in the least bloodthirsty and feared the shadow of any illegality; moreover, they understood that it was to the interest of the Versailles government that the Commune's hands be stained with blood.[2]

When the soldiers of the regular army entered Paris, the massacre of Fédérés began immediately. As early as the 23rd of May, to avenge the memory of Generals Lecomte and Clément Thomas, the soldiers shot 42 men, 3 women, and 2 children chosen at random along the rue des Rosiers. Forty-seven victims to propitiate the shades of two generals: such was the balance of justice. One woman refused to kneel: 'Show these wretches that you know how to die standing up,' she said.[3]

5. "The symbols of the enemy cannot be spared." The burning of the Palais des Tuileries, from an *image d'Epinal* by Pellerin.

6. "Repression struck at random." The summary execution of a pétroleuse at the Louvre, from the *Illustrated London News*, June 10th 1871.

At Les Batignolles, in the Place Clichy, on the outer boule-vards, on the Place de l'Hôtel de Ville—everywhere—the butchery went on. A man who was particularly hostile to the Commune tabulated how many murdered bodies he had en-countered while out for a stroll on the 24th of May. At the Quai d'Orsay, across from La Bourdonnais, 47 shot (9 women and 38 men); at the Pont de l'Alma, 16 shot (5 women, 11 men); at the Pont des Invalides, in front of the tobacco factory, 8 shot (2 women, 6 men); at the Esplanade des Invalides, 12 shot (1 women, 11 men); at the Pont de la Concorde, 2 shot; at the Cour du Télégraphe, ten delivery-vans, with 40 shot in each: 400 bodies; at the Place de la Concorde, 2 women, for having killed an officer; opposite the Conseil d'Etat and the Légion d'Honneur, 60 shot (10 women, 50 men). And this only accounted for a tiny fraction of Paris, during a single day.[4]

During the course of this dreadful bloodshed, the Fédérés executed, for their part, 84 hostages.[5] But the execution of the Archbishop of Paris, the execution of Jesuits, of Dominicans, and of the Comte de Beaufort, who was considered to be a traitor—these weigh more heavily in history than the thousands of nameless murders perpetrated by the soldiers of the govern-ment: bootmakers, stonecutters, carpenters, masons, day labourers, or seamstresses—small fry, neglected by history. Mme de Lamballe's head on the end of a stick weighs much more in the traditional balance of history than the sacrifice of thousands of unknowns. Right-thinking people were indignant at the former, but considered the latter insignificant. The masses form the vile matter of history. A hundred thousand infantry-men are not worth the death of a general.

Women were involved in these executions. Maxime du Camp, once more, accused them of having driven on and excited the men, of having sometimes delivered the first blows. One of the men active in the Commune, Da Costa, expressed the same opinion.[6] Thus, by means of a sort of latent antifeminism, the enemies and the supporters of the Commune shifted the res-ponsibility for the summary executions on to women. But in this matter too, the fact seems to be that they had only secondary roles; they were neither better nor worse than the men around them, neither more pitiable nor more ferocious.

On the 29th of June 1872, the Sixth Council of War sentenced a girl, Marceline Expilly (*femme* Adolphe) to death. She was a foundling, left at the Auxerre hospital in November 1848. She was brought up by various people, and married a man who, like herself, had been illegitimate and a foundling. However, she left him after six months. It was under the name of one of her friends, Amélie Célestine Clairiot, whose identity card she had borrowed—to find, she said, a job as a housemaid—that she was arrested and sentenced. On the 26th of May 1871, a man dressed in a white shirt (there was a rumour that the policemen were dressed that way) was arrested in the Place de la Bastille and taken to La Petite Roquette. A summary trial condemned him to death, and he was led in front of the Grande Roquette wall to be shot. Marceline Expilly, rifle slung over her shoulder, was in the courtyard beside the fountain where she was playfully splashing some Fédérés with water. Did she really ask to command the firing squad? We do not know, and the court proceedings do not clear things up. She herself claimed that she had gone into La Roquette only to meet her lover. However that may be, she was condemned to death under the name of her friend Amélie Clairiot, then transferred to Guiana to do a sentence of hard labour.[7]

The *cantinière* Marguerite Lachaise—admired, as we have seen, by her comrades in the 66th Battalion for her courage—was also tried in January 1872. She was accused of having taken part in the murder of the Comte de Beaufort. This authentic count, who became a captain of the Fédérés, was a strange person. There were hovering suspicions about his loyalty to the Commune.[8] The 66th Battalion held him responsible for the losses it had suffered during the course of various sorties. After certain acts of indiscipline—so common in the Federal army—he had been heard to say, 'I must purge this battalion.' On the 24th of May, Beaufort was arrested, at the instigation of Marguerite Lachaise, by the guards of the 66th Battalion. He was taken to the office of Commandant Genton. Having heard his explanations, Genton stated that he was not qualified to continue the interrogation (the Versailles officers, at that very moment, were not being so scrupulous about their prisoners). Someone said: 'You can't shoot a man for a remark he made.' Old Delescluze, supported by two or three members of the Commune, also intervened on behalf of the prisoner. Three times he got up on to a bench to appease the mob. But the cries continued: 'Death, death! He's a traitor. He's a nobleman and a count. He could only be among us to betray us. He has to be shot.' Marguerite Lachaise was supposed to have said to Delescluze: 'If you don't have him shot, I'll shoot him myself.'

Finally the mob took Beaufort on to a piece of waste ground at the corner of the Avenue Parmentier and the rue de la Roquette. A witness claimed to have heard Marguerite Lachaise say, 'That's good . . . there aren't enough like that. . . . I'm so glad I could wet myself.' But another asserted that she added her pleas to those of Delescluze, that she asked for two hours' respite to examine the charges weighing upon Beaufort, and that she began to cry when she saw the mob leading him off to be shot.

Confronted with these contradictory accounts, one hesitates to delineate the features of Marguerite Lachaise. It is certain that she was brave; she showed that at Issy and Meudon, and her comrades in the 66th Battalion admired her and asked that she be cited for bravery. But then courage can be found in a harpy. However, there are indications that Marguerite Lachaise was not the shameless shrew that a witness thought he recognized her to be. On the afternoon of the 24th of May, at La Roquette, Commandant Genton asked for men from the 66th Battalion, in order to execute the Archbishop of Paris and other hostages. Marguerite Lachaise went into La Roquette, despite the opposition of a captain of the 207th Battalion:

'You know very well that women can't come in here.'

'I'm not a woman, but a man, since I'm a victualler.'

And she opposed 'her' battalion's participation in the execution of hostages:

'Already this morning they have shot a Federal officer,' she explained. 'This is too much. I don't want "my" battalion being called murderers.'

And she left La Roquette, taking with her the guards of the 66th Battalion. Yet Marguerite Lachaise was condemned to death for having taken part in the Comte de Beaufort's execution, whereas this had not really been proved. She, too, was deported to Guiana.[9]

A girl was said to have participated in the murder of the Dominicans of the community at Arcueil (25th of May) who had been accused of having surrendered Le Moulin-Saquet to Versailles.[10] Among the fourteen accused, only one woman, Pauline Octavie Lecomte (*femme* Buffo), figured in this trial. She was a seamstress, the wife of a stonecutter who was a guard in the 101st Federal Battalion. No other charge was sustained against her except that some dessert-spoons bearing the monogram of the Pavillon de l'Horloge had been found in her lodgings. She replied that she had been given them by her daughter, a year before, and that she did not think they had any value. Pauline Buffo was acquitted.[11]

On the 26th of May, driven to despair by the ruthless murders committed by Versailles, a mob executed forty-seven hostages on the rue Haxo, despite the intervention of members of the Commune. There too, women were involved and witnesses accused one of them of having been the first to fire.[12] Vallès gives an account of the conversation he had with one of these women who was shouting 'Death!' in the crowd. She had a sister who had been seduced, and then abandoned, pregnant, by a curate. The *cantinière* who gave the signal to fire was the daughter of a man arrested during the Empire, denounced by an *agent provocateur*; he had died in prison. Vallès said that these women had no ideas about 'the Social State'; rather, they were there because they had suffered under the established order.[13]

One woman sentenced to hard labour for life, for complicity in the rue Haxo massacre, was Pauline Lise Séret, wife of a sculptor, Bourette, born in Paris in 1825. She was charged with having propagandized for the Commune, gone looking for defaulters, threatened a man who was hiding two policemen, and incited the mob to the murder of the hostages. The Government commissioner even added that she 'had outraged the corpses of the victims.' Even though she had 'no previous criminal record,' and even though the information obtained about her by the police commissioner was favourable, she was considered a 'dangerous woman.' Later, at Auberive, she proved to be hard-working, obedient, and 'worthy of interest,' according to the prison governor. Her husband, who had not participated in the Commune, was nevertheless arrested, and went mad on the hulks.[14]

By the 27th of May, all was lost. Taking advantage of the disorder, the prisoners held at La Roquette escaped. Four of them, Monsignor Surrat (the vicar-general of the archdiocese), the Abbé Bécourt, Father Houillon, and a policeman named Chaulieu, were arrested at a barricade on the Boulevard Voltaire, where the Fédérés were still fighting doggedly. They were led back to La Roquette. An ambulance nurse, Marie Wolff, *femme* Guyard, took part in their execution. She was a character out of *Les Mystères de Paris*. Born in Bar-le-Duc in 1849, the rag-picker Marie Wolff had been sentenced for theft and for vagrancy. What misery, what rancour, what despair was she avenging when she shouted: 'If you don't shoot them, I'll do them in myself.'[15] A washerwoman in her neighbourhood, called as a witness, formally identified her:

She was carrying a red banner and wore a belt with weapons stuck into it. She was dressed in a grey skirt and jacket, and a very faded blue apron. She wore her hair braided on her head, with a band around it; and wore hobnailed boots which she later threw away at Saint-Lazare, when she saw that I recognized her; for I had done her laundry three or four times during the Siege. I said that what she was doing was bad, and that it would get her into trouble. She replied, as she went back down the street, by threatening to do me in.[16]

She was condemned to death on the 24th of April 1872; her sentence was commuted to hard labour for life.[17]

An inn-servant, Marie Cailleux, was implicated in the same affair. But nothing could be sustained against her except that she had worked at building the barricade at Père-Lachaise, and that she had fired her rifle. She was sentenced to deportation to New Caledonia, where she married another deportee of the Commune.[18]

14

THE MAJOR TRIALS

THE TRIAL OF LOUISE MICHEL—called 'the new Théroigne,' 'the Inspirer,' 'the revolutionary breath of the Commune' by the newspapers—was awaited with interest.

On the 16th of December 1871, she appeared before the Sixth Council of War. The spectators' hopes were not let down. More courageous than most of the Commune members, Louise Michel assumed total responsibility, before the tribunal and before history, for her acts. Dressed in black, she lifted back her veil; beneath her magnificent forehead her large dark eyes looked steadily at her judges. She seemed to be the very incarnation of the vanquished insurrection, of eternal revolution. The lawyer Haussmann was in attendance, but she meant to handle her own defence on all of the counts of which she was accused: conniving in the arrest and execution of Generals Lecomte and Clément Thomas; planning to assassinate Thiers; organizing both the *Union des Femmes* (which was false) and the Vigilance Committees (which was true); drafting the famous appeal 'In the name of the Social Revolution that we acclaim . . .'; being president of the *Club de la Révolution*; professing before her pupils doctrines of 'free thought'; fighting 'in the front lines' at Issy, Clamart, Montmartre; rallying the deserters; belonging to the International, and so on. In all of this, the prosecution saw only one motive: pride. They evoked her hardheartedness (those who knew her called her 'the good Louise'): 'Her mother may, perhaps, have gone without bread; but what matter?' (we know how Louise Michel loved her mother, and that she gave herself up to save her). 'As guilty as Ferré, whom she is so strangely protecting, and whose mind, to use one of her expressions, is a challenge flung to conscience and her answer, a revolution,' she stirred up the passions of the mob, preached ruthless war, and, a 'she-wolf hungry for blood,' provoked the execution of the hostages 'by her infernal machinations.'[1]

This time it was no poor, trembling, unaware woman, stupefied by poverty, whom the officers of the Council of War had before them, but an intelligent, ardent woman, in harmony with herself. No chasm cut between her action and her thought: everything that she had done, she had fully desired to do.

I do not want to defend myself; I do not want to be defended. I belong entirely to the Social Revolution, and I declare that I accept full responsibility for all my actions. I accept it entirely and unreservedly. You accuse me of having taken part in the execution of the generals? I should answer yes to that, if I had been in Montmartre when they wanted to have the people fired upon; I would not have hesitated, myself, to fire at men who gave such orders. But I do not understand why they were shot when they were prisoners, and I regard that action as arrant cowardice.

As for the fires in Paris, yes, I took part in them. I wanted to set up a barrier of flames before the invaders from Versailles. I have no accomplices in that act.

It does not seem that Louise Michel actually took part in the burning of Paris; but she wanted to take upon herself all the charges that were made against the Commune.

I have been told that I am an accomplice of the Commune. Certainly, yes; for the Commune wanted, above all else, the Social Revolution, and the Social Revolution is the dearest of my desires. Even more, I am honoured in being one of the promotors of the Commune.

But, Louise Michel asserted, the Commune had had no hand in the executions and fires.

Why should I defend myself? I have already announced that I refuse to do so. You are men who are going to judge me. You are before me; your faces are revealed. You are men, and I am only a woman; yet I look you in the eye. I know very well that nothing I might say to you will change your sentence in any respect.

And, proudly, she flung into the military judges' faces:

We never wanted anything but the triumph of the great principles of the Revolution. That I swear, by our martyrs who fell at Satory; by our martyrs whom I hail aloud here, and who, one day, will surely find an avenger. Once more: I am yours. Do with me what you will. Take my life, if you want it. I am not the woman to argue with you for an instant.

Then the interrogation began. When she had heard of the execution of Generals Lecomte and Thomas, she had said: 'They have been shot. That's good.' Did she, then, approve of these executions?

'That is no proof,' she replied. 'I did say this, but the intention behind my words was to avoid stemming the onrush of revolutionary zeal, and no more.'

She had contributed to newspapers that called for the confiscation of ecclesiastical property, and other subversive measures.

'Of course. But we never wanted to take the property for ourselves. We had no thought but that of giving it to the people, to increase their well-being.'

She had demanded the abolition of the magistracy.

'That's because the examples of their mistakes were always before my eyes.'

She acknowledged having wanted to assassinate Thiers.

Her answers aroused the indignation of the public benches composed of Versailles partisans. (The Commune partisans had been arrested, hidden, or terrorized.) But Louise Michel did not seem to notice this; once or twice, however, she turned around and smiled scornfully.

The witnesses did not add any information that was not already known, for Louise Michel admitted everything of which she was accused, and more besides. Captain Dailly, delivering the indictment, demanded that an accused woman who represented a permanent danger to society be cut off from it. Her lawyer declined to plead, since Louise Michel did not want to be defended, and relied 'upon the wisdom of the Council.' Then, one last time, Louise Michel spoke out:

What I demand of you, who call yourselves a Council of War, who sit as my judges, and who do not disguise yourselves as the Commission for Pardons; you, who are military men, and who deliver judgment before the eyes of everyone: what I demand of you is Satory, where my brothers are already fallen. I must be cut off from society; you have been told to do so. Well, the Commissioner of the Republic is right. Since it seems that every heart that beats for freedom has no right to anything but a little slug of lead, I demand my share. If you let me live, I shall never cease to cry for vengeance; and I shall avenge my brothers by denouncing the murderers of the Commission for Pardons. . . .

The presiding judge interrupted her: 'I cannot allow you to speak if you go on in that manner.' Louise Michel: 'I have finished. If you are not cowards, kill me.'

The room, so hostile at the outset, was caught by emotion. Louise Michel was sentenced to transportation to a penal settlement. When the clerk of the court informed her that she had at her disposal twenty-fours hours during which to lodge an appeal, she merely answered:

'No. There is no appeal. But I would have preferred death.'[2]

Sophie Poirier, the president of the 18th arrondissement Vigilance Committee and the *Club de la Boule Noire*, was also sentenced to transportation to a penal settlement. In the eyes of society, her past was irreproachable. She does not seem to have voted for the death of the Archbishop of Paris, at the time when the Versailles government was refusing to hand over Blanqui. But she had enlisted ambulance nurses. 'And,' details the indictment, 'it is known that these ambulance nurses were willing to turn into barricade-fighters and *pétroleuses*. Consequently, *Citoyenne* Poirier in this situation, was doing nothing but carrying out the plan of the *Union des Femmes pour la Défense de Paris*.' To obtain quarters for the *Club de la Boule Noire*, she had had an occupied apartment requisitioned in the rue des Acacias. She had transmitted to the Police Commissioner of the Commune information that allowed him to proceed with requisitions and arrests. She had organized an assembly of more than twenty persons, and had incited to civil war.

Sophie Poirier defended herself circumspectly. It was not she who had signed the documents attributed to her. It had been

for the Government of National Defence, and with the authorization of Clemenceau, the mayor of Montmartre, that she had
organized a sewing workshop of seventy-five or eighty working
women. And she had sought to turn them into ambulance nurses
because they had no more work under the Commune. The
Vigilance Committee, she said, had no purpose but that of
allocating work, giving aid, and visiting the sick and the poor.
As for the *Club de la Boule Noire*, it was not she who had founded
it; she had only used it as a place to meet her workers. But the
Council of War did not admit any of these explanations. Its
opinion was that she had exerted a 'deplorable influence upon
that portion of the feminine population of Paris which later
found itself disposed to lend its incendiary support.'³

Béatrix Excoffon, the vice-president of the *Club de la Boule
Noire*, also appeared before the Council of War. It was she who
had requisitioned the apartment in the rue des Acacias, and she
had played an important role in the Vigilance Committee and
the *Club de la Boule Noire*. Béatrix Excoffon used the same
method of defence as had Sophie Poirier. The Vigilance Committee's sole purpose was to provide jobs for women who were
out of work. Certainly, she had attended almost all the Club's
meetings, but she had spoken there only three or four times, and
always to exert a moderating influence. But Béatrix Excoffon,
by way of her family and that of her 'companion,' belonged to
a revolutionary background. In her neighbourhood she was
called 'La Républicaine'—a serious charge in the eyes of these
'republican' judges. Therefore, on the 13th of October 1871,
she was sentenced to transportation to a penal settlement.⁴

Imprisoned at Auberive, she was at first considered 'a dangerous woman, having a bent for rebellion, and pushing others
into it.'⁵

But she seems gradually to have come around to 'more wholesome' ideas. And soon the Government Commissioner was of the
opinion that her sentence could be reduced. On the 28th of
March 1872, it was lightened to ten years' imprisonment.
Indeed Béatrix Excoffon wrote some remarkably platitudinous
letters from the Rouen prison. She expressed her sincere

repentance 'for everything I might have done, being too young to be able to distinguish good from evil, and not having wanted to take into account the advice of my parents, as well as M. Excoffon's.' She painted the situation: her widowed mother, the deaths of her only child and of a little brother-in-law that she had brought up. Her lover, whom she had been about to marry, had been subjected to such psychological blows that he was mentally deranged for eight months.[6] On the 28th of September 1874, in another letter to the President of the Republic, she fell back upon the same tone:

I was only twenty-one years old when I was arrested; knowing nothing and not believing I was doing wrong, I threw myself into the whirlwind that was carrying Paris to its ruination, not having cared to listen to the advice of the father of my children, who had never wished to get mixed up in it, and who wanted me to do likewise. But I, child that I was, without understanding anything, did not pay attention to him, and I kept on.

But now she had returned to a more wholesome vision of the world. In another letter, to Mme de Rémusat, who had already intervened on her behalf, the atheistic 'Républicaine' wrote: 'I should, at the time of that ordeal, have thought of my great, God-given duty of motherhood. Alas, I did not do so. Every day I ask God to pardon me for this, and I thank Him for having, in His bounty, put generous hearts along my path.'[7] And so on. The governor of the Rouen prison voiced some doubts about the sincerity of this conversion.[8] But the Vice-President of the Chamber of Deputies, the deputy of the Eure-et-Loire, and Clemenceau intervened on her behalf. Was it as a result of all these interventions that the prison governor changed his mind? Béatrix Excoffon gave the other prisoners an example of submissiveness. She seemed to have returned to 'the right path.' As the overseer of the workshop, she gave 'good advice' to her companions. Her correspondence with her family showed that she now understood 'the duty of women in society.' She showed great respect for the nuns, whose exhortations seemed to have had 'the best possible influence' upon her. In

short, the *Communarde* apparently turned into a model of virtue:
the rest of her sentence was remitted on the 26th of November
1878, as an encouragement to the other prisoners.[9]

On the 29th of December 1871, another member of the Montmartre Vigilance Committee, Jaclard's wife, Anna Korvina
Krukovskaya, was sentenced *in absentia* to hard labour for life.
Her political activity was not in the least emphasized; instead,
oddly enough, this general's daughter was accused of 'complicity in the fraudulent removal of various objects, at the
expense of M. de Polignac.'[10] Commune partisans always had
to be put on the same footing as common criminals.

After the insurrection, Victor Jaclard stayed hidden for some
time, and was then arrested. Anna's sister and brother-in-law,
Professors Sophie and Vladimir Kovalevsky—the three had
been reunited during the Commune[11]—had General Krukovsky
come to Paris. In fact, they had remembered that the General
had formerly met Thiers, at some watering spot. They were all
upright people. The General obtained an audience with the
statesman concerning this rather compromising family. But
Professor Kovalevsky made a more radical decision. He helped
his brother-in-law to escape, and sent him into Switzerland with
his own passport. Accompanied by her father, Anna went to the
Jura, near Bern, to rejoin her husband. In 1874, the Jaclards
returned to Russia, where Anna took up her pen once more.
She wrote several more short stories. But, undermined by the
privations of the Siege and the Commune, she died in Paris in
1887 at the age of forty-four. Louise Michel was present at her
funeral. At her request, no speeches were made over her grave.
A friend quietly recalled 'her qualities of courage and devotion,'
and the intelligent support that she constantly gave her husband
and her friends during 'their political tasks and struggles.'[12]

Paule Minck and André Léo also took refuge in Switzerland
and returned to their propaganda on behalf of the defeated
Commune. They tried to make its meaning and its grandeur
understood to audiences whose opinions were poisoned by the
Versailles press. André Léo was invited to the Peace Congress
being held in Lausanne in September 1871. She tried to open

the eyes and ears of the placid Swiss, so far removed from revolutionary struggle:

Who is so deaf that he has not heard the cannons of Paris and Versailles? And the rattling fire of executions in the parks, the cemeteries, the waste-lands and the villages around Paris? Who is so blind that he has not seen those wagon-loads of corpses being taken off, first during the day, and then by night? Those prisoners—men, women, children—being taken to their death by the hundreds, under the fire of artillery and *mitrailleuse*?

Certainly André Léo would not defend the 'blindness' and 'incompetence' of most of the men of the Commune, whom she never ceased to denounce. But 'these mistakes became honourable in comparison with the orgy of infamy that followed them.' She explained things and corrected false impressions. The law on hostages was administered by the mob only after the 23rd of May, when the Commune no longer existed and when Versailles had begun its mass slaughter. The fires had been caused as much by the Versailles shells as by the need for defence. The Commune had killed sixty-four; the number of murdered *Communards* mounted to fifteen or twenty thousand (and here André Léo, always scrupulous, estimates far lower than the actual figure). Thus, it was the murderers who were making the accusations. On the one side were all the defenders of privilege; on the other were the democrats. But the latter remained divided, for, as André Léo explained, some preferred liberty, and others equality. Well, 'there can be no equality without liberty, nor any liberty without equality.' And it was that which separated the socialists from the liberal bourgeoisie. But André Léo noted—and it is even more true today—that the middle- and lower-income bourgeoisie suffered as much as the common people from a capitalist government. 'The law of capital is aristocratic by nature,' she went on. 'It tends increasingly to concentrate power in the hands of the few; it inevitably creates an oligarchy, which is master of the nation's power. . . . It pursues the interest of a few as against the interest of all. . . . It is opposed to the new conception of justice. . . . It holds in servitude, not only the poor, but the great majority of the bourgeoisie who live by their work and their ability'—and who, perhaps even more than manual labourers, were dependent upon the whim of the capitalists. Therefore it was to the interest of the working class, and to that of a great portion of the bourgeoisie, to abolish the law of capital; and it was necessary to find a way of doing so. The Revolution of the 18th of March had been guided, not by the socialists, but by 'bourgeois Jacobinism.' André Léo wanted all factions of democracy to unite so as to establish a common programme that would include all freedoms (press, assembly, etc.), communal liberties, a single and graduated tax, the organization of a citizens' army, and a free, democratic and universal education. 'As long as a child is poor . . . as long as he grows up with no ideal but the tavern, no future but the day-to-day work of a beast of burden, most members of humanity will be deprived of their rights . . . equality will be only a decoy, and war—the most horrible, the most desperate of all wars, be it unleashed or latent—will desolate the world and dishonour humanity.'

This explanation, this perspective on civil war, provoked violent interruptions; the president of the Congress for Peace forbade André Léo to go on with her speech. 'I had come to this Congress with hope, and I left it with profound sadness,' she concluded. The bourgeoisie, even the liberal bourgeoisie, could not permit itself to be reminded of the existence of the 'class struggle.'[13]

The women who had guided the *Union des Femmes* also came to different fates. Nathalie Lemel, before the Council of War, assumed entire responsibility for her actions. After the defeat of the Commune, she had tried to kill herself in despair. She was arrested the next day (21st of June 1871), and appeared before the Fourth Council of War on the 10th of September 1872.

Like Louise Michel, she acknowledged all acts of which she was accused.

Yes, she and Varlin had founded the co-operative *La Marmite*, for the purpose of eluding the whims of frightful eating-house cooks, and meeting to eat together like a family. Yes, she had been active in politics, but until the Siege of Paris she had been concerned solely with the problems of working women. Yes, under the Commune she had taken part in the insurrection:

'I drew up a manifesto with four other women. I drafted an appeal to working women. I co-operated in building the barricades. I spoke in the clubs. . . .'

She acknowledged having run the *Union des Femmes*, along with Elizabeth Dmitrieff. She acknowledged the document: 'In the name of the Social Revolution that we acclaim . . .' She acknowledged that she had gone, on the orders of the Commune, with about fifty women to defend the barricades of Les Batignolles and the Place Pigalle. But she had not been armed:

'I was satisfied with passing ammunition to the fighters, and giving first aid to the wounded.'

A bookbinder, Mme Clémenceau, witness for the prosecution, stated that she had heard the accused speaking in the Clubs, calling upon women to defend the barricades and to care for the wounded. She had run into her in the street, when the fires were burning:

'It's nothing important,' Nathalie was supposed to have replied to her. 'It's only the Tuileries and the Palais Royal. Since we don't want any more kings, we don't need any palaces.'

Another bookbinder, Mme Hubert, came to testify on her behalf:

'For six months I saw her eating nothing but bread and cheese, so that she could feed her children.'

But the Police Commissioner remarked that Nathalie Lemel read nothing but 'bad newspapers,' about which she had spoken in the workshops before her comrades. Despite her 'frank and unaffected' attitude, which was emphasized by Joly, who was defending her, Nathalie Lemel, like Louise Michel, was sentenced to transportation to a penal settlement.

She refused to lodge any appeal. Upon learning that the director of the La Rochelle house of detention, where she was imprisoned, had decided to postpone her deportation because he had heard no news of her petition for reprieve, she proudly wrote to the *préfet*: 'I formally declare that not only have I made none, but I disclaim that which was made unbeknown to me, as well as any which might be made in the future. My sentence is irrevocable. . . .'[14]

Elizabeth Dmitrieff was more fortunate. She succeeded in escaping, and the police searched for her in vain. At the *Union des Femmes*, they had found papers signed by her: a commendation for good citizenship for *citoyen* Henri Colleville; a request addressed to the municipal council of the 11th arrondissement, for obtaining chairs, candelabra, and candles from the church of Saint-Ambroise, to be used for a meeting; the order to muster the women of the committee to go to the barricades. But what was she doing before the 18th of March? The police did not know. And, after the 'Week in May,' they were unable to lay their hands on her. It was thus a spectre that the Sixth Council of War sentenced *in absentia* on the 26th of October 1872, to transportation to a penal settlement 'for incitement to civil war.' This spectre, who seems not to have had 'any previous criminal record,' was, moreover, later pardoned, with the condition of expulsion from France.[15]

Elizabeth could not have cared less; she had taken refuge in Switzerland. Lissagaray, in *Les Huit Journées de Mai*, speaks admiringly of the Russian revolutionary: 'Tall, golden-haired, wonderfully pretty, smiling, she supported the wounded man (Frankel), whose blood flowed on to her elegant dress. For several days, she had worked unstintingly at the barricades, caring for the wounded, finding unbelievable strength in her noble heart. . . .'[16] But much later, in 1897, in an interview for *La Revue Blanche*, the old *Communard*, bitter, disappointed, out of touch with his youth, affected an irony which would not have been displeasing to Maxime du Camp:

Another, who was called Dmitrieff, had an imagination with a sense of tragedy. She came from Russia, where she had left her husband in the lurch. . . . One saw her, during the Commune, dressed in a magnificent red gown, her belt bristling with pistols. She was twenty years old, and very pretty. She had admirers. Whether it was that 'the bare-armed people' were not, *in camera*, very pleasing to her, or that love was, for her, an exclusively feminine sport, no man could melt this iceberg. And when, at the barricades, she took the wounded Frankel into her arms, she did so chastely. For she was at the barricades, where her bravura was charming. Mark the outfit, entirely of black velvet. . . .

He continued in the same bantering vein, describing the residence of the beautiful 'Russian princess' in Switzerland:

She was very rich, and kept a house at the lakeside, where she extended her hospitality to refugees; in her salons there was a brilliant society of 'hard labour,' with a sprinkling of death sentences, and other exotica. Then she went back to Russia to rejoin her husband; he died shortly thereafter. There was a trial, at which she appeared as a witness. It seems that milord had been poisoned. The steward was sent to Siberia, where she hastened to join him. There has been no news of her since.[17]

All this information is as suspect as it is spiteful. Elizabeth Dmitrieff did indeed go back to Russia, and she was involved in a trial. Marx used his influence with Professor Kovalevsky to help her find a laywer. 'I have learned that a Russian lady who has given great service to the Party cannot find a lawyer in Moscow, because she has no money.'[18] Elizabeth married a deportee in Siberia, where she died, but nothing indicates that this deportee was the murderer of her husband, as Lissagaray rather snidely asserts. Time passes, youth dies, and political solidarity does not operate to women's advantage.

What became of the other women of the *Union*? Doubtless many, like Blanche Lefebvre, died at the barricades; but the others? Neither the Archives of War at Vincennes, nor the National Archives, have preserved complete files on the sentenced *Communards*. How was the choice made? What criteria were applied for those that were destroyed? Historians always work with a mere fraction of the material, left to them by chance or by arbitrary choice.

Louise Michel had been sentenced, not as a teacher, but as a fighter. But Marguerite Tinayre was sentenced as a schoolteacher, for having had a job under the Commune. She had

been appointed Inspector of Schools in the 12th arrondises-
ment, and as we know, had taken part in the secularization of
the schools in her area. This was all that could be sustained
against her. Her previous conduct had given no cause for any
unfavourable attention, but she had always manifested revolutionary ideas, and, it was said, was affiliated with the International. Arrested on the 26th of May, and then released, she
was sentenced *in absentia* to transportation to a penal settlement
'for having been in communication with the leaders of insurrec-
tionary groups, and for having involved herself in public
functions without having the right to do so.' Her brother,
Antoine Ambroise Guerrier, manager of the tobacco factory at
Reuilly, was given the same sentence, also for having held an
office under the Commune.[19] He was able to take refuge in
London, where he died. As for Marguerite Tinayre's husband,
the peaceable notary clerk who was never interested in politics,
he made the mistake of going to look for his wife, in the midst
of the turmoil, and was therefore, as we have seen already, shot
at Le Châtelet, without any further trial.

Accompanied by her five children, Marguerite Tinayre went
first to Geneva, where she continued to fight her battle: she
was seen presiding at a 'civil baptism.'[20] But she had to keep
her five children alive. First, in Saxony, she held a position as
housekeeper for a large family, then—exile upon exile—reached
Budapest where she was able to gain acceptance by virtue of
her conscientiousness and her industry. The French ambassador
wrote concerning her that the exiled woman had 'the most
perfectly honourable outward behaviour one might find.' Her
irreproachable bearing and conduct earned her everyone's
respect. In 1879, she learned that women who had suffered
under extraordinary tribunals could return to France. But she
was excluded from this ruling because, at Geneva, she had been
involved in 'socialistic and internationalistic intrigues.' This
was, for her, a catastrophe: it would make people in Budapest
believe that she was a common criminal. She would lose her
pupils, on whom she depended to support herself and her
children. On the 15th of October 1879, she wrote a letter to *La*

Marseillaise, in which she drew the attention of the public to the punishment which the justice of her country had a second time imposed upon her:

I am a schoolteacher, that is, I am in that peculiar situation in which it is indispensable to have a good name. Not wanting to take advantage of anyone's good faith, I declared openly that I was banished (in this country, no one is shocked by that). Hungarian society accepted me, therefore, as a woman who had perhaps been led astray into extreme causes, but essentially as a respectable woman. Families and schools opened their doors to me, my classes were attended by girls belonging to what is conventionally called 'the best society.' In short, I earned enough to pay for the upbringing of my four sons and my daughter. Now, the Government's proclamations class me among the worst criminals. . . .

Six years' efforts were destroyed. 'You can imagine the retrospective horror that the mothers of my pupils have felt, thinking that they could have entrusted their daughters to an habituée of magistrates' courts or even to a woman sullied by "vile crimes."' What could she do? She still had two children to bring up, and two to support until their studies were completed. Her eldest son had begun to work, but conscription could take him from her. She was a widow in fact, but not in law; for 'the Council of War which executed my husband no doubt forgot (we can't think of everything) to ask him his name. Neither I nor his family have been able to obtain any proof of his decease.' Should she ask to be pardoned?—but that would be to admit that she had been guilty. 'And guilty I was not, nor can I desire to appear so before children to whom I owe the example of strength and constancy in the face of ill fortune.' And besides, would they restore her civic rights, without which she could not teach in her own country?

But it seemed that Marguerite Tinayre was worried for no reason (administrative mail travels slowly). On the 3rd of September 1879, the Head of the Sûreté Générale had authorized Marguerite Tinayre to return to France for three months. On the 29th of November, the rest of her sentence was remitted.[21]

Other women, like Marguerite Tinayre, suffered for having

accepted teaching jobs under the Commune. Thus it was that a
'young and pretty person, nineteen years old, with soft eyes,'
appeared before the tribunal on the 16th of December 1871.
Anne Denis and her mother ran a bookshop on the rue Monge.
One of their clients, Stanislas Blanchet, a Commune member,
had offered her a position as teacher in the convent school on the
rue Gracieuse, which had been taken in charge by Mme Da
Costa. Anne Denis demurred that she had no diploma. But
Blanchet answered that that was not necessary for teaching
children between the ages of six and eight.

'And your method of instruction consisted of teaching little
girls patriotic songs?' the presiding judge asked her.

'They used to sing the *Marseillaise*,' the young woman answered sweetly. 'But they knew it already: I did not have to
teach it to them.'

She was also accused of having solicited funds for the *Union
Pour la Propagande Républicaine*. She had praised the Commune,
and her 'fanaticism' had earned her a position as schoolteacher:
six days in prison.[22]

Anne Denis got off lightly.

Other women—women against whom nothing could be
sustained except that they had proclaimed aloud their sympathy
for the Commune—were severely punished. For Marie Ségaud,
deportation. She was a humble seamstress, born in Cronat-sur-
Loire, Saône-et-Loire, in 1828. She had married a Pole,
Jean-Edouard Orlowsky; since 1849 he had been a mechanic
for the *Chemins de Fer de l'Ouest*. He was a hard worker, earning
five francs a day. A member of the National Guard during the
Siege, he remained in the 91st Battalion during the Commune,
but concerning him there were no grounds for prosecution. His
wife, on the other hand, was an ardent *Communarde*; she was
called 'La Mère Duchêne' in the neighbourhood. In her house
were found Commune newspapers, a red sash, and a rough
draft of a denunciation of Versailles agents. Marie Ségaud
affirmed her convictions aloud:

'I wanted the Republic more than anything, and I thought
that only the Commune could give it to us.'

She was accused of having read Commune newspapers aloud.

'No; I don't read well enough.'

She was further accused of having denounced two neighbours, of having urged men to fight and women to build barricades, and of having frequented the *Club Saint-Michel*. In short, 'the accused seems to us to belong to that category of dangerous women who, without taking an active part in the fighting, definitely helped to give it the odious character that it had, particularly during the final days.' (But who threw the first stone? The Council of War preferred not to mention that.) Marie Ségaud was thus sentenced to transportation, for nothing more than having propagandized for the Commune.[23] The same thing happened to Anne Collot, *femme* Gobert, who had insulted the soldiers of the Versailles army, and had 'incited' the insurgents, 'including her husband, a sergeant under the Commune, who has disappeared'[24]—a euphemism meaning that he was probably shot without a trial.

Five years in prison for Jeanne Petit, *veuve* Gauthier, born in Heines-les-Plates, Nièvre, in 1831, because her wine-shop had turned into a sort of revolutionary Club.[25] The same for Agathe André, *femme* Joliveau, who belonged to a family of insurgents —her husband had been taken prisoner by Versailles on the Châtillon Plain; her father had been shot at the Butte-aux-Cailles barricade. Driven to despair by the arrest of her husband, she had drafted a petition, the gist of which was that policemen's wives were to be forced to march in front of the National Guards who were about to enter battle. Five years in prison, therefore, although the petition had had no effect.[26] Two years in prison for a laundress, Marie Mortier, born in 1818 in Monterne-Silly, Vienne. She was the wife of Régent Cretin, a captain in the 26oth Federal Battalion, who had been sentenced to transportation; she had insulted Versailles supporters, and tried to drag two Fédérés back into the fight, when, on the 22nd of May, they were running away on the rue Royale.[27] And again, two years in prison, augmented by a fine of 200 francs, for the tailoress Rosalie Kosakowska, *femme*

Niemic, who had turned her lodgings into a meeting-place for Polish refugees.[28]

FURTHER SENTENCES

AMONG THE DOSSIERS that have come down to us, we find those of several *cantinières* of the Commune. Various sentences were meted out to them, ranging from hard labour to a year in prison.

For one *cantinière*, Elisa Rousseau, *femme* Cabot, born in Louviers in 1832, fifteen years' hard labour: she had followed the 84th Battalion, and had brought about the arrest of a member of the National Guard, who was executed for treason. And finally, she was alleged to have stated that she had fired fourteen cannon shots.[1] Adèle Desfossés, *femme* Boulant, born in Péronne in 1832, was sentenced to transportation to a penal settlement. She had been a *cantinière* with the 238th Battalion, and had taken part in the fighting at Issy. But she was also accused of looting, for found among her things had been a stuffed otter and stuffed birds, several embroidered chair-covers, a dressing case, and a chamber-pot, all of which had come from the Couvent des Oiseaux, where her battalion had been quartered.[2]

Marie Schmitt, born in Obreck, Moselle, in 1837, was the wife of a military outfitter. She followed her husband, Gaspard, who was in the National Guard, to the 101st Battalion. She had been seen dressed in a uniform and carrying a rifle, firing in the defence of La Butte-aux-Cailles. She was a former prostitute, and her brazen attitude at the hearing antagonized the Council of War:

'I am sorry,' she said, 'that I did not do everything I am accused of.'

She, too, was sent to New Caledonia.[3]

Sentenced to 'simple' deportation,* Marie-Delphine Dervillé,

---

* As distinct from transportation to a penal settlement.—*Trans.*

femme Dupré, was also exiled to New Caledonia. She had been a *cantinière* in the 73rd Battalion, to which her husband belonged, and had gone along with the Fédérés in their sorties. But she was also accused of having illegally confined two nuns who had been removed from the Picpus convent. 'She was fanatically devoted to the Commune.'⁴

The linen-draper Célestine Gallois, wife of the manual labourer Jean-Baptiste Vayeur, was born in Naives, Meuse, in 1830; she was sentenced to simple deportation, and to the loss of her civic rights. (Her police record was rather lengthy.) At Courbevoie she had boasted of having 'forced her milksop commander to lead back the Fédérés under the fire coming from Mont-Valérien.' She had brought about the arrest of her neighbour, a former policeman who was released three hours later. 'She is a dangerous woman, whom it is important to keep at a remove from society.' But at Auberive, as in the Rouen prison, she displayed 'good conduct' and also 'right opinions.' Her sentence of exile was commuted to ten years' imprisonment, in November 1875, then reduced by a year in 1877, and by six months in 1879. She wrote to the minister on the 29th of January 1879, to ask him for a full pardon:

I am writing, Monsieur le Ministre, to present my apologies to you, and to place at your feet the mistakes that I made in being involved in the Commune, begging you to grant pardon to a poor woman of forty-nine years who has become a widow since entering prison (my husband died at Belle-Isle, at sea, also a prisoner, leaving a sixteen-year-old son without support), and who has a very old mother whom she wants to see again, since she is always ill. . . .⁵

The laundress Marie-Virginie Vrecq, *femme* Bediet, born in Bougival, in 1846, was known by the name of her lover Captain Vinot of the 170th Battalion, who soon became colonel in the Vengeurs de Paris. 'La Colonelle' went with her lover to the barricade near the church of Saint-Ambroise, and when he was wounded, helped him to escape from the Versailles soldiers. She was unwarrantedly accused of being mixed up in the rue Haxo executions, but in the end nothing was sustained against her except that she had taken part in the insurrection: she was sentenced to simple deportation.[6] If 'La Colonelle' seemed energetic, violent, awesome, nothing would have given any indication that Jeanne Bertranine, *femme* Taillefer (born on the 4th of July 1831, in Lasseubetat, Basses-Pyrénées), would join the ranks of the Commune. 'Gentle and quiet, she had never before been the object of any unfavourable comment,' we read in her dossier. The Commune transformed her. For two months, she followed her husband in the 118th Battalion, in the uniform of a *cantinière*, pistol at her waist. She was in all the sorties, and, on the 23rd of May, she went along with the armed National Guards to summon the tenants of her house to the barricade on the Place Maubert. She was arrested at Ménilmontant and sent to New Caledonia. The gentle and quiet Jeanne Bertranine, who sold fried fish, was too proud to lodge an appeal for pardon.[7]

It was also for the purpose of following her husband, a machine-adjuster, that Lucie-Euphrasie Boisselin, *femme* Leblanc, accompanied the 84th Battalion armed with a small rifle. She had worked at the rue de Bussy barricade, but she tried to exonerate herself: she had not served the Commune out of political conviction. She wrote in her plea for pardon:

Under the Government of National Defence she had accepted the position of *cantinière* with the 84th Battalion of the National Guard, and had had to keep this job after the 18th of March in view of the total lack of work, and because she had no other resources. . . . It had never entered her mind to harm the Government, but at that time seeing no other means of subsistence, and unaware of the events that were taking place and of their consequences, she believed that she was doing no wrong by keeping the insignificant job that she had held under the Government of National Defence.

At L'Ile-des-Pins, in New Caledonia, she worked hard to bring up her two children, and gave the penitentiary administration no cause for reproach.[8]

Other *cantinières* were sentenced to between one and five years in prison.

As for the women whom we saw building barricades, they too received various sentences. Marie-Augustine Gaboriaud, *femme* Chiffon, 'who had always displayed the greatest sympathy for the Commune,' was sentenced to twenty years' hard labour.[9] Elodie Duvert, *femme* Richoux, was sentenced to transportation to a penal settlement.[10]

The journeywoman Marguerite Fayon appeared before the Council of War on the 16th of October 1871. She was a small, fragile, slightly deformed woman; only thirty-five, she appeared to be fifty. She seemed 'endowed with great energy.' 'And the way she looked at the witnesses who came to give evidence against her makes sufficiently clear what she must have done when she found a firm support among the National Guards of the Commune, over whom she seems to have exercised a certain authority,' wrote the reporter of the *Gazette des Tribunaux*. She was accused of having denounced a policeman's wife, and of having detonated Orsini bombs.* But in the end all that could be sustained against her was that she had handed out cartridges to the Fédérés during the Bloody Week fighting. She was sentenced to simple deportation.[11] The same sentence went to the hairdresser Eugénie Bruteau, née Rousseau, who had led men, women, and children to the barricades.[12] Twenty years of confinement for Joséphine Courtois, *veuve* Delettra, who was already called 'Queen of the Barricades' in 1848, at Lyon.[13] For the others, the sentences varied from a year to five years.

The Commune had had to create its own army, courts, and police. The denunciations of Versailles agents appeared, to the Versailles government, crimes which could be dealt with under ordinary criminal law. It is certain that denunciations are always very unpleasant, even if the circumstances seem to justify them. Police tasks are repugnant to our sense of morality.

One Commune decree had compelled all men from nineteen to forty years of age to enter the National Guard. Women were given the responsibility of tracking down defaulters, as well as any Versailles agents remaining in Paris whose activities might

---

* Mercury fulminate bombs, named after an Italian patriot, Felice Orsini.—*Trans.*

be feared (and rightly so). The women's battalion organized in the 12th arrondissement was specifically charged with this task. And it was for having been party to an illegal arrest—illegal in the eyes of Versailles, legal in those of the Commune—that the seamstress Marie-Catherine Rogissart was arraigned and found guilty. We have seen her earlier speaking at the *Club Saint-Eloi*, and wearing an armband, taking part in the women's battalion, of which she was the flagbearer. Found in her room were a red poster having to do with the organization of that battalion, an oil-lamp, and a quantity of petroleum-oil so small that it was obviously only for the purpose of filling the lamp. But she had had one of her neighbours arrested.

'It is true that I had Lutz arrested, but not as a defaulter. One day he was making a noise in the house where I live. He was drunk. He had a rifle in his hand, and it went off. I had him arrested because he was disturbing the peace and quiet of the house.'

And Lutz confirmed this, to bursts of laughter from the court: 'One day, I came back home somewhat befuddled with drink . . .' But another witness testified that Marie-Catherine Rogissart had denounced him to the Central Committee as a Versailles spy. He had been released after his house had been searched.

Marie-Catherine Rogissart had always given vent to opinions favourable to the Commune: 'Although without education, she had a facile tongue, and misused it by talking politics,' a neighbour declared. And she urged the men to fight:

'I'll make you all go, you're nothing but a bunch of lay-abouts,' she had said. 'Me, I'm a woman, and I have more courage than any of you. Like it or not, you're going to fight the Versailles murderers. . . .'

Although she had no previous criminal record, and could scarcely be accused of anything except living 'in concubinage'; although the arrest of Lutz was warranted by his drunken state; although she could be accused of no active participation in the 'crimes of the Commune'—she was sentenced to seven years' hard labour.[14]

Sidonie Marie Herbelin, *femme* Letteron, was a member of the *Club de l'Eglise de la Villette*, which she used to call 'the Black Crows' barn.' She was accused of having invaded a policeman's house, of leading a battalion of women, and of looting. She had been seen with a red banner at the burial of a *cantinière*. 'Having done everything she could to ensure the triumph of the insurection', Sidonie Marie Herbelin was sentenced to transportation to a penal settlement.[15]

Elise-Louise Keinerknecht, née Neckebecker, also belonged to the women's battalion, in which she held the rank of captain. She had also been seen at the *Club de l'Eglise Saint-Eloi* and the *Club de l'Eglise Saint-Bernard*, where she had taken up a collection; five years in prison, and ten years' surveillance by a parole board.[16]

Other women who do not seem to have participated in the 12th arrondissement battalion or in the *Union des Femmes* (their names are not to be found listed there) were prosecuted for denouncing policemen and their wives. For these simple women of the people—seamstresses, laundresses, journeywomen and prostitutes—the shameful regime was concentrated in the authority of the policeman, entirely devoted to the Versailles government by virtue of the function he performed.

There was a former prostitute, Joséphine Poinbœuf, or Allix, born in Theillay, Loir-et-Cher in 1841; her lover had taken her out of a house of prostitution. Her feelings for the Commune were well known, and she had brought about the arrest of a policeman who was taken to the *mairie* of the 17th arrondissement. However, he was released immediately. Fifteen years' hard labour for Allix.[17]

Ten years' hard labour for the cook Mélanie Jacques, *femme* Gauthier, born in Briare in 1820, for denouncing the wife of a policeman. 'Assuming that the government of the Commune was a legal one, she believed that she was doing a patriotic deed by denouncing the woman Zehr.'[18]

The same sentence went to a trousers-maker, Claudine Lemaître, *femme* Garde, born in 1836 in Onlay, Nièvre; she had caused the arrest of a lady named Meyer, the wife of a former

police commissioner—an 'informer,' Claudine said—and a
Mme Luchaire, the widow of a policeman. Luchaire's uniforms,
papers, and decorations were defenestrated, to the great delight
of the spectators gathered in the street. Claudine Lemaître
acknowledged having taken part in these arrests, but not in the
looting.[19]

Five years' hard labour for Rosalie Joséphine Delavot,
femme Gaillardot, who reported a lieutenant and a policeman's
wife as Versailles agents.[20] Transportation for a concierge,
Marie-Anne Dumoulin, *femme* Ajame, who had chased after the
wives of policemen, threatening them. Apart from this, she was
considered a worthy and respectable woman; but she was
utterly loyal to the Commune and thought that, in so doing,
she was serving it.[21]

Marie Audrain, *femme* Vincent, born in 1821 in Donges,
Loire-Inférieure, was a charwoman whose employers gave her
'good references,' and whose neighbours attested to her
'irreproachable way of life and morality.' But she had taken up
with the federal colonel Laporte, who commanded the 6th
sector. A staunch supporter of the Commune, she attempted to
enroll men, and also women of the neighbourhood 'to go and
avenge their husbands and brothers who were being struck
down.' She denounced the wives and sons of policemen. She
was first arrested for seditious remarks, and then released. But
after a fresh case had been prepared against her, she was
arrested anew, and sentenced to hard labour for life. She
appealed and her trial was quashed for faulty procedure; at the
retrial Marie Audrain was sentenced to only ten years' reclusion—an adequate indication of how arbitrary were the sentences imposed upon the Commune supporters. At Auberive,
Marie Audrain retained her convictions, and showed no signs
of any 'repentance.' She was even condemned to two months'
solitary confinement for insolence toward the Inspector-
General, the Baron de Watteville.[22]

The denunciations did not concern merely the bulwarks of
the traditional order and their families, but also Versailles
agents and defaulters.

The journeywoman Thérèse Lecomte, born in Bazeilles, Ardennes, in 1836, was sentenced to five years' hard labour and twenty years' surveillance by a parole board, for having accused a woman from her neighbourhood of being in communication with Versailles. But a federal officer refused to take the responsibility for this arrest. The denounced woman was released after two days. Thérèse Lecomte also denounced her concierge, and it is not hard to believe that this was only a question of private vengeance. But on the day of the fighting at the barricades on the Boulevard Mazas, she brought the men who were taking flight to the attention of the Fédérés.[23]

A laundress, Suzanne-Augustine Preu, *femme* Dutour, who had had a man named Costes arrested, was condemned to simple deportation. The man had said that the Versailles government ought to send all the *Communards* to Cayenne. His arrest came to nothing; however, rifles and military clothing were found at the Dutours' house.[24]

Simple deportation again, for the laundress Victorine Gorget, born in 1843, in Paris, who had taken the floor at the *Club Saint-Michel des Batignolles* to demand a strong organization and the mobilization of all the nation's able-bodied men; and she had said to one of her neighbours that 'the women ought to take up arms to guard the ramparts while the men go out on sorties against the Versailles troops.' On the 23rd of May, she had stated that she was going to fetch the National Guard to 'arrest the loafers who are hiding out.' But she had been unable to go any farther than the command post.[25]

The same sentence for Anne Collot, *femme* Gobert, journeywoman, against whom nothing could be sustained except that she had insulted 'the decent folk' who stood up for Versailles, and had encouraged her husband to take up arms. But when they came to arrest her, she dared to say that they had no right to make arrests at night, and called the agents 'rabble, butchers, acting in the name of a government of butchers, which lets decent people die of hunger or else shoots them.'[26]

Anne Collot could scarcely be accused of anything except her remarks. By contrast, Joséphine Semblat, née Taveau, got five years in prison; on the 26th of May, leading a group of Commune sailors, she went to arrest some defaulters hidden in her house.[27] Five years' imprisonment or reclusion were handed out to many others for similar 'offences.'

Finally, one last category included a certain number of sentences for 'theft and looting.' Certain of these thefts could legitimately be subsumed under criminal law, although armies, on whichever side, have always had the tendency to consider abandoned or gutted houses as property that no longer belongs to anyone.

Henriette-Marie Dellière and Octavie Cornet were sentenced by the 13th Council of War to two years in prison and five years on parole, the one for having accepted jewels from her lover, the other for having taken a sewing machine.[28] But the sentences were heavier when it came to the Palais des Tuileries or Thiers' own private house. Ten years' hard labour for the seamstress Alexandrine Théodore Simon, *veuve* Godin; she had received a fur coat belonging to General Trochu.[29] Twenty years' hard labour and 5,000 francs' fine for Ernestine Garçon, *femme* Coleau, at whose house had been found a New Testament, a magnifying glass, and a paper-knife belonging to Thiers. This was rather stiff. But Ernestine Garçon took refuge in Belgium; for the same 'crime', however, her lover was sentenced to only two years in prison.[30]

These cases are hardly political in nature. But another affair seems much more significant. This had to do with, not an individual theft, but a 'legal' requisition, in the context of the redistribution of property.

Marie-Joséphine Miguet, *femme* Parfond, a button worker born in 1848 in Saint-Maurice-sur-Fessard, Loiret, was sentenced to five years' reclusion on the 19th of February 1872, for complicity in the looting of a shop 'in a gang, and by open force.' Some grocers on the rue des Amandiers had left Paris on the 18th of March, and had abandoned their shops without a watchman. During the last days of the Commune, some members of the National Guard, led by the Police Commissioner of

7. "Humble women thrown into a great cause."

(a) Joséphine Marchais, Eugénie Suétens, Elizabeth Rétiffe, drawn in prison by Daniel Vierge.

(b) Louise Michel, photographed in prison at Versailles in 1871.

8. "Angels and devils, gentle girls and keen-tongued shrews." Women of the Commune, photographed by Appert at the prison des Chantiers.

the Père-Lachaise district, called in a locksmith to open the door. The Fédérés had said that the grocer was a traitor to the Commune, and that they were going to take away his merchandise 'to give it to poor people who don't have anything.'

The ambulance nurse Marie Parfond went along with them, and voiced her approval: 'Yes, that's very fair. When I think that I have a husband who is under fire, and that, at a time like this, there are people who run away to get out of doing their service. . . .'

All the commodities were taken to the church in Ménilmontant to be distributed. One of the grocers, however, later found some bottles that the Fédérés had not emptied, despite the reputation they have been given as drunkards. At Marie Parfond's lodgings a package was also found containing toilet articles belonging to the grocer's wife. In her defence, Marie Parfond asserted that she had not entered the shop, and she had picked up the package in the street; she had intended to return it to its owner. Marie Parfond had no previous criminal record. But in spite of her denials before the Council of War, one can easily imagine that she had indeed participated in an operation which had no other purpose save that of distributing commodities that had been left behind by Versailles supporters.[31] This activity belongs to a social policy which the Commune conducted with the most extreme circumspection (we know that the Commune did not tackle the Banque de France, and that individual property was, in general, left untouched; the demolition of Thiers' house belongs to the realm of symbols).

But like every government in time of war, the Commune effected 'requisitions' of commodities, horses, and stores. The *Union des Femmes*, in the context of the reorganization of work, had the task of looking for workshops abandoned by their owners. This it did, with great attention to legality.[32] But this revolutionary legality could not, obviously, be acceptable to the Versailles government. This is why the Councils of War always subsumed under 'civil crimes' those deeds which most often grew out of activity that was revolutionary, and hence political.

Victor Hugo, who understood everything, was well aware of this and had the daring to say it. Interceding for those condemned to death, he wrote:

These wretches . . . have nothing to do with politics. Everyone is in agreement on this point. They are common delinquents, guilty of the ordinary misdemeanours provided for by the penal law in any period. Let us be perfectly clear on this point. It makes absolutely no difference to me that everyone is of one mind concerning the excellence of these sentences. When it comes to judging an enemy, let us guard against the raging consensus of the mob, and against the cheering of our own party. . . . Let us challenge certain phrases, such as 'common misdemeanours,' 'civil crimes'—these phrases are pliant, and easy to stretch to excessive sentences; they have the inconvenient quality of being useful. In politics, what is useful is dangerous. To confuse Marat and Lacenaire is easy, and has far-reaching consequences. It is certain that if the *Chambre Introuvable**—that of 1815, I mean—had come twenty years earlier, and if by chance it had triumphed over the Convention, it would have found excellent reasons for declaring the Republic to be a villainous thing; 1815 would have declared 1793 subject to common jurisdiction; the September massacres, the murders of bishops and priests, the destruction of public monuments, and the seizure of private property, would certainly not have been left out of its indictment; the White Terror† would have ordered legal proceedings against the Red Terror; the Royalist Chamber would have proclaimed the members of the Convention guilty in fact and in law of ordinary misdemeanours specified in, and punishable by, the criminal code. . . . In Danton it would have seen a cut-throat, in Camille Desmoulins an inciter to murder, in Saint-Just a killer, in Robespierre a felon pure and simple. It would have cried at all of them: 'You are not men of politics.' And public opinion would have said: 'It's the truth'—until such time as the human conscience said: 'It's a lie.'[33]

---

* See note, p. 41.—*Trans.*

† A series of rebellions shortly after the restoration of Louis XVIII, committed by Catholic Royalists in southern France against former supporters of Napoleon Bonaparte and the Republic, as well as against rich Protestants.—*Trans.*

Now the fighters of the Commune were also 'revolutionary fighters'; they, too, could only be accused of 'political deeds.'

We must agree that these lines, written in 1871, lack neither perspicacity nor grandeur—and both were rare at that time.

FROM AUBERIVE TO
NEW CALEDONIA

'IN MY MIND'S EYE, I see Auberive again, with its narrow walks winding under the fir trees, its large dormitories where the wind whistled as if on board ship, and its silent columns of prisoners who, with their white *coiffes* and tuckers, looked like peasant women of a hundred years ago.'[1]

In these terms Louise Michel described the prison where, one by one, the other sentenced women joined her: Nathalie Lemel; Sophie Poirier; Béatrix Excoffon; Mme Richoux; Mme Bruteau, 'who looked like a marquise, with her white hair sweeping back from her young face'; Marie Chiffon who, as she put her prison number on her arm, cried 'Long live the Commune!'; and old Mme Delettra, 'who had already fought at Lyon, during the period when the workers in the silk factories wrote "Live working, die fighting."'[2]

To the condition of prisoner imposed upon her, Louise Michel's response was that of a poet. She wrote poetry about Ferré—whom she may have loved, and who was shot—about her dead friends, and about the defeated Revolution:

> Blow, O winter winds; and fall yet more, O snow,
> Beneath your icy veils we're closer to the dead,
> Endless be the night, and shortened be the day,
> In winter we're as one with the cold friends we mourn. . . .

In August, 1873, Louise Michel and nineteen other women left Auberive for New Caledonia. They went aboard an old sailing frigate, the *Virginie*. The prisoners were locked up in iron cages, but they were permitted to take an occasional stroll on deck. The sea enchanted the captive Louise Michel, offering her an escape from the iron cells. She who had known nothing but Chaumont, Paris, and the countryside of her childhood, passionately discovered the savage grandeur of the ocean. In those days the route went by way of Cape Horn: 'We saw the southern polar sea, where, in the dead of night, snow would fall upon the deck.'[3] Here Louise Michel approaches the same experience as Melville's.

Rochefort was being deported in the same vessel, and exchanged poems with Louise Michel—a strange flirtation between prisoners.

From Rochefort:

> When today we saw that seal,
> I was reminded of the Past:
> Bald Rouher with his greasy hands.
> And those sharks they were fishing for
> To me seemed like the lopped-off members
> Of the Commission for Pardons. . . .[4]

Louise Michel answered this in a loftier tone:

> The sight of these abysses makes me drunk.
> Higher, O waves, and stronger, O winds,
> Life itself becomes too dear
> So vast, here, are one's dreams. . . .[5]

Though herself suffering from the utmost deprivation, Louise Michel gave away the little that she possessed. The captain, seeing her barefoot, sent her a pair of slippers by way of Rochefort, assuming that from Rochefort she would accept them. But three days later she had again given her footwear away, and was once more running barefoot on the deck. Forgetting that she was a prisoner, she was outraged at seeing sailors catching albatrosses with a baited hook, and made them stop such a cruel form of hunting.

Finally they arrived at New Caledonia. The prison governor wanted to send the women to a penitential colony run by nuns. But Louise Michel protested: since they had been sentenced as men, it was right that they should suffer the same penalty.

So Louise Michel and Nathalie Lemel, like Rochefort, were
sent to the Ducos peninsula. The deportees had straw huts for
shelter; the food was bad and the water brackish. The food was
cooked in the Polynesian manner: a hole dug in the ground, and
stones heated to a red-hot intensity in the fire; no soap; clothes
shredded to tatters; chains and the whip for punishment. Many
prisoners died from their privations.

Since they had demanded that the ordinary code be applied
to them, the women were subject to the same regulations as men.
But they had furthermore to submit to the abuse of the warders
and the insults of the governor. Several were young and pretty,
but never, one of their companions tells us, were these women
who were imprisoned with eight hundred men 'a cause of
scandal or of brawling or of dispute.'[6]

Louise Michel, Nathalie Lemel, Marie Schmitt, Marie
Cailleux, and two other women received the order to leave the
Numbo Camp for the West Bay. Nathalie Lemel protested.
She did not refuse to live in the hut assigned to her, but she
called attention to the fact that she was ill, in which state it was
impossible for her personally to undertake her removal, or to
gather and cut her own wood; that she had built two henhouses
and tilled a portion of land; and that, finally, 'pursuant to the
law concerning deportation which says that deportees may live
in groups or in families, and which leaves them the choice of the
people with whom they please to associate, Deportee Duval,
femme Lemel, refuses community life, unless it be under these
conditions.'[7] Louise Michel protested, in her turn, and asked if
this was to be a new outrage inflicted upon them. The transfer
of the women prisoners took place notwithstanding, and they
obtained permission to divide the large hut provided for them
into smaller cabins, so that they could live with what women
they chose.[8]

Because of the richness of her personality and the strength of
her character, Louise Michel bore up better than the others
under the conditions of exile. For one thing, the beauty of the
land accorded with her romantic soul. Cyclones sent her into
transports of wonder:

Sometimes a huge red lightning-flash rends the darkness, or reveals a single purple glow upon which the black waves float, as if in mourning. The thunder, the roughness of the sea, the alarm gun in the harbour, the noise of the water pouring down in torrents—it is all one single, immense, superb sound, the orchestra of savage nature.

Moreover this woman who had studied natural sciences, who had once taken up the discipline of Claude Bernard, studied the Caledonian flora and fauna and the camouflage devices of insects. She tried to apply the principle of vaccination to diseased papaw trees. An intelligent governor, M. de la Richerie, authorized her to experiment on the trees in the area.

Finally, and particularly, there were the people. Whereas many of the deported *Communards* shared the other whites' scorn of the natives, Louise Michel made friends with a Polynesian employee of the penitentiary administration, 'who wanted to learn the things the whites know.' She gave him lessons; in exchange, he taught her the rudiments of the Polynesian dialects. Then she plunged deep into the jungle to look for tribes still practising cannibalism; she succeeded in gaining the confidence of one of these, and collected its legends and its music. She did not share Rousseau's theoretical admiration for the 'noble savages,' but neither did she subscribe to 'civilized' scorn for them. She studied them as an ethnographer, and loved them because they were a part of humanity. When, in 1878, a native revolt broke out, some of the *Communards* joined the army of repression; but Louise Michel took the part of the Polynesians and secretly aided them. The insurrection was drowned in blood. As for the Arab deportees from Algeria, 'they were simple and good, and of great justice,' remarked Louise Michel.

But at the same time, she fought for the well-being of the deportees, wrote to an Australian magazine to make known the punishments to which they were subjected, and demanded that she and her companions be treated with dignity.⁹

In 1879, those deportees who had a trade obtained permission to settle in Nouméa. There Louise Michel resumed her profession as schoolteacher. At first her only pupils were deportees' children, but the mayor soon entrusted her with teaching music and drawing in the girls' schools.[10]

There had been marriages among the sentenced men and women. Henri Place married Marie Cailleux, and Langlois, Elizabeth Deguy.[11] Most of these women behaved 'well' according to the rules of bourgeois, penitentiary morality. At L'Ile-des-Pins, Lucie Boisselin (Mme Leblanc) worked hard, took good care of her children, 'behaved well,' and had 'right ideas.'[12] So, too, did Marie Braun (Mme Testot), who lived with her husband and worked as a laundress.[13] Anne Collot, *femme* Gobert, was able to save, from her work, a sum of 600 francs.[14] Marie Gaboriaud lived with her husband Jules Chiffon, who manfully tilled his concession. She washed the linen of the staff, and 'behaved well.'[15] Victorine Gorget, despite her 'fanatical' nature, proved to be submissive and prompted by 'good sentiments.'[16] Jeanne Petit, a houseworker at Nouméa, did not associate with the prisoners, and had 'very good behaviour,' but her 'fanaticism'—that is, her loyalty to the ideas of the Commune—did not cease to trouble the penitentiary administration.[17] Suzanne Preu, *femme* Dutour, lived 'on very good terms' with her son, and displayed 'good morality.'[18]

On the other hand, Marie Cailleux had only 'passable behaviour,' and 'bad opinions.'[19] Marie Schmitt, *femme* Gaspard, was 'actuated by ill-will.' Her conduct and morals were suspect, and she spent her time with a male deportee (with whom, moreover, she had been living since she had arrived there).[20] As for Louise Desfossés, *femme* Boulant, she was often drunk, and had 'disgusting morals.'[21] Marie Leroy, generally suspect, had reached her third husband, and was unfavourably regarded even by the deportees.[22]

Here too, the characters of this story retain their individuality. The women of the Commune were of every description.

Those women who were sentenced to death and whose sentences had been commuted, were sent to Guiana, whose climate was known for its unhealthiness. There we find the *cantinière* Lachaise, Marceline Expilly, and the '*pétroleuses*' Joséphine

Marchais, Elizabeth Rétiffe, and Eugénie Suétens, as well as Anne-Marie Menand and Marie-Jeanne Moussu. In 1871, the Governor of Guiana complained that these women produced 'incessant demands' on the penitentiary personnel, and created 'perpetual complications.' But since they had to serve their sentences in Guiana, it was impossible to send them back to France into central prisons. The Governor of Guiana therefore asked the Naval Minister for permission to give them a conditional release, as was done for the native women.[23]

The Governor of Guiana's 'complications' were not to last much longer. A partial amnesty was passed in 1879; the full amnesty for all the sentenced men and women of the Commune—at least, those who were still alive—was passed in 1880.

A report by Captain Briot, Deputy Public Prosecutor of the Fourth Council of War, tried, in its own way, to give an outline of women's participation in the Commune.[24] There were, he said, 1,051 women brought before the Councils of War. In 850 cases there were no grounds for prosecution. The others, as we have seen, suffered penalties ranging from the death sentence (which was always commuted) to prison terms. Seeking the causes which led women to participate in the Commune, Captain Briot indiscriminately listed: the state of concubinage, depravity, and dissolution; the flaws in the regulation of prostitution; the lack of surveillance by special police squads; the admittance into Saint-Lazare, and consequent maintenance in the capital, of persons whose past history and whose corruption posed a permanent danger to public peace and morality; socialistic theories, which led to dissoluteness; the meetings and the Clubs; immoral and obscene publications; the machinations of the International; and the organization of the Central Committee of the *Union des Femmes*.

The fact that a great number of women who took part in the Commune had lovers—'lived in concubinage,' as the police so elegantly put it—had nothing in itself to predispose them to revolution. As we have seen, *union libre* was the form of marriage most current in the working class, owing to their indifference towards ordinances, either religious or civil; but in no way did it exclude the possibility of lasting faithfulness. Many of the women whose trials we have considered bore the name of their lover as they would have borne a husband's, and followed him into battle in the same manner. It is curious to note how these 'irregular' situations, though highly fashionable in the bourgeoisie during the Second Empire and considered by the literature of the period with an amused complacency, became yet another crime in the eyes of the chaste military gentlemen of the tribunals, whose purpose it was to demonstrate the 'immorality' of the working class.

The number of prostitutes or former prostitutes (still according to Captain Briot), was said to have been 246, out of 1,051 women arrested. This ratio, which seems very high, is not borne out by the files that have come down to us. However that may be, low wages were, as we have seen, the primary cause of prostitution in the nineteenth century. For many women, such work was the sole means society offered them of 'earning a living,' or of compensating for wages that were often uncertain, and always inadequate. Yet it is understandable that such women, who are the first to suffer under the social order, should have a hand in a revolutionary movement aimed at changing that order. A prostitute taking part in a revolutionary movement is performing an act of human dignity. However, we must admit that most of them, degraded for good by their 'profession,' much more often than not collaborated with the police, and were 'respectful' of the established order. We must also admit that the virtuous indignation of the Councils of War with regard to prostitution was simply one more social hypocrisy. Officially condoned and codified in law, prostitution would not have existed had it not been for the men who were its instigators, beneficiaries or users.

Captain Briot put socialist and revolutionary propaganda on the same level as 'immoral and obscene publications'—a juxtaposition that does not seem worth discussing. In general, socialist morality bears the stamp of puritanism, as the motions made in the Clubs indicate on several occasions.

Many women who joined the ranks of the Commune do not seem to have been motivated by ideological considerations. Some of them were content to go along with their husbands or lovers in the ranks of the Fédérés. But others, on the contrary, were for the first time performing a political act, were for the first time participating in political life, from which they had always been excluded. Viewed in this light, the *Union des Femmes*, which implicitly defended the equality of men and women in society and demanded an equal salary for the same work, was obviously a scandal—as the Government Commissioner strove to demonstrate in a patently ridiculous manner during the trial of the *'pétroleuses.'*

Like the Fédérés themselves, these women of the Commune were recruited primarily from the working class. The Parisian working and artisan class claimed 756 of them: seamstresses, embroiderers, journeywomen, laundresses, linen-drapers, dressmakers, bookbinders, and so forth. We find only one woman of property, four schoolteachers, thirty-three proprietresses of hotels or cafés, eleven shop- or workroom-owners; 246 are 'without profession.'

But, with a few exceptions, the women who played a real role during the Commune—such as Louise Michel, Marguerite Tinayre, André Léo, or the Russian women Elizabeth Dmitrieff and Anna Jaclard—came from comfortable backgrounds and embraced the cause of socialism from intellectual motives. They furnish proof, once again, that although opinions and attitudes are most often conditioned by social affiliation, there exists a margin of freedom which allows *the choice of a cause* to each man or woman. Now whatever were the mistakes and shortcomings of the Commune and its supporters, the cause remained—that of a society in the process of transformation, a society in which equality, freedom, and justice were no longer to be words devoid of meaning. However mediocre they may often have been, the *Communards* nonetheless embodied a hope which transcended them, a hope of which they were the agents, the witnesses, and the martyrs.

We shall leave the task of turning the women of the Commune into chaste heroines to the hagiographers of revolutions. But it would be equally untrue to make them into the despicable harpies described by Maxime du Camp and other reactionary historians. At the level of the masses, as at the apex, history is composed of individuals, whose essential natures are difficult to grasp. Good or bad, as Diderot would have said, cowardly or brave, who knows? We can try to grasp them only through their actions, and they constantly elude us, for their actions are ambiguous and capable of various—and contradictory—interpretations. Nonetheless, 'mass movements' are achieved by men and women, each one unique, each one different. Angels and devils, models of virtue and harpies, all rub elbows in the crowds of the Commune, no more and no less so than in the courts of kings. The historians who lean toward sociology, of course, are interested only in the totality. For my own part, I have tried to do something else—probably not entirely successfully: to break up the masses into their elements, to reach the individual cells that compose them. The documents are incomplete, sketchy, and inadequate. I have come across names and actions, but who were Elizabeth Rétiffe, Eugénie Suétens, Eulalie Papavoine—those humble women hurled into a great cause? In the end, no one will ever know.

And it is at this point, perhaps, that myth is closer to truth than is history—the poetic myth that Victor Hugo, Rimbaud, and Verlaine helped to forge.

Jean-Baptiste Clément's *Le Temps des Cerises*, which for so long was sung by all the boys and girls in Paris, and which became the melancholy refrain of the last barrel-organs, was dedicated to a Commune ambulance nurse.

And the women of the Commune also cropped up in other popular songs. In Emmanuel Delorme's *Pimprelette*:

> One day they put up the barricades,
> The two of them went down the stairs . . .[25]

Eugène Pottier was the composer of the most famous and widespread song, *L'Internationale*:

> Even in their mothers' wombs
> The kids are *pétroleurs* already,
> To put an end to thievery
> No methods are too arbitrary.
> . . . Even a pregnant girl was taken,
> And so we had to shoot for two
>> Shoot 'em down,
>> Shoot 'em down,
> For the love of God, shoot 'em down.[26]

Trohel, a Blanquist, and the typographical worker Achille Le Roy honoured Louise Michel:

> You won't forget that modern Joan . . .[27]

or:

> She stood and faced the troops of Versailles . . .[28]

But we are indebted to Hugo, Verlaine, and Rimbaud, for having offered the greatest tribute.

Victor Hugo, who never made any distinctions between his poetic and his civic activity, did not limit himself to interceding for the Commune supporters condemned to death. He put his pity and his genius at the service of the vanquished, as he had already done in *Les Châtiments*. For him, the use of words was no empty game; his poetry was at the service of 'practical truth.' Therefore, he put into (alas, not always good) verse the news that reached him at Brussels. He drew the world's attention to the terrible repression that followed the Commune:

> The prisoner passes, she's wounded, her brow
> Bears the mark of who knows what confession.
>> And now
> She's reviled . . .

Whatever, impelled her to ally herself with the insurgents? Hunger, no doubt, or the love of a man. And Hugo contrasts the wounded woman's misery with the obscene delights of the men of Versailles, and of their wives who, 'with the carved handle of their silk parasols,' poke about in the wound of the captive woman.[29]

In his poem to Louise Michel, he is no longer describing
poor, wretched, helpless women, but a lucid and courageous
revolutionary who totally accepted the fate that she had
chosen:

> Because you had seen the vast slaughter, the battle,
> The People crucified, Paris reduced to tatters,
> An awe-inspiring pity filled the words you spoke.
> What all the great, wild spirits do, you did:
> You fought and dreamed and suffered. 'I have
>   killed,' you cried,
> For, weary of all this, you wanted now to die.

Hugo evokes the whole trial of Louise Michel, the accusation
of the Paris fires, which she admitted to:

> Terrible, more than human, you lied against
>   yourself . . .
> 'I burned the palaces,' you said for all to hear,
> You glorified all those who are accused and trodden
>   underfoot.
> You cried, 'Since I have killed, kill me . . .'

And the judges hesitated before the 'severe, guilty woman.'
Then the poet brings his personal evidence to bear. He had
known her since her youth, in the far-off time when, at Vroncourt, she still called herself Mlle Demahis. Thus he recalls:

> Your days, your nights, your cares, the tears you
>   shed for all,
> Your self-forgetfulness in giving others aid,
> Your word that was akin to the Apostle's flame,

and also her poverty, her goodness, her pride in being a 'woman
of the people.'

> You were so high, you seemed estranged from all
>   these quarrels;
> For all the creatures here are trivial and squalid,
> And nothing irks them more than two commingled souls,
> The holy turbulence of things that are bestarred
> Reflected in the deeps of a great, starry heart,
> A ray of light seen bursting, blazing to a flame.. . .[30]

Much later, in 1886, Verlaine, too, paid tribute to Louise Michel, in a ballad reminiscent of Villon:

> Madame and Pauline Roland,
> Charlotte, Théroigne, and Lucile,
> Almost Joan of Arc—a jewel
> In the idiot rabble's crown;
> Heavenly name and heart, exiled
> By bourgeois France of supple spine:
> Listen, good-for-nothing wretches,
> Louise Michel belongs to a great line . . .[31]

And Rimbaud exalts the struggle of the entire working class, in *Les Mains de Jeanne-Marie*:

> The hands of Jeanne-Marie are strong,
> Dark hands tanned by summer's heat,
> Hands as pallid as the dead.
> —Are these the hands of Juana?

> . . . At Madonnas' ardent feet
> Have they scattered golden blossoms?
> Within their palms there burst and sleeps
> The black blood of belladonnas.

> . . . A miracle: they have gone pale
> Under the sun of burdened love,
> Upon the bronze artillery
> Throughout the town risen to arms.[32]

Hugo, Verlaine, and Rimbaud have woven crowns for the seamstresses, laundresses, journeywomen, and schoolteachers of the Commune. Is there any queen who can boast of having gathered such a court of poets about her?

NOTES

INTRODUCTION

1. Maxime du Camp, *Les Convulsions de Paris*, II, 86–90.
2. Charles-Aimé Dauban, *Le Fond de la société*, p. 21.
3. Alexandre Dumas *fils*, *Lettres sur les choses du jour*.
4. Benoît Malon, *La Troisième Défaite du Prolétariat français*, p. 272.
5. Hippolyte-Prosper-Olivier Lissagaray, *Histoire de la Commune de 1871*, p. 209.
6. Karl Marx, *La Guerre Civile en France, 1871*, pp. 88, 98.

CHAPTER I

1. Henriette Vanier, *La mode et ses métiers*, p. 194.
2. Jules Simon, *L'Ouvrière*, p. 212.
3. Vanier, *op. cit.*, p. 219; *Journal des Demoiselles*, February 1865.
4. Simon, *op. cit.*
5. *Ibid.*, p. 269.
6. Victorine Brochon, (B . . .), *Souvenirs d'une morte vivante*, pp. 62–63.
7. *Ibid.*
8. Julie Daubié, *La femme pauvre au XIXᵉ siècle*, vol. II, 2.
9. Simon, *op. cit.*, p. 298.
10. Brochon, *op. cit.*, p. 71.
11. *Ibid.*, p. 71.
12. Maurice Dommanget, *Hommes et choses de la Commune*, pp. 194–200; A.N. BB 24, 792, 4380, S. 73; A.G. IV, 688; *Gazette des Tribunaux*, the 11th of September 1872.
13. A.G. Council of War III, 1416; A.N. BB 24, 852, 732, S. 79.
14. Jules Paty, *Un Rêve de femme* and *La Marguerite*.
15. Paty, *La Marguerite*.
16. *Ibid.*, p. 265.
17. Paty, *Un Rêve de femme*, preface, p. ii.
18. *Ibid.*, II, 109.

19. *Ibid.*, p. 110.
20. *Ibid.*, p. 118.
21. Simon, *op. cit.*, pp. 400 ff.
22. Victor Hugo, *Carnets intimes*, pp. 44–45.
23. On Louise Michel, consult the study by Irma Boyer. *Les Mémoires* and *La Commune* by Louise Michel. Her dossier in the Archives de la Guerre: Council of War VI, 135; her reprieve dossier in the Archives Nationales BB 24, 822, 4922, S. 76; her dossier in the Archives de la Préfecture de Police BA 1183; also the *Gazette des Tribunaux* for the 17th of December 1871.
24. Louise Michel, *Mémoires*, pp. 134–139.
25. A.G. VI, 135.
26. Michel, *Mémoires*, p. 146.
27. A.P. BA 1183, The Declaration of Louise Michel in *La Marseillaise*, the 21st of January 1869.

CHAPTER 2

1. A.P. BA 1183, Louise Michel's reply to an article in *Le Figaro*, the 7th of December 1861, published in *Justice*, the 13th of August 1880.
2. Maria Deraismes, *Œuvres complètes: Nos principes et nos mœurs. L'ancien devant le nouveau.*
3. Gustave Lefrançais, *Souvenirs d'un révolutionnaire*, pp. 296–297.
4. Marc de Villiers, *Histoire des clubs de femmes et des légions d'amazones*, p. 381; A.N. BB 24, 807, 5065 and 843, 8604; Krystyna Wyczańska, *Polacy w Komunie Paryskiej 1871. . . .*
5. Lefrançais, *op. cit.*, pp. 322–323.
6. A. Perrier, 'Grégoire Champseix et André Léo,' in *L'Actualité de l'Histoire*, January–March 1960; A.P. BA 1008.
7. Lefrançais, *op. cit.*, p. 298.
8. *Ibid.*, p. 301.
9. *Ibid.*, p. 302.
10. Villiers, *op. cit.*, p. 381.
11. Victorine Brochon, *Souvenirs d'une morte vivante*, p. 84.
12. Jules Vallès, *L'Insurgé*, p. 120.
13. Louise Michel, *La Commune*, p. 29.
14. Karl Marx, *La Guerre Civile en France, 1871.*
15. Michel, *La Commune*, p. 14.

16. *Ibid.*, pp. 61–62; *Mémoires*, pp. 163–165.
17. Brochon, *Souvenirs d'une morte vivante*, p. 115.
18. Michel, *La Commune*, p. 68.

CHAPTER 3

1. Victorine Brochon, *Souvenirs d'une morte vivante*, pp. 126 ff.; *Journal Officiel*, the 18th of January 1871.
2. *Journal Officiel*, the 19th of January 1871.
3. Brochon, *op. cit.*, p. 135.
4. *Complainte et récit véridique des maux soufferts par la population parisienne pendant le siège.* Paris: published by Matt, 7 rue des Deux-Gares (B.N., Estampes).
5. Louise Michel, *La Commune*, p. 132; A.N. BB 24, 792, 4380, S. 73; A.G. Council of War IV, 688.
6. Brochon, *op. cit.*, p. 122.
7. Michel, *op. cit.*, p. 131; A.N. BB 24, 781, 11.688, S. 72; A.G. Council of War XXVI, 101.
8. A.G. Ly 23.
9. Michel, *op. cit.*, p. 129.
10. Brochon, *op. cit.*, p. 138.
11. *Ibid.*, pp. 145, 152.
12. G. de Molinari, *Les clubs rouges pendant le siège de Paris*, pp. 173–174.
13. A.N. BB 24, 845, 11.147, S. 77.
14. A.N. BB 24, 751, 5051, S. 72.
15. André Léo: article in which she gives an historical account of the situation, *La Sociale*, the 12th of April 1871, and *La Commune*, the 14th of April 1871.
16. A facsimile of the poster is in M. de Villiers' *Histoire des clubs de femmes et des légions d'Amazones*, pp. 383–385.
17. André Léo, *op. cit.*
18. Michel, *Mémoires*, p. 169.
19. A.G. Council of War XXVI, 101.
20. A.P. BA 1183, the 27th of November 1870.
21. Michel, *Mémoires*.
22. A.N. BB 24, 792, 4380, S. 73.
23. Molinari, *op. cit.*, pp. 74–75.
24. *Ibid.*, p. 197.

25. *Ibid.*, p. 255.
26. Michel, *La Commune*, pp. 73–75; and *Mémoires*, pp. 185–186.
27. *Ibid.*
28. Michel, *La Commune*, p. 130; *Mémoires*, pp. 186–187; Victor Hugo, *Carnets intimes*, pp. 75–76.
29. Michel, *La Commune*, pp. 97, 161; Molinari, *op. cit.*, p. 263.
30. Michel, *ibid.*, pp. 102–103; and A.P. BA 1008.
31. Molinari, *op. cit.*, p. 266.
32. H.-P.-O. Lissagaray, *Histoire de la Commune*, p. 85.
33. *Enquête Parlementaire sur l'insurrection du 18 mars*, II, 364, the statement by Denormandie.
34. Michel, *La Commune*, p. 121; Augustine Blanchecotte, *Tablettes d'une femme pendant la Commune*, p. 2.

CHAPTER 4

1. Louise Michel, *La Commune*, p. 139.
2. Gaston da Costa, *La Commune vécue*, I, p. 11.
3. Michel, *op. cit.*, pp. 139–140.
4. *Ibid.*
5. Da Costa, *op. cit.*, p. 11.
6. *Ibid.*, p. 12.
7. *Enquête Parlementaire sur l'Insurrection du 18 mars 1871*, II, p. 434, statement of General d'Aurelles de Paladine; *ibid.*, p. 472, statement of M. Ossude.
8. *Ibid.*
9. H.-P.-O. Lissagaray, *Histoire de La Commune*, p. 99; P. Lanjalley and Paul Corriez, *Histoire de la Révolution du 18 mars*, pp. 27–31.
10. Da Costa, *op. cit.*, pp. 21–25.
11. *Ibid.*
12. *Ibid.*, pp. 152–158.
13. *Le Vengeur*, the 30th of March, 1871.
14. Lissagaray, *op. cit.*, p. 171.
15. Lanjalley and Corriez, *op. cit.*, p. 190.
16. *L'Action* and *Le Cri du Peuple*, the 4th of April.
17. The account by Béatrix Excoffon in Louise Michel, *Mémoires*, pp. 406 ff; A.G. IV, 57.
18. Béatrix Excoffon's account.
19. *La Commune*, the 6th of April.

20. *La Sociale*, the 5th of April; *Le Cri du Peuple*, the 5th of April.
21. *Ibid.*, and the 6th of April.
22. *Le Cri du Peuple*, the 6th of April.
23. *L'Action*, the 6th of April.
24. A. Blanchecotte, *Tablettes d'une femme pendant la Commune*, p. 42.
25. *Ibid.*
26. *Le Cri du Peuple*, the 6th of April.
27. Lissagaray, *op. cit.*, pp. 296, 291–292; Benoît Malon, *Troisième défaite*, p. 330; *Enquête Parlementaire* . . ., statement by M. Gerspach, II, p. 258.
28. Malon, *op. cit.*, p. 272.
29. *Journal Officiel de la Commune*, the 20th of April.
30. *Procès-Verbaux de la Commune*, I, p. 162.
31. Arthur Arnould, *Histoire populaire et parlementaire de la Commune*, II, pp. 124–125.
32. *Journal Officiel*, the 11th of April; *La Commune*, the 11th of April; *La Sociale*, the 12th of April.
33. *Journal Officiel*, the 14th of April; *Le Cri du Peuple*, the 16th of April.
34. Lanjalley and Corriez, *op. cit.*, p. 385.
35. *Ibid.*, pp. 410–411; *Journal Officiel*, the 8th of May; there is a facsimile in Jean Bruhat, Jean Dautry, and Emile Tersen, *La Commune de 1871*, p. 179.

CHAPTER 5

1. Benoît Malon, *Troisième défaite*, p. 274.
2. *Enquête Parlementaire*, II, pp. 261, 362.
3. A.G. Council of War VI, 683.
4. Ly 23.
5. Vassili Soukholmine, 'Deux femmes russes combattantes de la Commune,' *Cahiers internationaux*, May 1950; P. Tchérednitchenko, 'La vie généreuse et mouvementée d'Elise Tomanovskaïa, *Etudes Soviétiques*, June 1955.
6. *L'Affranchi*, the 14th of April; *Journal Officiel*, the 17th of April; *Le Cri du Peuple*, the 22nd, 23rd and 28th of April.
7. A.G. Ly 23, Report signed by Elizabeth Dmitrieff.
8. *Ibid.*, *Statuts de l'Union des Femmes*; *La Sociale*, the 20th of April 1871.

9. A.G. Ly 23.
10. *Ibid.*; A.S. V *bis*, 388.
11. *Ibid.*; J. Bruhat, J. Dautry, and E. Tersen, *Histoire de la Commune de 1871*, p. 180.
12. *Le Réveil du Peuple*, the 1st of May.
13. A.G. Ly 23.
14. *La Montagne*, the 16th of April.
15. Maxime Vuillaume, *Mes Cahiers rouges*, II, p. 56.
16. H.-P.-O. Lissagaray, *Les huit journées de mai*, p. 292.
17. P. Fontoulieu, *Les Eglises de Paris sous la Commune*, p. 48.
18. *Rapport sur la délégation de Levy-Lazare et Evette à l'habillement militaire et les conclusions de Léo Frankel* in *Journal Officiel*, the 13th of May; Dauban, *Le fond de la société*, pp. 250–252.
19. A.G. Ly 23.
20. *Journal Officiel*, the 7th of May.
21. A.G. Ly 23.
22. A.G. Ly 23, *Adresse du Comité central de l'Union des Femmes à la Commission du travail et d'échange*, signed by Elizabeth Dmitrieff.
23. A.G. Ly 23, Central Committee of the *Union des Femmes*.
24. A.G. Ly 23, Commune. Organizational plan for the Ministry of Public Works, Labour and Exchange.
25. *Le Cri du Peuple*, the 18th of May.
26. *Le Vengeur*, the 14th of May.
27. *La Sociale*, the 11th of May; *Journal Officiel*, the 17th of May.
28. A.G. Ly 23.
29. *Ibid.*, text written by Elizabeth Dmitrieff; *Journal Officiel*, the 18th of May.
30. *Le Cri du Peuple*, the 22nd of May.

CHAPTER 6

1. Vassili Soukholmine, 'Deux femmes russes . . .'; A.P. BA 1123.
2. A.G. Ly 23.
3. *Le Cri du Peuple*, the 26th of April.
4. *Le Cri du Peuple*, the 2nd of May.
5. Account by Béatrix Excoffon in *La Commune* by Louise Michel, p. 407.
6. *La Révolution politique et sociale*, the 16th of May.

7. Maxime du Camp, *Convulsions de Paris*, IV, pp. 250–251.
8. *Journal Officiel*, the 5th of May.
9. Benoît Malon, *Troisième défaite*, pp. 269–271.
10. Lissagaray, *Histoire de la Commune*, pp. 297–299.
11. Article in *The Times*, dated the 4th of May 1871; reprinted in *L'Etoile*, the 10th of May.
12. P. Fontoulieu, *Les Eglises de Paris sous la Commune*, p. 288.
13. *Les Femmes célèbres*, I, p. 307.
14. Fontoulieu, *op. cit.*, pp. 254–256.
15. A.N. BB 24, 861, 4567; Krystyna Wyczańska, *Polacy w Komunie Paryskiej 1871*. . . .
16. *La Sociale*, the 6th of May; *Journal Officiel*, the 6th of May.
17. Fontoulieu, *op. cit.*, pp. 163–165.
18. A. Blanchecotte, *Tablettes d'une femme pendant la Commune*, p. 202.
19. *La Vérité*, the 28th of April.
20. *Ibid.*, the 29th of April.
21. *Ibid.*, the 2nd of May.
22. Fontoulieu, *op. cit.*, p. 160.
23. A.N. BB 24, 746, 4082, S. 72.
24. A.N. BB 24, 756, 5761, S. 72.
25. A.N. BB 24, 799, 981, S. 74.
26. *Journal Officiel*, the 16th of May; *Le Populaire*, the 17th of May.
27. Abbé Coullié, *Saint-Eustache pendant la Commune*, pp. 46, 79–80.
28. *Ibid.*
29. *Le Vengeur*, the 12th of May.
30. Fontoulieu, *op. cit.*, p. 13.
31. *Ibid.*, pp. 182–184.
32. *Gazette des Tribunaux*, the 11th of September 1872.
33. *Le Cri du Peuple*, the 10th of May.
34. A.G. Ly 22.
35. Fontoulieu, *op. cit.*, p. 63.
36. A.N. BB 24, 781, 11568, S. 72; AG.. XX, 528.
37. Fontoulieu, *op. cit.*, pp. 270–275; Marc de Villiers, *Histoire des Clubs des Femmes*, p. 307.
38. Fontoulieu, *op. cit.*, p. 111.
39. *Ibid.*, p. 175.
40. A.N. BB 24, 761, 6809, S. 72; A.G. XXVI, 212.
41. Fontoulieu, *op. cit.*, p. 80; Da Costa, *La Commune vécue*, pp. 213–220; A.G. VI, 135.

42. *La Commune*, the 7th of May.
43. Fontoulieu, *op. cit.*, p. 224; A.G. Ly 22.
44. A.N. BB 24, 768, 8345, S. 72.
45. BB 24, 760, 6427, S. 72 and 4826, S. 76; A.G. XV, 419.
46. A.G. Ly. 22.
47. Fontoulieu, *op. cit.*, pp. 228–229.
48. A.G. IV, 57.
49. *Ibid.*; A.N. BB 24, 736, 1046, S. 72.

CHAPTER 7

1. Louis Barron, *Sous le drapeau rouge*, quoted in H. d'Alméras, *La Vie parisienne pendant le Siège et sous la Commune*, p. 489.
2. *Journal Officiel*, the 5th of May.
3. *La Sociale*, the 9th of May.
4. P. Fontoulieu, *Les Eglises de Paris sous la Commune*, p. 217.
5. *L'Etoile*, the 10th of May.
6. A.G. Ly. 22.
7. *Enquête Parlementaire*, III, p. 204.
8. *Le Cri du Peuple*, the 20th of May.
9. *Journal Officiel*, the 19th of May.
10. *Ibid.*, the 18th of May.
11. *Procès-Verbaux de la Commune de 1871*, II, pp. 446.
12. Louise Michel, *La Commune*, p. 248; Maurice Dommanget, *Hommes et Choses de la Commune*, pp. 200–205.
13. A.G. Ly 22, *Club Saint-Ambroise*.
14. A.G. Ly 22, *Club des Prolétaires*.
15. *La Sociale*, the 5th of April.
16. *Le Cri du Peuple*, the 7th of April.
17. C.-A. Dauban, *Le fond de la société sous la Commune*, p. 205.
18. Benoît Malon, *Troisième défaite*, p. 209.
19. A.G. Council of War XX, 528; A.N. BB 24, 781, 11.568, S. 72.
20. A.N. BB 27, 107–109.
21. A.N. BB 24, 773, 9263, S. 72.
22. A.N. BB 24, 745, 3884, S. 72.
23. A.N. BB 24, 744, 3375, S. 72.
24. A.N. BB 24, 748, 4425, S. 72.
25. A.N. BB 24, 772, 9167, S. 72.
26. A.N. BB 24, 781, 11.470, S. 72.

NOTES 217

27. A.G. Ly 22, *Club Saint-Ambroise.*
28. A.G. Ly 22, *Club Révolutionnaire.*
29. *Le Cri du Peuple,* the 25th of April.
30. Victor Hugo, *Les Misérables,* III, pp. 284–286, 289–290.
31. George Sand, *Spiridion.*
32. *Le Cri du Peuple,* the 19th of May.

CHAPTER 8

1. *Journal Officiel,* the 2nd of April; *La Sociale,* the 5th of April.
2. *Le Réveil du Peuple,* the 23rd of April; *L'Affranchi,* the 24th of April.
3. *Journal Officiel,* the 14th of April; *La Sociale,* the 28th of April; *Le Réveil du Peuple,* the 29th of April.
4. *Journal Officiel,* the 30th of April.
5. A.G. Council of War VI, 135.
6. A.G. Ly 23.
7. *Journal Officiel,* the 15th–17th of May.
8. *Journal Officiel,* the 20th of April.
9. *Journal Officiel,* the 30th of Arpil.
10. *Ibid.*
11. P. Fontoulieu, *Les Eglises de Paris,* p. 49.
12. *Journal Officiel,* the 12th of May.
13. *Gazette des Tribunaux,* the 16th of December 1871.
14. A.G. Council of War III, 1416; A.N. BB 24, 852, 732, S. 79.
15. A.G. Ly 23, Schools.
16. Jean Allemane, *Mémoires d'un Communard,* p. 73.
17. *Journal Officiel,* the 16th of May.
18. *Le Vengeur,* the 3rd of April.
19. *Journal Officiel,* the 8th of May.
20. *Journal Officiel,* the 13th of May.
21. *Le Cri du Peuple,* the 21st of May.
22. *Journal Officiel,* the 22nd of May; A.P. BA 1123.

CHAPTER 9

1. Benoît Malon, *Troisième défaite,* pp. 273–274.
2. *La Sociale,* the 9th of April.

3. *La Commune*, the 10th of April; *La Sociale*, the 3rd of May; Malon, *op. cit.*, pp. 169–173.
4. *La Commune*, the 22nd of April; *La Sociale*, the 23rd of April.
5. *La Sociale*, the 16th of May.
6. *La Sociale*, the 18th of April.
7. *La Sociale*, the 21st of April.
8. *La Sociale*, the 22nd of April.
9. Louis-Nathaniel Rossel, *Mémoires, Procès, et Correspondance*, pp. 250–252.
10. *La Sociale*, the 14th of May.
11. *La Sociale*, the 15th of May.
12. *La Sociale*, the 28th of April.
13. *La Sociale*, the 30th of April.
14. *La Sociale*, the 6th of May, the 8th of May, the 9th of May.
15. *Le Vengeur*, the 8th of May; *L'Etoile*, No. 4.
16. A. Blanchecotte, *Tablettes d'une femme pendant la Commune*, p. 181.
17. Maxime Vuillaume, *Mes Cahiers rouges*, III, p. 234; *L'Avant-Garde*, the 5th of May.
18. *Le Vengeur*, the 8th of May; *L'Etoile*, No. 4.
19. *La Vérité*, the 22nd of May.
20. Vuillaume, *op. cit.*, II, p. 129; Gustave Labarthe, *Le Théâtre pendant les jours du Siège et de la Commune*, pp. 127–130.

CHAPTER 10

1. Louise Michel, *La Commune*, pp. 188–189.
2. *Journal Officiel*, the 14th of April.
3. *Le Cri du Peuple*, the 26th of April; A.G. Ly 23.
4. *Le Cri du Peuple*, the 28th of April.
5. *Le Cri du Peuple*, the 30th of April.
6. *Journal Officiel*, the 12th of May.
7. Jean Allemane, *Mémoires d'un Communard*, p. 81.
8. *La Vérité*, the 13th of May; *Journal Officiel*, the 22nd of May.
9. *La Sociale*, the 25th of April.
10. *La Sociale*, the 22nd of April.
11. Michel, *op. cit.*
12. *Ibid.*
13. A.G. Ly 23.

14. Account by Béatrix Excoffon in Louise Michel's *La Commune*, pp. 401–407.
15. *Ibid.*
16. Vuillaume, *Mes Cahiers rouges*, IV, p. 113.
17. Victorine Brochon, *Souvenirs d'une morte vivante*, pp. 122–127.
18. *Les Milliet: La Commune et le second Siège de Paris. Alix Payen ambulancière*, pp. 67–99.
19. *La Sociale*, the 13th of May; *Le Cri du Peuple*, the 21st of May.
20. *Procès-Verbaux de la Commune*, II, p. 380.
21. *La Sociale*, the 6th of May.
22. *La Sociale*, the 7th of May.
23. *La Sociale*, the 9th of May. The first woman to receive a medical degree was an Englishwoman, Miss Garrett, in 1870; the second was an American, Miss Putnam, in 1871. Lipinska, *Les Femmes et le progrès des sciences médicales*.
24. *La Sociale*, the 8th of May.
25. *Le Cri du Peuple*, the 20th of May.
26. A. Blanchecotte, *Tablettes d'une femme*, p. 186.
27. B. Malon, *Troisième défaite*, p. 279; A.N. BB 24, 756, 5805, S. 72.
28. *La Justice*, the 15th of May; *La Discussion*, the 15th of May.
29. *Ibid.*
30. Gaston da Costa, *La Commune vécue*, I, p. 373.
31. *L'Affranchi*, the 13th of April, *Le Vengeur*, the 12th of April.
32. *Le Vengeur*, the 12th of April.
33. *La Commune*, the 14th of April.
34. *Le Cri du Peuple* and *La Vérité*, the 18th of May.
35. *Le Vengeur*, the 12th of April.
36. *La Commune*, the 20th of April.
37. *Le Cri du Peuple*, the 8th of April.
38. *La Commune*, the 18th of April; *L'Avant-Garde*, the 19th of April.
39. *Le Cri du Peuple*, the 22nd of May.
40. *Journal Officiel*, the 17th of May.
41. A.N. BB 24, 759, 6263, S. 72.
42. *Journal Officiel*, the 9th of April.
43. *La Commune*, the 12th–13th of April.
44. Louise Michel, *Mémoires*, p. 70.
45. Jules Clère, *Les Hommes de la Commune*, pp. 88–89.
46. A. J. Dalsème, *Histoire des Conspirations sous Commune*, p. 127; Maxime du Camp, *Les Convulsions de Paris*, II, p. 102.
47. Louise Michel, *La Commune*, p. 192.

48. *La Montagne*, the 16th of April; *Journal Officiel*, the 20th of April.
49. Michel, *La Commune*, pp. 161–162.
50. *Ibid.*, p. 189.
51. *Journal Officiel*, the 10th of April.
52. Michel, *La Commune*, pp. 192–193, 219.

CHAPTER II

1. *La Sociale*, the 20th of April.
2. H.-P.-O. Lissagaray, *Huit Journée*, pp. 29–30.
3. *Bulletin Communal*, 3 Prairial, 79 (As the days of the Commune drew to a close, the French Revolutionary Calendar came increasingly into vogue. This was the 23rd of May.—*Trans.*)
4. Jules Vallès, *L'Insurgé*, p. 255.
5. Lissagaray, *op. cit.*, p. 50.
6. *Ibid.*
7. A. Blanchecotte, *Tablettes d'une femme*, pp. 257–258.
8. A.N. BB 24, 765, 7603, S. 72.
9. A.N. BB 24, 746, 3960, S. 72.
10. A.N. BB 24, 787, 779, S. 73.
11. A.N. BB 24, 735, 837, S. 72.
12. A.N. BB 24, 753, 5271, S. 72.
13. A.N. BB 24, 798, 62, S. 74.
14. A.N. BB 24, 782, 12096, S. 72.
15. A.N. BB 24, 748, 4540, S. 72.
16. A.N. BB 24, 778, 11072, S. 72.
17. A.N. BB 24, 758, 6120, S. 72.
18. A.N. BB 24, 799, 981, S. 74.
19. A.N. BB 24, 798, 60, S. 74.
20. A.N. BB 24, 738, 1493, S. 72; A.G. IV, 62.
21. A.N. BB 24, 775, 10096, S. 72.
22. A.N. BB 24, 737, 1149, S. 72; BB 27, 107–109.
23. A.G. IV 688.
24. Lissagaray, *Huit Journées*, p. 61.
25. *Ibid.*, p. 63.
26. A.G. VI, 683.
27. Louise Michel, *La Commune*, p. 266.
28. Camille Pelletan, *Le Comité central*, pp. 162–166, quoted in Georges Bourgin, *La Commune*, p. 174, note 3.

29. B. Malon, *Troisième défaite*, p. 410; Karl Marx, *La Guerre Civile*, p. 65.
30. Malon, *op. cit.*, p. 432.
31. Lissagaray, *Huit Journées*, p. 93.
32. Lissagaray, *Histoire de la Commune*, p. 340.
33. J. Allemane, *Mémoires d'un Communard*, pp. 130–131.
34. A. Blanchecotte, *Tablettes d'une femme*, p. 274.
35. Malon, *Troisième Défaite*, p. 461.
36. *Ibid.*; Lissagaray, *Huit Journées*, the 27th of May.
37. Arsène Houssaye, *Les Comédiens sans le savoir*, quoted in Henri Alméras, *La Vie Parisienne pendant le Siège et sous la Commune*, pp. 519–522.
38. M. Vuillaume, *Mes Cahiers rouges*, I, 78, note 1.
39. Lissagaray, *Histoire de la Commune*, p. 382.
40. Lissagaray, *Huit Journées*, p. 170.
41. *Ibid.*, pp. 297–298, note 5; *Histoire de la Commune*, pp. 526–527.
42. *The Times*, the 29th of May.
43. Maxime du Camp, *Les Convulsions de Paris*, II, 419.
44. Lissagaray, *Huit Journées*, p. 202.
45. Michel, *La Commune*, pp. 295–300.
46. *Ibid.*, Béatrix Excoffon's account, p. 407.
47. *Ibid.*, p. 306.
48. *Ibid.*, p. 309.
49. Mme C. Hardouin, schoolteacher, *La détenue de Versailles en 1871*.
50. Lissagaray, *Histoire de la Commune*, p. 401.

CHAPTER 12

1. *L'Avant-Garde*, the 27th of May 1871.
2. H.-P.-O. Lissagaray, *Huit Journées*, pp. 248–253; *Histoire de la Commune*, p. 392.
3. Gustave Lefrançais, *Souvenirs*, p. 568.
4. Lissagaray, *Huit Journées*, p. 253.
5. *Ibid.*, p. 97.
6. Maxime du Camp, *Convulsions de Paris*, II, pp. 401–403.
7. Louise Michel, *La Commune*, p. 274.
8. Lissagaray, *Histoire de la Commune*, pp. 533–534.

9. M. Rubel, 'Deux interviews de Karl Marx sur la Commune,' *Le Mouvement Social*, March 1962.

10. *La Sociale*, the 20th of April; A.G. Ly 23.

11. Lissagaray, *Histoire de la Commune*, p. 286.

12. *Enquête Parlementaire sur l'insurrection du 18 mars 1871*, II, pp. 362–364.

13. A.N. BB 24, 731, 5412, S. 71.

14. A.N. BB 24, 748, 4503, S. 72, and 733, 89, S. 72. *Gazette des Tribunaux*, the 1st of October.

15. A.N. BB 24, 780, 11441, S. 72; A.G. IV, 639.

16. A.G. IV, 21.

17. *Ibid.*

18. A.N. BB 24, 730, 3975, S. 71.

19. A.G. IV, 21, evidence of her landlord, Verry.

20. *Gazette des Tribunaux*, the 4th–5th of September 1871.

21. *Ibid.*

22. *Ibid.*

23. *Ibid.*

24. A.N. BB 24, 730, 3975, S. 71.

25. A.G. IV, 21; A.N. BB 24, 764, 7519, S. 72.

26. *Ibid.*

27. A.G. IV, 21; A.N. BB 24, 730, 3975, S. 71.

28. *Gazette des Tribunaux*, the 4th–5th of September 1871.

29. A.G. IV, 21.

30. *Gazette des Tribunaux*, the 6th of September.

31. *Ibid.*

32. *Ibid.*

33. Victor Hugo, *Depuis l'exil, 1871–1876*, pp. 17–18.

34. *Ibid.*, p. 16.

35. *Gazette des Tribunaux*, the 15th of December; A.N. BB 24, 730, 3975, S. 71.

36. Du Camp, *Convulsions de Paris*, III, pp. 113–114.

37. *Ibid.*, pp. 122, 481.

38. A.G. IV, 439, Evidence of Ignace Langlet.

39. A.G. IV, 439; A.N. BB 24, 762, 6976, S. 72.

40. *Ibid.*

41. A.G. IV, 439.

42. *Ibid.*

43. Du Camp, *Convulsions de Paris*, III, pp. 113–114.

44. A.G. IV, 439; A.N. BB 24, 744, 3312, S. 72.

45. *Gazette des Tribunaux*, the 17th of April, 1872.
46. A.N. BB 24, 764, 4082, S. 72.
47. A.N. BB 24, 762, 6976, S. 72.

CHAPTER 13

1. *Journal Officiel*, the 6th of April.
2. *Procès-Verbaux de la Commune de 1871*, II, p. 388.
3. Lissagaray, *Histoire de la Commune*, p. 325.
4. A.N. AB XIX, 3353, dossier 10.
5. Pierre Lévêque, 'Le nombre des victimes de la Commune,' *L'Information Historique*, November–December 1960.
6. Maxime du Camp, *Convulsions de Paris*, IV, p. 209; Gaston da Costa, *La Commune vécue*, p. 474.
7. A.N. BB 24, 761, 6771, S. 72; A.G. VI, 549. *Gazette des Tribunaux*, the 3rd of July 1872.
8. Lissagaray, *Histoire de la Commune*, pp. 338, 532.
9. A.N. BB 24, 759, 6263, S. 72; *Gazette des Tribunaux*, the 10th–11th of January 1872; Da Costa, *op. cit.*, II, p. 2.
10. Du Camp, *op. cit.*, I, 299.
11. *Gazette des Tribunaux*, the 14th–18th of February, 1872.
12. *Gazette des Tribunaux*, the 13th of March 1872.
13. Jules Vallès, *L'Insurgé*, pp. 285–287.
14. A.N. BB 24, 782, 11788, S. 72.
15. A.N. BB 24, 759, 6314, S. 72; 747, 4186, S. 72.
16. *Gazette des Tribunaux*, the 24th of April 1872.
17. *Ibid.*
18. A.N. BB 24, 759, 6314, S. 72; 747, 4186, S. 72.

CHAPTER 14

1. *Gazette des Tribunaux*, the 17th of December; A.G. VI, 135; A.N. BB 24, 882, 4922, S. 76.
2. *Gazette des Tribunaux*, the 18th of December 1871.
3. A.N. BB 24, 781, 11688, S. 72.
4. A.G. IV, 57; A.N. BB 24, 736, 1046, S. 72.
5. *Ibid.*
6. *Ibid.*

7. *Ibid.*
8. *Ibid.*
9. *Ibid.*
10. A.N. BB 24, 862, 5156, S. 79.
11. *La Sociale*, the 12th of May.
12. V. Soukholmine, 'Deux femmes russes combattantes de la Commune,' *Cahiers Internationaux*, XVI (May 1950), p. 62; AP BA 1008.
13. André Léo, *La guerre sociale*, Neuchâtel, 1871; A.P. BA 1008.
14. *Gazette des Tribunaux*, the 11th of September 1872; A.G. IV 688; A.N. BB 24, 792, S. 73.
15. A.N. BB 24, 856, 2832; A.G. VI, 683.
16. H.-P.-P. Lissagaray, *Huit Journées*, p. 115.
17. Lissagaray, *Histoire de la Commune*, p. 534, Appendix.
18. P. Tchérednitchenko, 'La vie généreuse et mouvementée d'Elise Tomanovskaïa,' *Etudes Soviétiques*, June 1955.
19. A.N. BB 24, 862, 5738, S. 79.
20. A.N. BB 24, 852, 732, S. 79; A.G. III, 1416.
21. A.N. BB 24, 852, 732, S. 79.
22. *Gazette des Tribunaux*, the 16th of December.
23. A.G. XV, 419; BB 24, 760, 6427, S. 72, and 4826, S. 76.
24. A.N. BB 27, 107–109.
25. A.N. BB 24, 745, 3885.
26. A.G. XXVI, 155.
27. A.N. BB 24, 749, 5742, S. 72.
28. A.G. XV, 478; BB 24, 745, 3837, S. 72.

CHAPTER 15

1. A.N. BB 27, 107–109.
2. A.N. BB 24, 773, 9289, S. 72.
3. A.N. BB 24, 747, 4183, S. 72.
4. A.N. BB 24, 836, 2440, S. 77.
5. A.N. BB 24, 775, 10.287, S. 72.
6. A.N. BB 24, 822, 4512, S. 76; BB 27, 107–109, supplement.
7. A.N. BB 24, 838, 2812, S. 77.
8. A.N. BB 24, 786, 70, S. 73.
9. A.N. BB 24, 775, 10096, S. 72; BB 24, 732, 5705, S. 71; A.G. IV, 142.

10. A.N. BB 24, 753, 5271, S. 72.
11. A.N. BB 24, 738, 1493, S. 72; A.G. IV, 62. *Gazette des Tribunaux*, the 16th–17th of October.
12. A.N. BB 24, 737, 1149, S. 72.
13. A.N. BB 24, 778, 11072, S. 72.
14. A.N. BB 24, 781, 11568, S. 72; A.G. XX, 528; *Gazette des Tribunaux*, the 7th of August, 1872.
15. A.N. BB 24, 761, 6809, S. 72; A.G. XXVI, 212.
16. A.N. BB 24, 756, 5805, S. 72; A.G. XXVI, 94.
17. A.N. BB 24, 762, 6961, S. 72.
18. A.N. BB 24, 744, 3375, S. 72.
19. A.N. BB 24, 748, 4425, S. 72.
20. A.N. BB 24, 773, 9209, S. 72.
21. A.N. BB 24, 755, 5676, S. 72.
22. A.N. BB 24, 773, 9263, S. 72.
23. A.N. BB 24, 780, 11297, S. 72.
24. A.N. BB 24, 781, 11470, S. 72.
25. A.N. BB 24, 768, 8345, S. 72.
26. A.N. BB 24, 776, 10384, S. 72.
27. A.N. BB 24, 771, 9112, S. 72.
28. *Gazette des Tribunaux*, the 16th–19th of May 1872.
29. A.N. BB 24, 783, 12217, S. 72.
30. A.N. BB 24, 856 B, 2793, S. 79.
31. A.N. BB 24, 756, 5756, S. 72.
32. *Gazette des Tribunaux*, the 18th of January 1872; A.G. Ly 23.
33. Victor Hugo, *Depuis l'Exil*, II, p. 17.

CHAPTER 16

1. Louise Michel, *La Commune*, p. 334; *Mémoires*, p. 205.
2. Michel, *Mémoires*, p. 343.
3. Michel, *La Commune*, p. 353.
4. Henri Rochefort, *Les Aventures de ma vie*, III, pp. 254 ff.
5. Michel, *La Commune*, pp. 354, 355; *Mémoires*, pp. 283–287.
6. Michel, *La Commune*, p. 440.
7. Michel, *Mémoires*, p. 306.
8. Michel, *La Commune*, p. 373.
9. Michel, *Mémoires*, p. 307.
10. Michel, *La Commune*, p. 387.

11. Michel, *La Commune*, p. 376.
12. A.N. BB 24, 786, 70, S. 73.
13. A.N. BB 24, 838, 2814, S. 77.
14. A.N. BB 24, 776, 10384, S. 72, and F 7, 12695–12696.
15. A.N. BB 24, 775, 10096, S. 72; BB 24, 732, 5705, S. 71.
16. A.N. BB 24, 768, 8345, S. 72.
17. A.N. BB 24, 760, 6407, S. 72.
18. A.N. BB 24, 781, 11470, S. 72.
19. A.N. BB 24, 747, 4186, S. 72.
20. A.N. BB 24, 747, 4183, S. 72.
21. A.N. BB 24, 773, 9289, S. 72.
22. Da Costa, *La Commune vécue*, I, pp. 402–403.
23. A.N. BB 24, 759, 6263, S. 72.
24. *Enquête Parlementaire sur l'Insurrection du 18 Mars*, III, p. 309.
25. *Les Poètes de la Commune*, p. 68.
26. *Ibid.*, p. 154.
27. *Ibid.*, pp. 41–43.
28. *Ibid.*, pp. 64–65.
29. Victor Hugo, *L'Année Terrible*, pp. 222–223.
30. Hugo, *Toute la Lyre*, I, 39. 'Victor Hugo à Louise Michel: Viro Major.'
31. Paul Verlaine, *Œuvres poétiques complètes*. Bibliothèque de la Pléiade. 'Ballade en honneur de Louise Michel,' p. 299.
32. Arthur Rimbaud, *Œuvres complètes*. Bibliothèque de la Pléiade, p. 83.

MANUSCRIPT SOURCES

Archives Nationales (A.N.): Fichier des Grâces de la Commune: BB 27, 107–109. Dossiers des Grâces: BB 24. Documents concernant les déportés et transportés: F 7, 12695–12698. Dessins accompagnés de légendes représentant des femmes de la Commune: AB XIX 3353, dos. 10.

Archives de la Seine (A.S.): Mairies de Paris: V *bis* 388.

Archives du Ministère de la Guerre (A.G.): Dossiers des Conseils de guerre de 1871. Documents concernant les clubs et les comités de femmes: Ly 22 et Ly 23.

Archives de la Préfecture de police (A.P.): BA 1008, 1123, 1183.

❧

NEWSPAPERS CONSULTED

L'Action.
L'Affranchi.
L'Avant-Garde.
La Commune.
Le Constitutionnel.
Le Cri du Peuple.
La Discussion.
L'Etoile.
Le Figaro.
Gazette des Tribunaux.
Journal Officiel de la Republique
    Française (La Commune).
La Justice.
La Marseillaise.
Le Moniteur des Citoyennes, 1870.
La Montagne.
La Patrie.
Le Père Duchêne.
Le Populaire.
Le Réveil du Peuple.
La Révolution politique et sociale.
Le Rouge, journal des Jeunes.
La Sociale
Le Siècle.
The Times.
Le Vengeur.
La Vérité.

BIBLIOGRAPHY

Adam, Mme Edmond. *Idées anti-proudhoniennes sur l'amour, la femme et le mariage.* Mme Juliette La Messine. Paris: A. Taride, 1858.

Allemane, Jean. *Mémoires d'un Communard. Des Barricades au Bagne.* Paris: Librairie socialiste, 1910.

Alméras, Henri. *La Vie parisienne pendant le Siège et sous la Commune.* Paris: Albin Michel, 1925.

Amodru, Abbé Laurent. *Annales de Notre-Dame des Victoires . . . publiées en 1871 et 1872 par . . . avec un supplément renfermant des documents inédits sur le Siège et la Commune.* Paris: Le Coffre, 1891.

Arnould, Arthur. *Histoire populaire et parlementaire de la Commune de Paris.* 3 vols. Brussels: Librairie Socialiste H. Kistemaeckers, 1878.

Audebrand, Philibert. *Histoire intime de la Révolution du 18 mars.* Paris: Dentu, 1871.

Audouard, Olympe. *Guerre aux hommes.* Paris: Dentu, 1866.

————. *Le luxe effréné des hommes.* Paris: Dentu, 1865.

B . . . (Victorine Brochon). *Souvenirs d'une morte vivante. 1848–1851, 1870–1871.* Preface by Lucien Descaves. Lausanne: Librairie A. Lapie, 1909.

Barron, Louis. *Sous le drapeau rouge.* Paris: A. Savine, 1889.

Bellessort, André. *La société française sous Napoléon III.* Paris: Perrin, 1960.

Blanchecotte, Augustine-Malvine. *Tablettes d'une femme pendant la Commune.* Paris: Didier, 1872.

Bourgin, Georges. *Histoire de la Commune.* Paris: Publications de la Société Nouvelle, E. Cornely et Cie, 1907.

————. *La Commune.* Paris: Presses Universitaires Françaises, 1953.

Boyer, Irma. *Louise Michel, la vierge rouge.* Preface by Henri Barbusse. Paris: Delpuech, 1927.

Bruhat, Jean; Dautry, Jean; and Tersen, Emile; eds. (with the collaboration of Pierre Angrand, Jean Bouvier, Henri Dubief, Jeanne Gaillard, and Claude Perrot). *La Commune de 1871.* Paris: Editions sociales, 1960.

Chevalier, Louis. *Classes laborieuses, classes dangereuses à Paris pendant la première moitié du XIXe siècle.* Paris: Plon, 1958.

Clère, Jules. *Les Hommes de la Commune. Biographie complète de tous ses membres.* Paris: Dentu, 1871.

Cluseret, General Gustave-Paul. *Mémoires.* 3 vols. Paris: L. Lévy, 1887–1888.

Cobb, Robert. 'Mentalité révolutionnaire,' *La Revue d'histoire moderne et contemporaine,* April–June, 1959.

Coullié, Abbé. *Saint-Eustache pendant la Commune, mars, avril, mai, 1871.* Paris: Imprimerie et Librairie administratives, 1871.

Da Costa, Gaston. *La Commune vécue, 18 mars–28 mai 1871.* 3 vols. Paris: Ancienne Maison Quantin, Librairie-Imprimerie réunies, 1903–1905.

Dalsème, Achille. *Histoire des Conspirations sous la Commune.* Paris: Dentu, 1872.

Dauban, Charles-Aimé. *Le fond de la société sous la Commune décrit d'après les documents qui constituent les Archives de la justice militaire avec des considérations critiques sur les moeurs du temps et sur les événements qui ont précédé la Commune.* Paris: Plon, 1873.

Daubié, Julie. *La femme pauvre au XIXe siècle.* Paris: Guillaumin, 1866.

Dautry, Jean and Scheler, Lucien, eds. *Le Comité central républicain des vingt arrondissements de Paris (septembre 1870–mai 1871) d'après les papiers inédits de Constant Martin et les sources imprimées.* Paris: Editions sociales, 1960.

Dayot, Armand. *L'Invasion, le Siège, la Commune 1870–1871, d'après des peintures, gravures, photographies, sculptures, médailles, autographes, objets du temps.* Paris: Flammarion, 1901.

Delmas, Abbé. *La Terreur dans l'Eglise en 1871.* Paris: Dentu, 1871.

Deraismes, Maria. *Œuvres complètes.* 4 vols. Paris: Alcan, 1895–1898.

Dommanget, Maurice. *Blanqui et l'opposition révolutionnaire à la fin du Second Empire.* Paris: Colin, 1960.

————. *Hommes et choses de la Commune.* Marseille: Editions de la Coopérative des Amis de l'Ecole émancipée, 1937.

Du Camp, Maxime. *Les Convulsions de Paris.* 4 vols. Paris: Hachette, 1878–1880. (Copy annotated by the author in the Library of the Archives Nationales.)

Dumas, Alexandre (fils). *Une Lettre sur les Choses du jour* (the 6th of June 1871) Paris: Michel Lévy, 1871.

————. *Nouvelle lettre . . .* (the 21st of January 1872), Paris: M. Lévy, 1872.

Duveau, Georges. *La vie ouvrière en France sous le Second Empire*. Preface by Edouard Dolléans. Paris: Gallimard, 1946.

Enquête Parlementaire sur l'insurrection du 18 mars 1871. 3 vols. Versailles: Cerf, Imprimerie de l'Assemblée Nationale, 1872.

Esquiros, Adèle. *L'amour*. Paris: 42 rue des Tournelles, 1860.

———. *Les amours étranges*. Paris: A. Courcier, 1853.

———. *Histoire d'une sous-maîtresse*. Paris: E. Pick, 1861.

———. *Un vieux bas-blue. L'amour au couvent*, in *Les Veillées Littéraires illustrées*. Paris: J. Bry aîné, 1849.

Excoffon, Béatrix. *Récit* in *La Commune* by Louise Michel.

Femmes célebrès (Les). 2 vols. Paris: Ed. Mazenod, 1960–61.

Fontoulieu, Paul. *Les Eglises de Paris sous la Commune*. Preface by A. de Pontmartin. Paris: Dentu, 1873.

Grousset, Paschal, and Jourde, Francis. *Les condamnés politiques en Nouvelle-Calédonie. Récit de deux évadés*. Geneva: Ziegler, 1876.

Hardouin, Mme C., schoolteacher. *La détenue de Versailles en 1871*. Paris: published by the author, 1879.

Hemday. *Bibliographie de Louise Michel, 1830–1905*. Brussels-Paris: Pensée et Action, 1959.

Héricourt, Jenny d'. *La femme affranchie, réponse à MM. Michelet, Proudhon, E. de Girardin, A. Comte et aux autres novateurs modernes*. 2 vols. Brussels: A. Lacroix, Van Meenen et Cie, 1860.

Houssaye, Arsène. *Les Comédiens sans le savoir*. Paris: Librairie illustrée, 1886.

Hugo, Victor. *L'Année Terrible*. Paris: Michel Lévy frères, 1872.

———. *Toute la Lyre*. 3 vols. Paris: J. Hetzel, A. Quantin, 1888–93.

———. *Depuis l'Exil, 1871–1876*. Paris: J. Hetzel, A. Quantin, 1892.

———. *Carnets intimes. 1870–1871*. Paris: Gallimard, 1953.

———. *Les Misérables*. 5 vols. Paris: J. Hetzel, A. Quantin, 1881.

Jeloubovskaïa, E. *La chute du Second Empire et la naissance de la Troisième République en France*. Moscow: Foreign Language Editions, 1959.

Labarthe, Gustave. *Le Théâtre pendant les jours du Siège et de la Commune*. Paris: Librairie Fischbacher, 1910.

Lamber, Juliette. See Adam, Mme Edmond.

Lanjalley, Paul, and Corriez, Paul. *Histoire de la Révolution du 18 mars*. Paris-Brussels: A. Lacroix, Verboeckhoven et Cie, 1871.

Lecour, Charles-Jérôme. *La prostitution à Paris et à Londres, 1789–1871, augmenté des chapitres sur la prostitution à Paris pendant le Siège et la Commune. . . .* Paris: Asselin, 1872.

Lefrançais, Gustave. *Souvenirs d'un révolutionnaire.* Preface by Lucien Descaves. Brussels: Les Temps Nouveaux, 1902.

Lenin, Vladimir Ilyich. *The Paris Commune.* Moscow: Foreign Language Publishing House, n.d.

Léo, André. *Un divorce.* Paris: Librarie Internationale, 1866.

————. *La femme et les mœurs, Liberté ou Monarchie.* Paris: Le Droit des Femmes, 1869.

————. *La Guerre sociale. Discours prononcé au Congrès de la Paix à Lausanne, 1871.* Neuchâtel: Imprimerie G. Guillaume fils 1871.

————. *Un mariage scandaleux.* Paris: Hachette, 1862.

————. *La vieille fille. Articles de divers journaux sur un mariage scandaleux.* Paris: Achille Faure, 1864.

Lepelletier, Edmond. *Histoire de la Commune de 1871.* 3 vols. Paris: Mercure de France, 1911–1913.

Levêque, Pierre. 'Le nombre des victimes de la Commune,' *L'Information historique,* November–December, 1960.

L'Huillier, Fernand. *La lutte ouvrière à la fin du Second Empire.* Paris: A. Colin, 1957.

Lipinska, Dr Melina. *Les Femmes et le Progrès des Sciences médicales.* Paris: Masson, 1930.

Lissagaray, Hippolyte-Prosper-Olivier. *Histoire de la Commune de Paris. Nouvelle édition precédée d'une notice sur Lissagaray par Amédée Dunois.* Paris: Librairie du Travail, 1929.

————. *Les huit journées de mai derrière les barricades.* Brussels: Bureau du Petit Journal, 1871.

Malon, Benoît. *La Troisième Défaite du Prolétariat français.* Neuchâtel: G. Guillaume fils, 1871.

Marx, Karl. *La Guerre Civile en France, 1871.* Paris: Bureau d'Edition, 1933.

————. 'Deux Interviews de Karl Marx sur la Commune,' (ed. M. Rubel). *Le Mouvement social,* January–March, 1962.

Michel, Louise. *La Commune.* 'Bibliothèque Sociologique No 22,' Paris: P.V. Stock, 1898.

————. *Mémoires.* Paris: F. Roy, 1886. Vol. I.

————. *A travers la vie, avec illustrations de l'auteur.* Paris: Librarie des Publications à cinq centimes, 1888.

Milliet (Les). Une famille de républicains fouriéristes, vol. X. Paris: Cahiers de la Quinzaine, Ser. XIII, No. 7, 1911.

Molinari, G. de. *Les clubs rouges pendant le siège de Paris.* Paris: Garnier frères, 1871.

Parent-Duchâtelet, Dr Alexandre Jean-Baptiste. *De la Prostitution dans la ville de Paris.* 2 vols. Paris: J.-B. Baillière et fils, 1857.

Paty, J. *La Marguerite. Un Rêve de femme.* 2 vols. Paris: 53 rue Saint-Anne, 1865.

Pelletan, Camille. *Question d'histoire. Le Comité central de la Commune.* Paris: M. Dreyfous, 1879.

———. *La Semaine de Mai.* Paris: M. Dreyfous, 1880.

Perrier, A. 'Grégoire Champseix et André Léo.' *L'Actualité de l'Histoire,* January–March, 1960.

Planche, Fernand. *La vie ardente et intrépide de Louise Michel, avec des documents inédits et de nombreux portraits.* Paris: Imprimerie La Slim, 1946.

Poètes de la Commune, Les. With a preface by Jean Varloot for the eightieth anniversary of the Paris Commune. Paris: Editeur Français Réunis, 1951.

Procès-Verbaux de la Commune de 1871. Critical edition by Georges Bourgin and Gabriel Henroit. 2 vols. Paris: A. Leroux and E. Lahure, 1924–1945.

Proudhon, Pierre-Joseph. *Amour et Mariage.* Paris: A. Lacroix, 1876.

———. *La Pornocratie ou les femmes dans les temps modernes.* Paris: A. Lacroix, 1875.

Ravailhe, Chanoine Romain Pierre. *Une semaine de la Commune de Paris.* Paris: V. Palmé, 1883.

Reclus, Elie. *La Commune au jour le jour. 1871, 19 mars–28 mai.* Paris: Reinwald-Schleicher, 1908.

Rimbaud, Arthur. *Œuvres complètes.* 'Bibliothèque de la Pléiade.' Paris: Gallimard, 1946.

Rochefort, Henri. *Les Aventures de ma vie.* 5 vols. Paris: Dupont, 1896–1898.

Rossel, Louis-Nathaniel. *Mémoires, Procès et correspondance, présentés par Roger Stéphane.* Paris: J.-J. Pauvert, 1960.

Rubel, M. (ed.). See Marx, Karl.

Sarcey, Francisque. *Le siège de Paris. Impressions et souvenirs.* Paris: E. Lachaud, 1871.

Schulkind, Eugène W., 'Le rôle des femmes dans la Commune de 1871,' *1848, revue des révolutions contemporaines,* Vol. XLII, February 1950.

Simon, Jules. *L'ouvrière.* Paris: L. Hachette, 1861.

Soukholmine, Vassili. 'Deux femmes russes combattantes de la Commune,' *Cahiers Internationaux,* XVI, May 1950.

Tchérednitchenko, P. 'La vie généreuse et mouvementée d'Elisa Tomanovskaïa . . . ,' *Etudes Soviétiques*, LXXXVII, June 1955.

Tchernoff, Iouda. *Le parti républicain au Coup d'Etat et sous le Second Empire, d'après des documents et des souvenirs inédits.* Paris: A. Pédone, 1906.

Vallès, Jules. *L'Insurgé.* Paris: Nouvelle Librairie de France, 1950.

Vanier, Henriette. *La mode et ses métiers. Frivolités et Lutte des classes, 1830–1870. Les Faits, la Presse, l'Opinion.* Paris: A. Colin, 1960.

Verlaine, Paul. *Œuvres poétiques complètes.* 'Bibliothèque de la Pléiade.' Paris: Gallimard, 1954.

Vermersch, Eugène. *Les Incendiaires.* London: 29 Frith Street (Soho), 1872.

Vésinier, Pierre. *Histoire de la Commune de Paris.* London: Chapman and Hall, 1871.

Villiers, Baron Marc de. *Histoire des clubs de femmes et des légions d'Amazones: 1793–1848–1871.* Paris: Plon-Nourrit, 1910.

Vuillaume, Maxime. *Mes Cahiers Rouges.* 10 vols. Paris: Cahiers de la Quinzaine: Ser. IX. Nos. 10–12, 1908; Ser. X. Nos. 7, 8, 11, 1909, Ser. XI, No. 9, 1910; Ser. XIII. No. 11, 1910; Ser. XIV. No. 11, 1910; Ser. XV. No. 9, 1914.

Weill, Georges. *Histoire du parti républicain en France de 1814 à 1870.* Paris: Alcan, 1900.

Wyczańska, Krystyna. *Polacy w Komunie Paryskiej 1871 r.* Wyd. Warszawa 1: Wydaw. Ministerstwa Obrony Narodowej, 1957.

INDEX OF NAMES

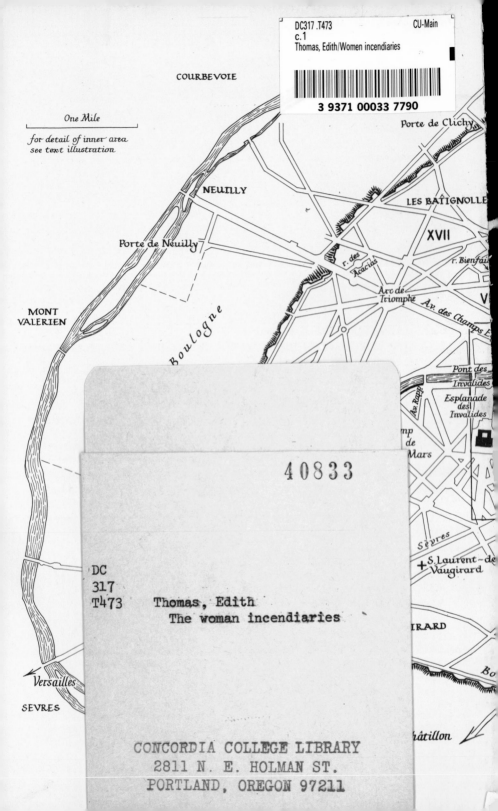

COURBEVOIE

One Mile

*for detail of inner area
see text illustration*

Porte de Clichy

NEUILLY

LES BATIGNOLLE

Porte de Neuilly

XVII

r. des
Acacias

r. Bienfais

MONT
VALERIEN

Boulogne

Arc de
Triomphe

Av. des Champs E

V

Pont des
Invalides

Av. Rapp

Esplanade
des
Invalides

mp
de
Mars

40833

Sèvres

S. Laurent-de
Vaugirard

DC
317
T473

Thomas, Edith
The woman incendiaries

IRARD

Versailles

SEVRES

Bo

hâtillon